OTHER PLACES, OTHER TIMES

ROSEMARY NEERING
PETER GRANT

Consultants

Sandra Boulanger
Ken Cooper
Peter Massiah

 **gage** EDUCATIONAL PUBLISHING COMPANY
A DIVISION OF CANADA PUBLISHING CORPORATION
TORONTO ONTARIO CANADA

Copyright © 1986 Gage Educational
Publishing Company
A Division of Canada Publishing
Corporation
Toronto · Ontario · Canada

ISBN 0-7715-8163-7

Project editor: Bruce Bartlett
Book design: Michael van Elsen Design Inc.
Illustrations: Helen Fox
Maps and diagrams: James Loates *illustrating*

6 7 8 9 10 11 **BP** 96 95 94 93 92 91

Written, Printed, and Bound in Canada

Cover:
*When Heinrich Schliemann
uncovered this golden death
mask at Mycenae, he was
convinced this noble face could
only be that of the Greek hero
Agamemnon. Further research
was to indicate the mask
predates the Trojan War, yet the
name "Mask of Agamemnon"
remains.*

Acknowledgments

The publisher is grateful to the many individuals and organizations who assisted in the preparation of this book. In particular, the helpful suggestions made by the following are acknowledged:
Stephen Corry, Survival International;
Dr. David Pendergast, Royal Ontario Museum;
Dr. Paul Swarney, York University; and
Dr. John Topic, Trent University.

Acropolis Museum, Athens, 114; Paul Almasy/Canapress Photo Service, 317; Marcia and Robert Ascher, 233; James P. Blair © National Geographic Society, 262; David S. Boyer © National Geographic Society, 266; British Tourist Authority, 144; Canapress Photo Service, 5, 69, 285; Claudio E. Chehébar/Mammal Slide Library, 192; Photo Peter Clayton, 32, 92; Dr. Ludwig Delp, 46; Ekdotike Athenon S.A., front cover, 110, 133; Victor Englebert, 186, 217, 219, 220, 221, 222, 225, 242, 302, 305, 307, 308, 310, 313, 321; Jean Galt, viii; Dr. Georg Gerster/Photo Researchers, Inc., 30; Greek National Tourist Organization, 104, 128; Janet Gunn, 281, 283, 295; Robert Harding Picture Library Limited, 138; Hirmer Fotoarchiv, 41, 53, 109; Holle Bildarchiv, 108; From *Mandinko The Ethnography of a West African Holy Land* by Matt Schaffer and Christine Cooper, Copyright © 1980 by Holt, Rinehart and Winston, reprinted by permission of CBS College Publishing, 250, 251, 256, 265, 267; P. B. Kaplan/Photo Researchers, Inc., 270; Gary Kenny, back cover, 184, 230; Edward P. Leahy/Canapress Photo Service, 274; Norman R. Lightfoot/Photo Researchers, Inc., 272; Photo Dr. H. Stanley Loten, 191, 194, 195; Macmillan, London and Basingstoke, 129, 224, 228, 230; From *The Conquest of the Incas* by John Hemming, copyright 1970, Macmillan, London and Basingstoke, 240; Mansell Collection, 61, 123; Mexican Government Tourism Office, 202, 209; John Moss/Photo Researchers, Inc., 287, 288, 297; National Museums of Canada, National Museum of Man, ASC Cat. No. RI 72-21-8, 18; National Tourist Office of Spain, 144; The Newberry Library, 212; Lennart Nilsson/Black Star, 290; Diane Rawson/Photo Researchers, Inc., 259; Drawing by Hans Peter Renner, Stansstad/Switzerland, 52; From *Ibn Batuta, Travels in Asia and Africa*, by H. A. R. Gibb, copyright 1929, Routledge & Sons, London, 260; Courtesy of the Royal Ontario Museum, Toronto, Canada, 3, 22, 31, 43, 67, 70, 73, 75, 77, 83, 87, 98, 100, 101, 192; Schofield & Sims Ltd., 64; K. Scholz/Miller Services, 245; John Scofield © National Geographic Society, 265; Alfred H. Siemens, 196; Staatliche Museen zu Berlin, 53; From *The Book of Chilam Balam of Chumayel* by R. L. Roys, copyright 1967, University of Oklahoma Press, Norman, 211; Copyright, University Presses of Florida, photographs by Roy C. Craven, Jr., 189, 201, 210; From *The Men of Cajamarca* by J. Lockhart, copyright 1972, University of Texas Press, Austin, 237; Wadsworth Atheneum, Hartford, Gift of J. P. Morgan, 131; Robert Waldock, 192; Werner Forman Archive, 249, 255, 256, 263, 264; Robin J. S. White, 292.

Contents

Preface

All people are influenced by the world around them. Some of these influences come from our physical environment: we put on a coat when it is cold outside, and stay out of the rain if we can. Other influences come from our human environment, the people around us. Whether we realize it or not, our behavior is affected by other people. For example, we walk on the right side of a crowded hallway and line up in single file to pay for our purchases in a store. These behaviors are part of our culture, as are the way we dress, prepare food, earn a living, and think about things.

But, where does our culture come from? What influences help to create or shape a culture? These are ideas that will be explored in *Other Places, Other Times*. Each of the nine different groups of people you will see have different cultures. No two are alike, but all share some common features. Each group has developed ways of getting food, methods of making decisions, techniques for dealing with neighboring peoples, and so on. Each group has learned to live comfortably in the physical environment of their homeland.

One of the important ideas you will investigate is the relationship between the culture of the people and their physical environment. You will see that people use the natural resources in their environment to meet their needs. But, you will also see that the physical surroundings influence the people, and that the relationship between culture and environment changes over time.

Other Places, Other Times begins with a short chapter summarizing the scientific evidence we have about the early development of humans. This chapter covers a very long period of time, ending when people have developed agriculture. The next four chapters, Unit 1, are on those groups of people who have contributed in an important way to the culture of the western world, of which Canada is a part. Mesopotamia, Egypt, Greece and Rome are covered in this unit.

Unit 2 examines three other groups: the Maya of Central America, the Incas of South America, and the Mandinko of West Africa. While important cultures, these people did not contribute directly to our way of life. The final two chapters, which make up Unit 3, are on the Mbuti of the Ituri Forest, and the Yanomami of the Amazon Basin. These two groups have kept their traditional ways of life, and, until recently, have been little influenced by outsiders.

A Word about the Text

Several features have been included in this book to help you understand the ideas being considered. Words in **bold type** are explained at greater length in the glossary on pages 323-324. The index, beginning on page 325, is helpful for finding information about specific topics. International Metric System (SI) units have been used throughout the book.

Pronunciation keys are given for words which may be difficult to pronounce. The letters and signs used are given below. This book uses the same system as the *Gage Intermediate Dictionary*, and the *Gage Canadian Dictionary*.

a	hat, cap	j	jam, enjoy	TH	then, smooth
ā	age, face	k	kind, seek		
ä	barn, far	l	land, coal	u	cup, butter
		m	me, am	u̇	full, put
b	bad, rob			ü	rule, move
ch	child, much	n	no, in	yü	use, music
d	did, red	ng	long, bring		
				v	very, save
e	let, best	o	hot, rock	w	will, woman
ē	equal, be,	ō	open, go	y	young, yet
	y in pretty	ô	order, door	z	zero, breeze
er	care, bear	oi	oil, voice	zh	measure, seizure
ėr	term, learn	ou	out, loud		
				ə	represents:
f	fat, if	p	paper, cup		a in above, pillar
g	go, bag	r	run, try		e in taken, under
h	he, how	s	say, yes		i in pencil, tapir
		sh	she, rush		o in lemon, favor
i	it, pin	t	tell, it		u in circus, measure
ī	ice, five	th	thin, both		

There is much we do not know about early people. Even relatively recent evidence, such as Stonehenge, is difficult to explain. Why was this monument built? How was it constructed? These are questions that still puzzle scientists.

Chapter 1

Early People

INTRODUCTION

When we say "history," we usually mean the period of the past for which we have written records. Writing, however, has only been a part of human life for about five thousand years. The period before written history we call **prehistory.**

Prehistory includes a period of time so enormous that it is almost impossible to imagine. For a long time it was widely believed that the Earth was only a few thousand years old. Today, scientists think it is about four and a half *billion* years old! Human beings have been around for only an extremely small part of this time, perhaps two or three million years.

Here is a way of thinking about the age of the Earth. Imagine that each year of those four and a half billion years represents a single second.

- You were born twelve or fourteen seconds ago.
- Your great-grandparents were born a minute and a half or two minutes ago.
- Eight minutes ago, Columbus discovered America.
- About an hour and a half ago, the first cities (the ones you will study in the next chapter of this book) began.
- The first people in North America arrived eight or nine hours ago.
- Three or four days ago, people living in Africa and in the southern parts of Europe and Asia had just learned how to use fire.
- About three weeks ago, people in Africa began to use pieces of rock as simple hand tools.

- The first human-like creatures appeared three months ago, give or take a couple of weeks. These primitive people lived on wild fruits and berries, and did not know how to use tools.
- A little more than two years ago, the first mammals appeared, just as the dinosaurs were dying out. These tiny, furry, tree-living animals are not unlike the tree shrews that still exist today.
- About four and a half years ago, on our year-to-second time-scale, the first dinosaurs walked the Earth.
- Roughly seven years ago, early reptiles emerged from the sea. They were the first forms of animal life on land.
- Eleven or twelve years ago, the first vertebrate fish, those with skeletons, appeared in the seas.
- The first invertebrate sea creatures, much like the jellyfish, sponges and starfish found on beaches today, appeared some sixteen to nineteen years ago.
- The first forms of life on Earth, single-celled algae and bacteria, began sixty or sixty-five years ago.
- To arrive at the time when the Earth was formed, we have to go back still much further. Four and a half billion years, reduced to seconds, would be a period of about 142 years.

EARTH'S HISTORY

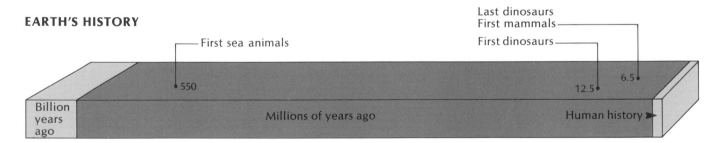

In this chapter, we will look at only a very small part of the total age of the Earth. We will begin about 1.75 million years ago, when the earliest people first began using small pieces of rock as tools. We will continue up until the time of the first civilizations. Humans developed a good deal during this period. In fact, some scientists say there were four major groups of people who lived during this period. From the earliest to the most recent, they are known to us as *homo habilis* (hō'mō hab'i lis), *homo erectus* (hō'mō i rek'təs), Neanderthal (nē an'dər tol') Man and Cro-Magnon (krō mag'non) Man. We will look at each one in turn.

EARLY PEOPLE

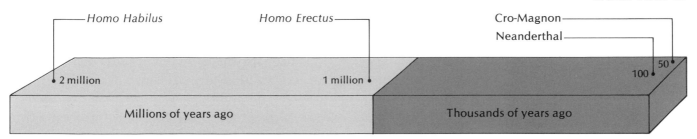

*Like early plant and animal life, much of our evidence of early humans comes from **fossils.***

Fossils are formed when the remains of plants and animals are changed into stone over millions of years. The remains must be buried undisturbed while this process goes on.

A Knife Edge

A Sidescraper

HOMO HABILIS

On the plains of eastern Africa, just south of the equator, lies a valley called the Olduvai Gorge (ōl′dù vī′ gôrj). If you had visited this place millions of years ago, you would have found a flat grassland beside a lake. Over a period of hundreds of thousands of years, nearby volcanic eruptions dumped lava and ash over the area. After that, a river cut a path through the hardened lava and ash, creating the steep-sided valley that is there today.

The Olduvai Gorge extends for some forty kilometres and is over one hundred metres deep in places. The river has eroded away the material so that now the walls of the Gorge show seven different layers of rock, each containing fossils. Scientists estimate that the deepest layer, the oldest one, was formed almost two million years ago.

In the 1930s, a British team, Louis and Mary Leakey, organized an expedition to the Olduvai Gorge. Encouraged by some earlier fossil finds in the area, they wanted to dig further. For the next four decades, the Leakeys supervised research at the Gorge.

At first, they uncovered many animal fossils and stone tools, but only a few fragments that could be identified as human. But in 1959, at one of the lower levels of the dig, Mary Leakey discovered an almost complete skull-fossil with definite human characteristics. Scientific tests showed that this skull was about 1.75 million years old!

A Primitive Hammer

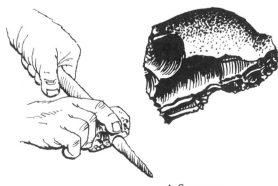

A Scraper

Until his death in 1972, Dr. Leakey conducted research on early people in eastern Africa. Here he explains his findings to a staff member of the Canadian television science show "The Nature of Things."

DIGGING UP AND DATING THE EVIDENCE

Fossils are the hardened remains of plants or animals, preserved in rock. A **paleontologist** is a scientist who finds and studies fossils.

Paleontologists take great care in digging up a site where fossils have been discovered. They use stakes, strings and surveying equipment to divide the site into numbered squares one or two metres in length. Then, the earth from each square is carefully removed.

Each bit of earth is passed through a sieve to be sure that no evidence is lost. Even very tiny pieces of information can be useful. Sometimes the discarded soil is reexamined for further evidence.

The fossils and tools are set back into place until they are mapped, numbered and photographed. They then are covered in plaster, or some other protective material, and sent to a laboratory.

In the laboratory, scientific equipment is used to calculate the age of the fossils.

Over the next few years, many more fossilized human bones were uncovered in the same area, along with stone tools and animal fossils. From this evidence, researchers think that the bones belonged to an early tool-using ancestor of modern people. Louis Leakey gave this ancestor the name *homo habilis*, Latin for "handy man."

Much of our understanding of early humans is based on fossil evidence. Using this information, scientists have put together a description of the way of life of homo habilis. *What tools did these people use?*

From the finds of the Leakeys and other paleontologists, we can put together a picture of what *homo habilis* must have been like. The skull fossils show that *homo habilis* had a much longer, flatter head than human beings today, with a brain only two-thirds as large. From the size of the leg- and thighbones, we think that adults were about 1.5 m tall and that they walked in a slightly stooped position.

Homo habilis people built shelters of branches and collected birds' eggs and wild berries for food. Animal fossils found with human ones show that they also ate meat. We think that when they hunted animals such as wild pigs, they would creep up in groups and pounce on the unsuspecting beasts. Or, they might have surrounded the animals, yelling and screaming until the frightened creatures backed into a rock crevice or hole and became stuck there. Because they did not have real weapons, hunters probably killed the animals with rocks or heavy branches. Using pieces of sharp stone, they would then hack up the meat and eat it raw. They broke open the bones in order to eat the soft marrow inside.

The people whose fossils we group together as *homo habilis* lasted for almost a million years (from about three weeks ago to about eleven days ago on our year-to-second time-scale). They first lived in eastern Africa, gradually spread into the north of the continent and then moved into some parts of southern Asia. They only lived in warm parts of the world. Because they did not make clothes and did not know how to use fire, *homo habilis* people could not have survived the winters of colder climates.

1. Here are some important words from the section you have just read on *homo habilis.* For each word, write a sentence that will make the meaning clear. If you do not understand some of the words, use a dictionary to help you.
    ancestor   estimate   expedition   fragment   gorge
2. Resources is the name given to those things that help people meet their needs. Make a list of the **resources** *homo habilis* found in the environment.
3. Using the picture on page 6, describe the ways sharp stones were used as tools to help get food.

HOMO ERECTUS

Years before the Leakeys' diggings at Olduvai Gorge, a Dutch scientist had already discovered early human fossils. Dr. Eugène Dubois found fossils at a dig on the tropical island of Java, now part of Indonesia.

In 1891, Dr. Dubois discovered the top of a skull and, nearby, a thighbone. The skull-fossil showed a head that was long, flat, and sharply angled at the back. It was neither apelike nor quite like a modern human skull. The thighbone, however, was practically identical to that of a present-day human being. Because of this, Dubois believed the creature had walked fully upright. He concluded that he had found the remains of a human ancestor.

Homo erectus walked in a more upright position than earlier ancestors. The word homo *is from the Latin for man and is the scientific term for humans.* Erectus *means they walked upright or erect.*

Other scientists laughed at Dubois's discovery; they claimed his fossils were nothing more than the remains of an extinct giant monkey. Dubois was so humiliated that he gave up his research. Later he even came to believe his critics were right.

Several decades later, a Canadian named Davidson Black was digging at Chau Kou Tien (chü kü tyen) ("Dragon Bone Hill") near Peking, China. He found skull and bone fossils amazingly similar to those of Dubois's "Java Man." Black used the name "Peking Man" to refer to the people he was studying.

By the 1930s, the new evidence forced paleontologists to take Dubois's earlier conclusions seriously. A German scientist named von Koenigswald (von kō′nigz wold′) took up in Java where Dubois had left off. Von Koenigswald found other fossils which, when matched with Dubois's earlier finds, provided a much more complete picture of "Java Man."

Paleontologists came to realize that "Java Man" and "Peking Man" were the fossils of early human beings that had lived about three-quarters of a million years ago. The bone structures showed that these human beings had walked fully upright. The scientific community gave them the name *homo erectus*, Latin for "upright man." From the presence of charred animal bones at some of the sites, we can conclude that these people cooked their meat. In other words, they were the first people to use fire.

It is difficult to know the exact time period when *homo erectus* lived. A well-preserved skull was found in northern Kenya in 1975. It has been dated back to 1.5 million years ago! Most of the *homo erectus* fossils, however, are no older than 1.25 million years, with the most recent dated at about 250 000 years. On our year-to-second scale, this would place *homo erectus* during the period from seventeen to three days ago.

Some of the human fossils dated between 1.25 and .75 million years ago have been classified by paleontologists as belonging to *homo habilis*, others to *homo erectus*. Still other fossils from this time period are partly *homo habilis*, partly *homo erectus*. No *homo habilis* fossils have been dated more recently than .75 million years ago. Therefore, most paleontologists believe that *homo erectus* was a descendant of *homo habilis*. They think that some groups of *homo habilis* remained unchanged for tens of thousands of years, and gradually died out. Yet, these scientists think that other groups of *homo habilis* gradually changed, developing into *homo erectus*.

It is likely early *homo erectus* people did not know how to make fire. They probably took burning branches from trees that had been struck by lightning, or coals from smoldering volcanic ash. Later on, some *homo erectus* groups did learn how to make fire. The heat of friction caused by rapidly twirling a short, sharpened stick in a wooden groove filled with wood shavings will start a fire.

This ability to make fire, not just to use it, made life much easier for the later groups of *homo erectus.* Fire-using *homo erectus* people adapted more successfully to their environment than those groups who were unable to make or to use fire.

Because they were able to use fire, some *homo erectus* groups could live in cold climates. Although most *homo erectus* fossils have been found in Africa, southern Europe and southern Asia, some have been found as far north as England and Germany.

Like *homo habilis*, a *homo erectus* adult was only about 1.5 m tall on the average. These people had great bony eyebrow ridges and almost no chin. The vocal tract of *homo erectus* was not well developed, compared to that of modern humans. If these people did talk, they did so in a very slow and halting way.

The tools used by *homo erectus* were much better than those of the earlier *homo habilis.* By using bones and rocks to chip

What evidence from the map shows homo erectus *was better able to adjust to different environments than was* homo habilis?

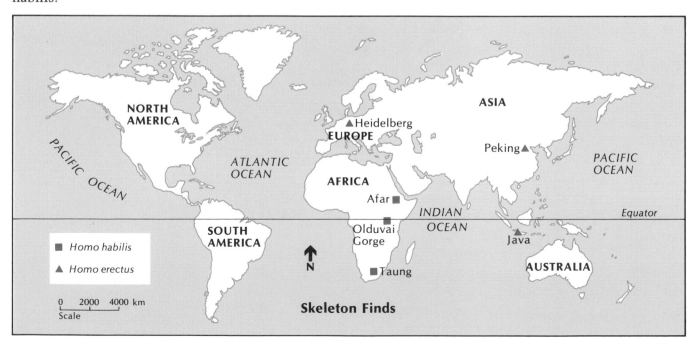

Skeleton Finds

■ Homo habilis
▲ Homo erectus

0   2000   4000 km
Scale

away at pieces of flint, they were able to make blades for cutting and scraping. The blades were also used for carving points onto wooden spears. The tips on the spears were then hardened by sticking them into the coals of a fire. *Homo erectus* used these spears to hunt wild animals, even elephants.

We can make guesses about how such elephant hunts took place. As the elephants passed near a swamp, the hunters set a fire in their path. The terrified animals stampeded into the swamp, wallowing deeper and deeper in the thick mud. Finally, they collapsed from exhaustion. Groups of hunters then killed the elephants by stabbing them with their spears. By staying on firmer ground, and building footbridges, hunters carried the meat back to the rest of the group.

Most scientists agree that such prehistoric big game hunts were a major event in human development. There was a lot of danger and difficulty involved in these hunts. The people had to plan their activities in advance, organize the hunters, and carry through the hunt successfully. Then, because there were so many people involved, they had to work out ways to be sure everyone got a fair share. Much skill, organization and quick thinking was required. Over tens of thousands of years, this mental activity made even more complex thinking possible.

By about 250 000 years ago, most *homo erectus* people were very different from those of a million years earlier. Scientists use a different name, *homo sapiens* (hō'mō sā'pē enz), for these late *homo erectus* groups. *Homo sapiens*, or "reasoning man," is the **species** to which all modern-day people belong.

A *homo erectus* skull

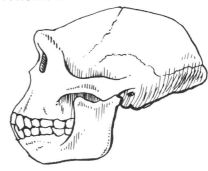

A modern human skull

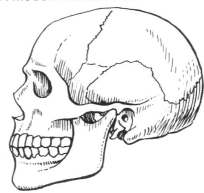

Compare these pictures. What differences do you notice?

1. Describe the changes in the use of tools from *homo habilis* to *homo erectus*.
2. List four uses of fire by *homo erectus*.
3. What activities would have taken up most of the time for early people?
4. Describe the differences in the physical appearance of *homo habilis* and *homo erectus*. Suggest reasons why the appearance of people might change over a long period of time.

NEANDERTHAL MAN

One of the first discoveries of prehistoric human remains happened completely by accident. In 1856, at a limestone quarry in the Neander Thal (Neander Valley) in Germany, a group of workmen were busily shovelling out a cave. The owner of the quarry, a Mr. Beckershoff, noticed some fossilized bones among the rubble being carted away. These bones looked human.

Beckershoff saved some of the bones, including a skull, and sent them off to some scientists. By estimating the age of the rock deposits in the cave, the scientists concluded that these bones were tens of thousands of years old, perhaps even older. They determined that these were the bones of a young male.

Neanderthal Man made tools and used fire. This technology allowed the people to survive in a wide variety of environments.

This discovery of "Neanderthal Man" created a great deal of controversy. At that time, even many educated people believed that human beings had existed for only a few thousand years. Many people refused to believe that these bones could be so old. Yet over the next few decades, similar discoveries of fossils just as old, if not older, were made at many other locations in Europe.

Today, paleontologists are still uncovering evidence of Neanderthal Man. Since Beckershoff's lucky accident, over one hundred different sites have been **excavated**, mostly in Europe and the Middle East. Some of these finds have dated the Neanderthals back to as early as 130 000 years ago. On our year-to-second scale, they existed from about a day and a half ago to eight or nine hours ago.

In appearance, the Neanderthals had characteristics similar to both *homo erectus* and ourselves. They were, on the average, about six centimetres taller than *homo erectus.* Neanderthal people still had thick eyebrow ridges, though less so than *homo erectus.* Some paleontologists say that if people from Neanderthal time suddenly showed up today, dressed in modern clothes, their appearance would not attract much attention.

Neanderthal people developed many tools. They had knives, **borers** and spear-sharpeners, all made from chipped rock. These simple tools were used for getting food, providing shelter, and for protection.

Animal hides were worn as clothes. They scraped away the fat from the inside of the hides, dried them, and then poked holes in the edges. By lacing strips of skin through the holes, they made simple coats.

Neanderthal people often lived in caves kept warm with fires. In some of these caves, skulls of enormous bears have been discovered. We think the Neanderthals hunted this creature by throwing burning branches into its cave to smoke it out. When the bear came rushing out, they killed it with spears and heavy rocks. The bear's meat was cooked and eaten, its hide used for clothing, and possibly its skull kept as a good luck charm.

Neanderthal people were the first to bury their dead. Paleontologists have discovered graves scooped into the floors of caves;

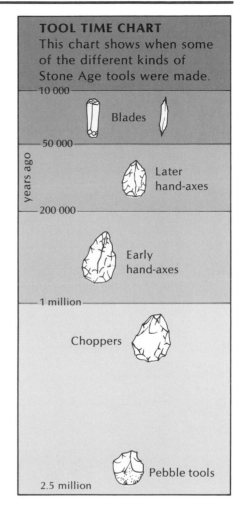

TOOL TIME CHART
This chart shows when some of the different kinds of Stone Age tools were made.

years ago

10 000

Blades

50 000

Later hand-axes

200 000

Early hand-axes

1 million

Choppers

Pebble tools

2.5 million

the skeletons have shown that the bodies were carefully prepared before being buried. At one such site in northern Iraq, fossilized pollen from the hollyhock flower was found in a grave. These Neanderthal people had even sprinkled their graves with flowers, just as we do today.

1. Make two lists, one to show the advantages of living in a cave for Neanderthal Man, and the other to show the disadvantages.
2. More than the earlier groups, Neanderthals changed and improved things found in their natural environment to make them more useful. Find several examples in the text to prove this point.
3. Why do you suppose the skull of a bear would be considered a good luck charm?

Engravings by Cro-Magnon Man give information about life in prehistoric times. What can be learned from these engravings?

CRO-MAGNON MAN

In the same year that Mr. Beckershoff noticed the bones at his limestone quarry, Louis Lartet was beginning to explore some caves in southern France. Over a number of years, Lartet collected a wide variety of stone tools and carved animal bones. The carvings on some of the bones were amazingly clear and detailed.

At the Paris Exhibition of 1867, Lartet's finds caused a great deal of public curiosity. It was agreed that whoever these prehistoric artists were, they had been people of considerable imagination and skill.

A year after the Paris Exhibition, railway workers were laying tracks in the same area where Lartet had found many of his prehistoric engravings. As they were clearing away earth from the back of a rock shelter locally known as Cro-Magnon, they noticed stone tools and pieces of skeleton imbedded in the dirt.

Hearing of this discovery, Lartet hurried to the scene. He carefully dug up the area, revealing several skeleton-fossils. Investigating further, Lartet found the skeletons to be those of four men, a woman and a premature baby. From marks on the remains, it became clear that the members of this prehistoric family had been brutally murdered.

During the next several decades, more evidence was found throughout southern France. Most of it was similar to that unearthed by Lartet. This group of people became known as the "Cro-Magnons," because of the location where the first remains were found.

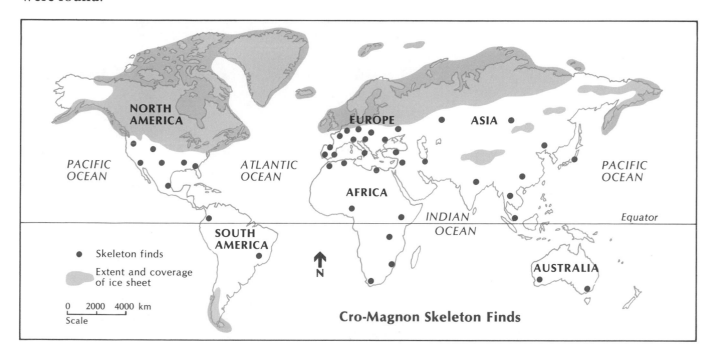

Cro-Magnon Skeleton Finds

- Skeleton finds
- Extent and coverage of ice sheet

0 2000 4000 km
Scale

The Cro-Magnons first appeared in Europe about 30 000 years ago. They probably followed the retreat of the glaciers at the end of the last ice age. Although concentrated there, Cro-Magnon fossils have been discovered on five continents. This widespread distribution shows they were able to adjust to many different climates. The most recent finds have been dated to about 10 000 years ago. On our year-to-second scale, this period would be from about eight and a half to about three hours ago.

The brain of Cro-Magnon Man was as large as that of a modern person. Adults were as much as two metres tall, more than the average height of people today. With their high foreheads and

Cro-Magnon skeletons have been found throughout most of the world. This indicated they were a people able to adapt to many environments, from deserts to rain forests.

prominent chins, the faces of Cro-Magnon people were unmistakably "modern." Since the Cro-Magnons' vocal system was identical to ours, it is a reasonable guess that their speech had the same range of sounds as ours does today.

Cro-Magnon cave paintings were first discovered in the middle of the last century. However, the greatest find of all did not come until 1940. On a September day in that year, some children from the town of Lascaux (las' kō) were chasing a runaway dog. Lascaux is in the Dordogne (dôr' dony') Valley, the same area as the Cro-Magnon rock site. When the dog disappeared into an underground cave, the children lit torches and went in after it. They found the dog, but they also found what has been called a "prehistoric art gallery."

On the walls of the cave were row after row of bright, multicolored paintings, preserved for thousands of years by the perfect conditions inside the cave. To make these remarkable pictures, the Cro-Magnons had used paints made from a mixture of colored rock-powder and animal fat. The brushes were made of

The fossil evidence shows distinct differences between homo erectus, Neanderthal Man and Cro-Magnon Man. Later peoples made and used tools more than earlier groups.

Homo Erectus   Neanderthal Man   Cro-Magnon Man

THE ICE AGE

Scientists call the period from about 1.75 million years ago to about 10 000 years ago the "Pleistocene" (plīs′tə sēn′) era. During this time, the Earth's climate was very unstable. Very cold periods lasting thousands of years alternated with warm spells. With each cold cycle, glaciers advanced from out of the north. During warm times, the glaciers retreated. The last of these cold periods, from about 80 000 to 10 000 years ago, was the most severe. Ice covered a great deal of North America, Europe and Asia.

Each time the glaciers covered the land, early people were forced to change their way of life. Often they migrated to warmer parts of the globe. Thousands of years later, as the climate warmed and the glaciers retreated, the people moved northward to the new lands.

The graph shows the alternating cold and warm periods of the Pleistocene era. The map on page 15 shows the extent of the ice cover during the last ice age.

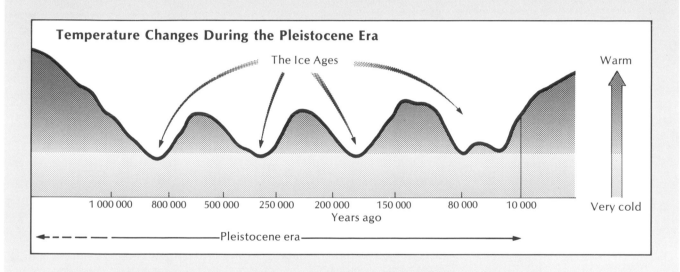

Temperature Changes During the Pleistocene Era

animal hair tied to small bones. These pictures have been dated to 30 000 years ago, near the beginning of the Cro-Magnon period. By looking at pictures of the Lascaux cave-paintings, we can make guesses about the life of Cro-Magnon people, especially about their hunting. People now think that the Cro-Magnons believed such paintings would bring them good luck when hunting.

Evidence of the earliest peoples comes from rock and cave paintings. This is an example of rock paintings found in British Columbia.

The Cro-Magnons developed more tools than did the Neanderthals. From flint they were able to make slim, sharp-edged blades that could be used as chisels, knives, and spearpoints. From deer antlers they made needles, fish-hooks, and barbed harpoon-heads. They made lamps by filling a stone bowl with animal grease and floating in it a wick of moss or fur. Snail shells and animal teeth were used to make necklaces. The Cro-Magnons even had flutes and whistles carved from animal bones.

Cro-Magnon people were not only artists and hunters, they were also fierce warriors. Many finds show evidence that whole groups of people had been ruthlessly speared, stabbed or beaten to death. Scientists have long wondered why the Neanderthals were disappearing from the scene just as the Cro-Magnons were arriving. Some people have suggested that the Cro-Magnons, with their more developed tools and greater strength, killed off the Neanderthals. Others argue that the Cro-Magnons adapted better to the ice age environment (see page 17) than the Neanderthals did. While the Cro-Magnons survived, the Neanderthals did not.

1. What part has "luck" played in finding information about early humans?
2. Make a chart in your notebook with the headings: *Homo habilis*, *Homo erectus*, Neanderthal Man, Cro-Magnon Man. For each group, record information about time span, tools, food, shelter, clothing, and art.

FROM HUNTING TO FARMING

As we have seen, *homo habilis*, *homo erectus*, the Neanderthals and the Cro-Magnons all survived by gathering wild plants and by hunting animals. None of these people grew their own food. They were always searching for food and animals, and never stayed in any one place for very long. They never built cities or towns, or even permanent shelters.

As the Earth warmed up at the end of the last ice age, about 10 000 years ago, some areas began to produce wild, edible plants in a greater abundance than ever before. Some bands of hunters and gatherers found that certain plants would grow again even after being picked. This abundant supply of food meant that they did not have to move as often.

By learning how and when to pick the plants, these bands of people could provide themselves with enough food for long periods of time. As they built small settlements in places where the edible plants grew well, they also began to tame certain animals.

By 5000 years ago, people in almost every **temperate** part of the world had established a pattern of simple farming. They all used plants and animals of the local environment. Agriculture did not develop as easily in those parts of the world where the environment is harsh—the northern areas and the dry lands. In the table on the next page are some examples of the first **domestic** plants and animals.

AREA	DOMESTIC ANIMALS	DOMESTIC PLANTS
eastern Mediterranean	goats, sheep	barley, dates
eastern Asia	chickens, water buffaloes	soyabeans, rice
western Africa		watermelons, yams
southern Europe	cattle, pigs	grapes, oats
southern portion of North America	turkeys	sunflowers, beans

These were the first attempts at farming. In the next chapter of this book, we will look at early farming and how this led to the development of cities.

SUMMARY

Although scientists estimate the Earth to be about four and a half billon years old, tool-using human beings have been around for only about 1.75 million years.

Homo habilis (1 750 000-800 000 years ago) were the first tool-using creatures, using pieces of rock to hack the meat of wild animals they had hunted. *Homo habilis* also gathered plants for food. Because they did not know how to use fire, *homo habilis* people lived only in warm climates.

Homo erectus (1 250 000-250 000 years ago) learned first to use and, later, also how to make fire. *Homo erectus* people used chipped pieces of flint for cutting and scraping. They hunted large animals, such as elephants, and cooked the meat.

The Neanderthals (130 000-30 000 years ago) were the first people who lived in colder climates. They wore animal hides and lived in caves kept warm with fires. They had a wide variety of stone tools, and were the first people to bury their dead.

The Cro-Magnons (30 000-10 000 years ago) were almost physically identical to modern people. They developed even more tools than the Neanderthals. Their caves were painted with scenes of the hunt. The Cro-Magnons were fierce warriors; it has been argued that they killed off the Neanderthals.

The first traces of farming date from about 10 000 years ago. By 5000 years ago, small patterns of farming had been established in most temperate parts of the world.

Chapter Review: Early Peoples

NEW WORDS AND IDEAS

1. Write a sentence to identify each of the following:
   (a) prehistory   (d) fossils
   (b) environment   (e) paleontologists.
   (c) resources

2. Give the Latin term for each of the following phrases:
   (a) handy man
   (b) upright man
   (c) reasoning man.

3. (a) Use the maps on page 10 and page 15 to list the parts of the world where evidence has been found of: (i) *homo habilis*, and (ii) Cro-Magnon Man.
   (b) What differences are there in the locations of the sites?
   (c) Suggest one or two reasons for the differences in site location.

4. Copy the following sentences into your notebook. After each sentence, write whether it is true or false. Rewrite the false statements so that they are true.
   (a) All of the early peoples knew how to make fire.
   (b) Scientists believe that Cro-Magnon and Neanderthal Man lived during the same time period.
   (c) Mary and Louis Leakey were anthropologists.
   (d) All early people lived in caves.
   (e) The dinosaurs died out before the first early humans appeared.

CHECKING YOUR UNDERSTANDING

5. For each statement, write whether it best describes: *homo habilis*, *homo erectus*, Neanderthal, or Cro-Magnon people.

   (a) Created cave paintings.
   (b) The first to bury their dead.
   (c) The first to use fire.
   (d) They made shelters from branches.
   (e) They walked fully upright for the first time.
   (f) Designs were carved on animal bones.
   (g) Their voice system was identical to ours.
   (h) Used knives made from chipped rock.
   (i) Fish-hooks and needles were made from deer antlers.
   (j) The first to use stone tools.

6. Record the scientific evidence given in the text that supports each of the following statements:
   (a) *Homo habilis* ate meat.
   (b) "Java Man" walked upright.
   (c) *Homo erectus* cooked meat.
   (d) Neanderthal people lived in caves.
   (e) Cro-Magnons created works of art.

7. In one or two sentences, explain how the use of stone tools changed the everyday life of early people. Do the same for fire and farming.

USING YOUR KNOWLEDGE

8. A paleontologist is planning to search for evidence that early people settled in the area of your community over 10 000 years ago. You find a crude clay pot, a hollowed-out log, and fish-hooks made of bone. How would you interpret your find?

9. Imagine that you had to survive for one year in the natural environment of your area. There are no industries, buildings, stores or means of transportation. Describe how you would use the natural resources available for: food, clothing, shelter, and tools.

UNIT 1

ANCIENT WESTERN CIVILIZATIONS

INTRODUCTION

For most of us, the word "civilization" has meanings that include things such as government, religion and economic activity. When we say a group of people is "civilized," we usually mean that their way of life includes laws, religious beliefs and methods of buying and selling goods. We also include a way of writing or recording of events that have taken place.

According to this meaning of the word, "civilization" exists practically everywhere in the world today. No matter how rich or how poor, all countries of the world today have some form of writing, law, religion and economy.

Before about 5500 years ago, there was no such thing as "civilization." Human beings had been around for hundreds of thousands of years, but they had lived as wandering tribes. In these small groups they did not need to develop written rules or laws because everyone grew up learning what was expected of them. Beliefs were shared mostly within their tribe, and the simple trading of items was the only economic activity. While these people shared a way of life, and passed their ideas along to their children, they did not have a "civilization" as we have defined the term in the first paragraph.

In different places and in different ways, starting about 10 000 years ago, some people established permanent villages. The size of villages grew slowly, and it was not until about 5500 years ago that the first cities appeared. It was in these early cities that systems of writing, government, religion and economic activity first became established. This makes it easy to understand why the words "civilization" and "city" come from the same origin. When we talk about the civilizations of ancient history, we are really talking about the earliest cities of history.

The first cities and civilizations arose in four areas, all of them around major rivers–the Tigris and Euphrates, Nile, Indus, and Yellow rivers. This was no coincidence. Cities need to be located where there is a good supply of food, and where transportation is easy. River environments have provided both.

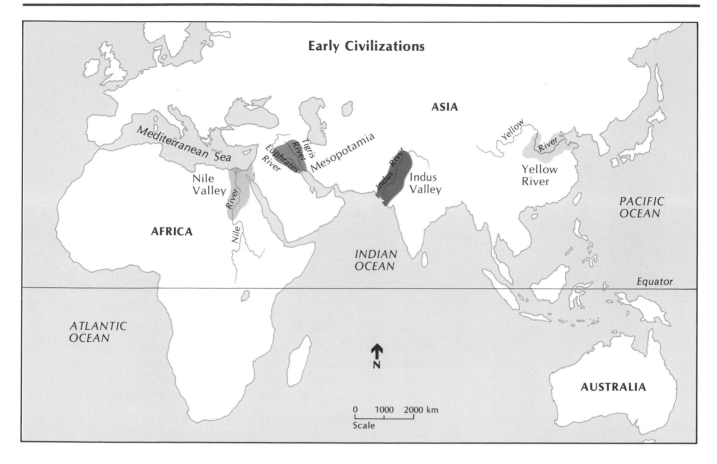

Early Civilizations

Soil that is near a river is usually fertile. Farming villages located on rivers could generally support larger numbers of people, and so grew in size. Food supplies, and other goods, could also be brought in from other areas by boats using the river. Rivers were for ancient civilizations what highways and air routes are for modern people.

If we say that the writing and recording of events signals the beginning of civilization, then the first of the four earliest civilizations began between 3500 and 3000 **B.C.** This was Mesopotamia, the land between the Tigris and Euphrates rivers, in what is today Iraq. The next civilization, a few hundred years later, was along the Nile Valley of Egypt. The cities of the Indus Valley, in present-day Pakistan, developed about 2000 B.C. Along the

As this map shows, river valleys were important environments for early civilizations. What other geographic characteristics do these civilizations have in common?

25

Yellow River of northern China, written records appeared about 1500 B.C.

Much of our knowledge about these early civilizations is uncertain. What we know comes mostly from the written records they left behind and the pieces of utensils and buildings that remain. Many of these finds have been uncovered only in the past century. They are often incomplete and difficult to understand. Since the evidence is so limited, historians often have to make guesses about what these early civilizations were really like.

These earliest civilizations had very little contact with each other. Barriers, such as mountain ranges or deserts, separated them. The Himalaya Mountains rose between the civilizations of China and India. The Syrian and Arabian deserts lay between Egypt and Mesopotamia.

Later civilizations did succeed in overcoming natural barriers. For example, Persia controlled an area covering Mesopotamia, Egypt, and even parts of the Indus Valley. This civilization lasted from about 550 B.C. to about 330 B.C.

Located just to the west of the Persian empire, the Greeks had managed to resist conquest by the Persians. In fact, by 323 B.C. under Alexander the Great, the Greeks were in control of all the lands of the Persian empire, and had expanded their lands even farther. Alexander's conquests helped to spread Greek influence throughout much of the ancient civilized world.

The next great civilization of the later ancient world was that of the Romans. At the time of Alexander, the Romans controlled central Italy. Three hundred years later, Rome was the centre of a civilization that covered the entire Mediterranean world, stretching as far west as the Atlantic Ocean. It lasted until the sixth century **A.D.**

These later civilizations were able to use the resources of their environment more effectively than earlier ones. They developed better crops, had improved metalworking, and built roads.

We know considerably more about Greece and Rome than we know about older ancient civilizations. Because they were more recent, written records are more abundant, better preserved and

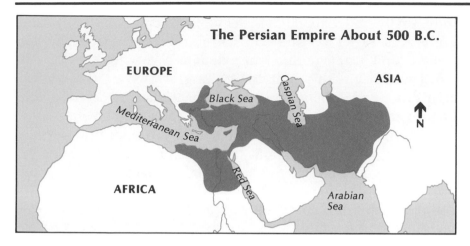

The Persian Empire About 500 B.C.

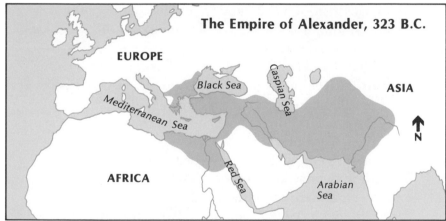

The Empire of Alexander, 323 B.C.

These maps show three large empires that developed near the Mediterranean Sea. From small homelands, they grew outwards. As they expanded, many of their ideas and ways of living were picked up by the people with whom they came into contact. Persian, Greek and Roman influences have been important in shaping our own society. Give some examples of their influence.

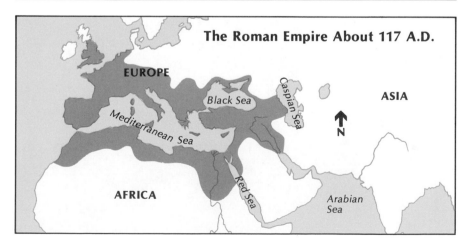

The Roman Empire About 117 A.D.

more easily understood. Other evidence, such as buildings and pottery, is easier to find and has not been damaged by the weather and people to the same extent as earlier finds.

We will begin this unit by looking at two of the earliest civilizations, Mesopotamia and Egypt. Then, we will study Greece and Rome, two civilizations of the later ancient world.

For each of the four civilizations, three different time periods will be described: an early one, a middle one and a later one. In this way, we will be able to observe the changes that took place during their development. Each civilization became a foundation or base for those that followed, and contributed much to our own way of life.

1. Read back through this section and write down the four earliest major civilizations of the ancient world, and the three major later ones.
2. Fertile land and transportation were important reasons why cities developed on rivers. Name three other ways a river would be important to a city.
3. Why do you think writing is considered to be a necessary part of civilization?
4. Why do you suppose later civilizations were able to overcome the natural barriers that had hindered the expansion of earlier civilizations?
5. What might be some reasons why we study ancient civilizations? What benefit could this be to our modern world?

Chapter 2

Mesopotamia

INTRODUCTION

The Tigris (tī′gris) and the Euphrates (yü′frā′tēz) spill from the mountains of Syria, then flow through hills and on to the flat plains of Iraq. Hundreds of kilometres from their sources, they empty into the Persian (pėr′zhən) Gulf.

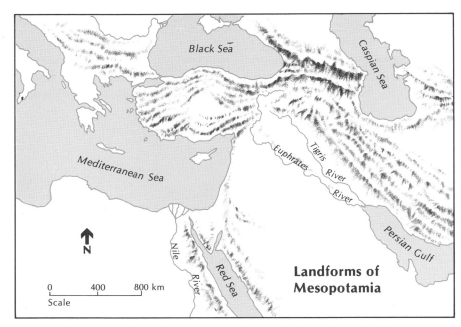

Landforms of Mesopotamia

The Tigris and Euphrates rivers flow down from the mountains and into a flat valley, eventually reaching the Persian Gulf. What other water bodies are shown on the map?

If you stand on the plain between the rivers today, you will be surrounded by sand dunes created by the wind. If you are near a river, you may see a grove of date palms clinging to the river bank. You might catch a glimpse of a camel caravan driven by desert Arabs, or a herd of donkeys urged on by a young boy. Far in the distance, across the sand, you might see the walls of a city.

29

Irrigation was necessary to make "the land between the rivers" produce enough food. Without irrigation, crops could not be grown during the dry summer months.

Five thousand years ago, the world's first great civilization rose here in the desert. We now call this civilization Mesopotamia, a word that means "the land between the rivers." This civilization lasted for almost 3000 years. Its people were the first to use many skills and inventions that we take for granted today. They irrigated their fields, devised a system of writing, developed mathematics, invented the wheel, and learned to work with metal.

We will look at three groups: Sumerians, Babylonians, and Assyrians. Together, they are called Mesopotamians. The geographic features and climate of the area encouraged the development of these civilizations.

UNCOVERING INFORMATION ABOUT MESOPOTAMIA

On the Mesopotamian plain and in the highlands, travellers sometimes see huge earth mounds. They are the remains of the cities of the Mesopotamians. For more than 100 years, **archaeologists** (är′kē ol′ə jists) have been digging into these mounds to discover what lies inside.

Thousands of clay tablets have been discovered among the ruins. The writing on these tablets has given us most of our information about Mesopotamia. Stones with picture-stories carved on them have given us further information.

As civilizations developed in neighboring areas, people there wrote about their contacts with the Mesopotamians. From these writings, we gather still more information. Modern-day aerial photographs show patterns on the land created thousands of years ago. These and observations of present-day life in the area let us draw more conclusions about life in ancient Mesopotamia.

An archaeological dig in Iran.

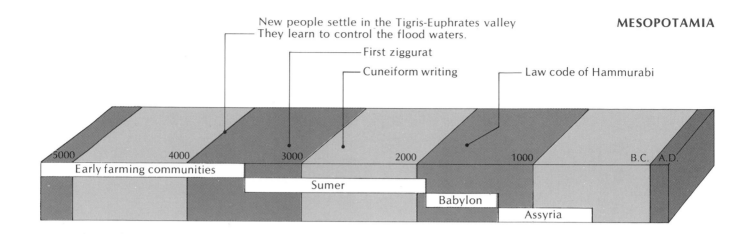

New people settle in the Tigris-Euphrates valley
They learn to control the flood waters.

First ziggurat

Cuneiform writing

Law code of Hammurabi

MESOPOTAMIA

5000   4000   3000   2000   1000   B.C.   A.D.

Early farming communities

Sumer

Babylon

Assyria

Warriors from Sumer were among the first to use wheeled chariots. The soldiers in the middle of the picture are prisoners.

This time line shows when each of these groups held power. When did each rise? When did each fall? How long did each last? How long did the civilization of Mesopotamia last?

MARDUK CREATES THE WORLD

Based on the evidence they have found, archaeologists, historians and geographers have built a picture of life in Mesopotamia. One of the tablets found in the ruins of a Mesopotamian city contained a story about the creation of the world by the Mesopotamian god Marduk. As you read this story, imagine that you are an archaeologist. You are trying to make some suggestions about life in Mesopotamia. What animals were raised? What were buildings made of? What parts of the natural environment were important to the Mesopotamians in building their civilization?

Marduk laid a reed on the face of the waters....
He formed mankind....
The beasts of the field and the living things he formed
The Tigris and the Euphrates he created and established
them in their place:
The grass, the rush of the marsh, the reed and the forest
he created,
The lands, the marshes and the swamps;
The wild cow and her young, the lamb of the fold,
Orchards and forests;
The he-goat and the mountain goat....
The Lord Marduk built a dam beside the sea....
Reeds he formed, trees he created;
Bricks he laid, buildings he erected;
Houses he made, cities he built....

The god Marduk as imagined by the Mesopotamians. What symbols of power are shown in the diagram?

SUMER

The River and the Plain: Base for a Civilization

The Tigris and the Euphrates begin in the mountains of Syria. As tiny streams join together and become rivers, they rush down the mountainsides towards the hills below. They cut deep channels and pick up a great deal of fine sand and earth, known as silt.

As these muddy rivers spill from the hill onto the plain, they change. Because the plain is almost totally flat, the waters in the rivers slow until they hardly seem to move at all. The Euphrates drops only fifty metres in its last 700 km, an average of only seven centimetres every kilometre.

Some of the silt sinks to the bottom of the river, building the bed higher. More silt is left along the banks of the river, so that they too become higher. The bed and banks eventually build so high that the river runs above the level of the plain.

On the southern part of the plain, the rivers split into smaller streams, to create a marshy area near the Persian Gulf.

Every April, snow in the mountains melts, sending great volumes of water down the Euphrates and the Tigris. The water spills over the banks of both rivers flooding large areas. Nowadays, the people of Iraq can measure the snowfall and rain and predict when the floods will come and how severe they will be. They can control the floods through dams near the mountains. But in ancient times, the arrival and size of the floods could not be predicted exactly. These factors depended on how much snow there was in the mountains and when it melted. They also depended on how much it rained in the hills where the streams that fed the Tigris flowed.

Summer on the plain is very hot and dry. Temperatures can reach 50°C, and there may be no rain for four months. The flood waters evaporate, leaving layers of silt behind them. In ancient times, this silt built a fertile soil, rich with **nutrients,** on the Mesopotamian plains.

As the river floods, sand and mud are deposited along the banks, building them higher and higher. The bottom of the river is also built up. The river may end up higher than the land in the valley.

Because of the heat and dryness, not much grows on the plain. Near the rivers, date palms sink their roots into any moist areas. Some scrub brush and grasses can grow in winter. Reeds grow thickly at the mouth of the river and in other marshy areas.

THE CLIMATE OF THE PLAIN

The figures in the chart below give average monthly temperatures and rainfall for Baghdad, Iraq. We think the climate in this area today is very similar to the climate on the plain of Mesopotamia five thousand years ago.

	Temperature (°C)	Precipitation (mm)
Jan	9.7	23
Feb	11.7	25
Mar	15.3	28
Apr	21.7	13
May	27.8	2
June	31.7	0
July	33.9	0
Aug	33.9	0
Sept	30.6	0
Oct	24.7	2
Nov	17.8	20
Dec	11.7	25

Read the chart to find out:

1. What was the highest average monthly temperature recorded in this area? the lowest?
2. Which months are usually the warmest? the coldest?
3. When does the greatest amount of rain fall? What is the total yearly rainfall? Do you think this is a lot of rain? How much rain falls each year where you live?

By 4500 B.C., people had settled in the hills surrounding the plain and on islands in the swamps at the mouths of the rivers. They lived in small villages, grew **crops** and other food and kept small herds of sheep and goats. The swamp-dwellers also relied on fishing for food.

The earliest inhabitants of Mesopotamia did not settle in the river valleys, but in the swamps near the mouths of the rivers or in the hills around them. Why would they have preferred these environments?

For many years, they did not move onto the plain. They did not know how to use this land where floods rolled over the river banks and rains rarely fell. Eventually, some of the hill- and swamp-dwellers decided to venture out onto the plain. They knew the plain would be good for farming. Flat land could be easily ploughed. The silt left behind by the river would be fertile. But to use this soil, farmers would have to find a way to control the floods and to bring water to their crops.

At first, the plains-dwellers lived on the banks of the rivers. They dug trenches through the banks in order to bring water to the fields where they would grow crops. They established villages and dug canals to bring water further from the river. To protect their fields from floods, they built dikes.

They were the first people that we know of to use irrigation instead of natural rain to make their crops grow. They had learned to change their physical environment in order to make better use of it.

In about 4000 B.C., new people arrived on the plain. We do not know where they came from or how they had lived. Perhaps they came from the hills to the north or from the swamps to the south. They took over the new settlements and made many improvements. We call them the Sumerians. The civilization they established is known as Sumer.

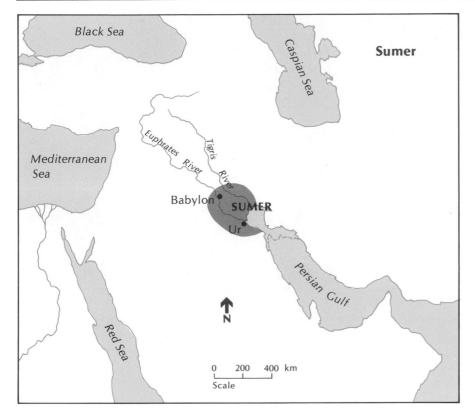

Sumer occupied the valley of the Tigris and Euphrates and the swamps where the rivers entered the Persian Gulf. Refer back to the map of Mesopotamia on page 29. What physical conditions to the north and south limited the size of Sumer?

1. Describe the conditions that limited the use of the land along the Tigris and Euphrates rivers.
2. Explain how flooding helps make good farmland.

Building a Civilization on the Plain

The farming of the plain provided the basis of the civilization of Sumer. The irrigated fields between and near the rivers produced huge crops. The Sumerians built an intricate network of canals, dikes, dams, reservoirs and drainage ditches to provide irrigation and flood control.

The main harvest took place in late spring, a time when floods surged down the rivers. To save their crops from the floods, the Sumerians built dikes that kept the water from spilling onto the fields.

INTERPRETING A SUMERIAN CLAY TABLET

This map is adapted from one found on a Sumerian clay tablet.

1. Locate and describe the farm fields.
2. Describe how water is brought to the fields.
3. Describe how people would get from one field to another.
4. Decide who owns each field. On what do you base your decision?

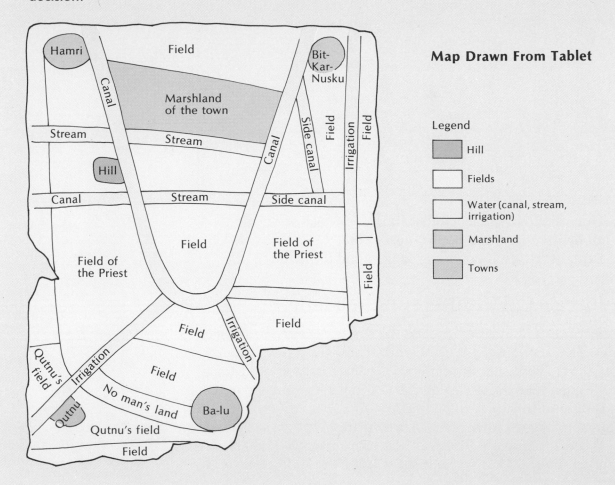

Map Drawn From Tablet

Legend

Hill

Fields

Water (canal, stream, irrigation)

Marshland

Towns

The Sumerians relied on three basic crops: barley, dates and sesame seeds. Wheat, millet, onions, cucumbers, and other fruits and vegetables were also grown.

The environment of the Sumerians provided fruits and vegetables for food. The people cultivated staple crops to ensure a plentiful food supply. What does this scene, taken from an ancient carving, show?

Barley, a type of grain, grew wild in the areas east and north of Mesopotamia. People who lived in these areas eventually learned how to grow this barley in their gardens. In Sumer, barley was the main crop. It was used mainly to make a flour or meal that was baked into a flat barley bread. This bread was the basic food of the Sumerians. Barley was also used to make a type of cereal and to make barley beer, a popular drink with the Sumerians.

Date palms grew wild along the river banks and in the marshes of Mesopotamia. Iraq is still the largest producer of dates in the world. The Sumerians not only picked these wild dates, but also planted their own large date orchards. They ate the dates raw or dried, or made them into wine. The leaves from the palm tree were used for house **thatching**, palm fibres for matting and the palm trunk wood for building.

The sesame plant is one of the oldest herbs known to people. It is valued for its seeds, used in baking and for seasoning, but most of all for oil. Sesame seeds are up to 50 percent oil. They were the major source of cooking oil for the Sumerians.

The Sumerians raised sheep, goats, pigs and cattle. The sheep were especially valued for their wool. In the early days of Sumer, people wore simple sheepskins as clothing. As time went on, they learned to card, spin and weave the wool into cloth that could be used for clothing or traded to other places.

The Growth of Cities and Trade

Because the Sumerians were very successful farmers, there was abundant food in Sumer. The population increased. Not everyone had to work on the farms to feed themselves. The villages became towns and then cities as people moved away from the farms to work in these communities. The Sumerians were the first city dwellers in the world. We think that some cities were home to as many as a quarter of a million people.

The people of the cities became artisans, workers skilled in making cloth, pottery and jewellery. Some worked as boatmen or traders, others worked in their own homes or in the households of the priests. As the cities developed, the economy of Sumer became more complicated.

Although the Sumerians had plenty of food, the plain provided no stone, metals, timber or grapevines. If they wanted these, they would have to get them somewhere else.

From early days, there had been much movement of peoples, ideas and goods between the plain and surrounding areas. Land routes led across the plain and into the hills. Water routes, via the Persian Gulf or the rivers, were easily accessible. The Sumerians were able to develop a trading system that brought them many goods. From the north, they obtained stone, metals, timber and a type of sticky petroleum oil called bitumen (bə tyü′mən). From the area to the south came copper and luxury goods such as pearls and ivory.

At first, the Sumerians traded surplus barley for these goods. But because the sacks of barley were large and heavy, it was difficult and expensive to send them over long distances. The Sumerians began to manufacture trading goods that they could transport more easily. They used wool to make woollen cloth. They traded the cloth for silver, gold and copper. Using their own ideas and those from other areas, they learned methods of mixing copper and tin to make bronze and improved methods of working these metals. They then made these metals into fine vessels and ornaments such as necklaces, statues and bowls. These, in turn, they could trade for timber, precious stones like rubies and sapphires, and other goods.

Inside Sumer, barley was still used as a method of payment. Housing, clothing or pottery could be traded for barley. Workers were paid in barley. A certain weight of barley was considered worth a certain number of hours of work.

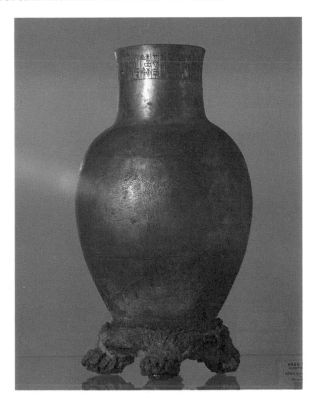

Surplus food meant not everyone had to work at farming. Some people became artisans, creating items like this silver vase crafted over 5000 years ago.

THE DEVELOPMENT OF WRITING

For hundreds of years, people in what was once Mesopotamia have used bricks from ancient cities to build their houses. They did not care that some of the bricks were oddly shaped and had strange markings on them. They did not realize these bricks had on them the first evidence in the world of written language.

The Sumerians developed this language in order to keep records of their farming and trading.

One mark indicates a number. The other mark indicates what is being counted. These are called pictograms because each mark is a picture showing a meaning.

A system of pictograms has limits. You would find it difficult to write a pictogram for 3000 sacks of barley. In time, the Sumerians began to use signs instead of pictures. Each sign represented a different word. These signs are known as ideograms.

Ideograms are also limited. Imagine how difficult writing would be if you had to memorize a different sign for each word. The Sumerians took another step forward. They began to use signs to represent sounds. This is known as phonetic writing. Phonetics are the

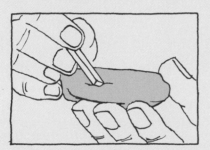

To make a crescent, insert a corner of the reed in the clay.

Here is how the crescent appears.

To make a wedge, insert a corner of the reed in the clay as before.

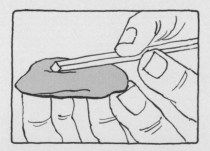

Then, lower the edge of the reed to mark the clay.

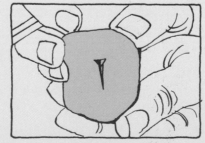

Here is how a wedge appears.

Crescents and wedges were the basic shapes in Sumerian cuneiform.

basis of our writing system and of most of the writing systems in the world.

The Sumerians wrote on wet clay tablets with the point of a **reed**. Once the tablet was full, it was allowed to dry and harden in the sun. This hardened tablet made a permanent record.

It is difficult to make curved symbols with a reed on clay. The symbols developed in Sumer are made up of long, thin triangles. They are known as cuneiform.

Because the Sumerian cuneiform system was not a simple system to learn, few Sumerians learned to read and write. Those who did studied for many years to master the system. When they graduated from school, they were given the title of "scribe."

The scribes of Sumer were important people. They served as priests in the temples, as record-keepers for the palace and the courts and as accountants in places of business.

1. What connections did the Sumerian writing system have to the natural environment? Did anything about the environment determine how the writing system developed? What?
2. Why were scribes important in Sumerian society?

A Sumerian clay tablet and envelope.

Original pictograph	Cuneiform	Early Babylonian	Assyrian	Meaning
				bird
				fish
				donkey
				ox
				sun day
				grain

Government and Religion in Sumer

In order to farm the plain of Mesopotamia, the Sumerians had to co-operate to control the rivers. The citizens of each area had to work together to dig canals, build dikes and clean out the mud and reeds that constantly clogged the canals. This co-operation was the basis of government in Sumer.

Voting was not the way in which the Sumerians decided how to co-operate. They did what they were told by the god of the city. In the early days of Sumer, a council of leading citizens decided what the god wanted them to do. As time went on, power passed to priests and to a main leader of the city. This leader came to be known as the *lugal*, a title which roughly means "king." Often a king would choose his son as his successor, saying that the city god had approved of his choice.

The gods played a big part in the government of Sumer. The Sumerians believed that all the gods lived on the distant mountaintops, and that they had created people to bring them food and do their work. Each god had control of certain things, and each city was ruled by a different god. In his or her city, a god's word was absolute.

The king and priests acted as the god's interpreters as they told the people what the god wanted them to do. They had interesting ways of deciding what the god wanted. One way was to examine the liver and lungs of a newly-killed sheep. The shape of these organs would tell the kings and priests whether or not to go to war, or whether to build a new canal.

The priests administered the land in and around the city on behalf of the god who owned the city. Sometimes, they rented out land to farmers in return for part of the crop. Sometimes, they hired workers to farm the land, paying them in barley, wool and sesame oil.

As the people of each city irrigated and used fields further and further away from where they lived, they clashed with people from other cities. Priests and kings from different cities argued about who had the right to certain areas or to the water from certain canals. Each city had a small army that could be used for defence against or for attacks on other cities. In times of war, the king could call up farmers or other citizens to fight for their city.

When the city won a battle, people believed that their victory was due to the strength of their city's god. When the city lost, it was because the god was too weak. A victorious city sometimes claimed that, since it had a stronger god, it had the right to rule its defeated enemies.

Almost every Sumerian city contained a **ziggurat** (zig′ù rat′), a large temple dedicated to the god of the city. The Sumerians believed that their gods usually lived on the mountaintops. Therefore, they built the ziggurat high above the ground to make it comfortable for the god. The priests, workers and artisans who worked for the gods lived in the area near the ziggurat.

Ziggurats, such as this one at Ur, were built to provide a high place for gods to live. The temple on top was a sacred place and only priests could enter.

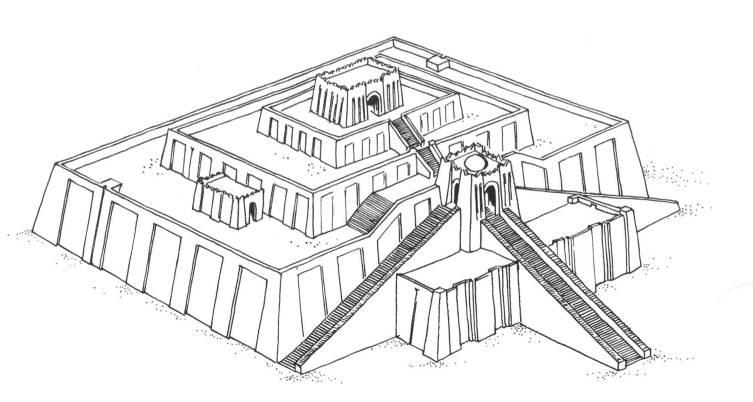

The stairway at the front of a large ziggurat. Notice the mud bricks that have been used in the construction of this temple.

The ziggurat was made of layer upon layer of mud bricks, in the shape of a pyramid with many tiers. It was solid inside, the dried mud held together with reed matting. One typical ziggurat was seventy-two by fifty-four metres at the base and twenty-six metres high.

The temple at the top, serving as the god's home, was decorated with beautiful materials such as ivory and gold. Stone figures of bulls and lions guarded the temple. Inside was a room where offerings of food and goods were made to the gods.

Everyday Life in Sumer

Imagine that you are standing in the middle of a plain in southern Mesopotamia. In front of you are green fields where barley is growing. You cross a canal on a bridge made of palm tree trunks. You see men and children working in the fields. Oxen strain along a path beside a big canal, pulling a raft loaded with goods upstream. A crew of men is cleaning reeds and digging mud out of another canal. A farmer is opening a gate to let water into the field.

There are a few huts scattered around the fields. They are round and made of reed matting bent inwards on a skeleton of reeds. Some of the people working in the fields are wearing capes made of sheepskins, with the fleece turned outwards. Most are dressed in simple tunics made of rough woollen cloth.

You walk on. Soon, you are entering a city through tall gates in a mud brick wall. The streets are narrow and twisting. On each side of you are the long walls of houses joined together, broken only by doors that lead inside. There are also small shrines to

The environment of Sumer provided a good living for the people. Nobles and priests enjoyed luxuries that most people did not get.

minor gods along the wall. At one of these shrines, a man is placing barley and asking the god to make his journey safe.

You walk through one of the doors into a Sumerian house. It is made of bricks of mud mixed with straw and dried in the hot summer sun. A passageway leads you to a central courtyard. At one side is a hearth–a place for the cooking fire–made of dried clay. A woman and a girl, dressed in tunics of woollen cloth, are by the hearth, making flat bread from barley flour. Not far away are huge pottery jars, full of water, sunk into the clay floor.

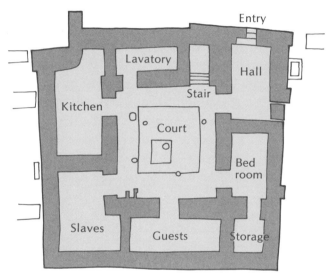

The floor plan of a wealthy person's house in Sumer. Much of the evidence we have about the past comes from the wealthier groups in a society. They could afford large houses built of permanent materials while average people built their homes of less durable substances. Compare this floor plan with that of a modern-day house.

Several open doorways lead from the courtyard. Inside one is a bedroom with a few low beds made of palm tree wood and bricks. In another room are several low platforms and chairs with backs made from woven reeds and a low table that looks like it might be used as a dinner table. Another doorway leads to a washroom. Water held in large clay jars is available for washing; a hole in the floor opens onto drains that lead to the river.

Going back outside and walking farther down the street, you come upon workshops. In some, artisans are pounding metal to make copper jars. Others are weaving cloth. Some are making pottery that will be fired in an oven to make it hard and strong.

The streets are getting steeper now. You arrive at the area near the ziggurat. The priests and king's servants wear fine robes made of woven wool. Priests are working in their kitchen preparing a meal for the god: mutton, bread, cakes, barley beer and turtledoves.

Nearby, you also see a room of boys who are all busy making marks on clay tablets with reeds. This is the schoolroom. When they have completed their training, these boys will become scribes or priests.

You climb to the top of the ziggurat: all is quiet. As an ordinary person, you cannot enter the temple. Instead, you turn and look out over the lands of the city that stretch for many kilometres across the plain. Then you begin to descend again into the hustle and bustle of everyday life in Sumer.

1. Group the items in the list below into two categories; those the Sumerians mainly grew or made for themselves, and those they mostly got from other people.

bitumen	grapevines	ivory	dates
timber	bronze vessels	pottery	
woollen cloth	barley	gold	

2. Under the title "Sumerian Crops" in your notebook, draw three columns. Write the headings "Barley," "Date Palms" and "Sesame Oil" at the tops of the columns. List the major uses of each crop.
3. Explain what irrigation is, and why the people of Sumer needed it.
4. In several sentences, explain what a ziggurat was used for, who lived there, and who worked there.
5. (a) Why did the Sumerians develop a system of writing?
   (b) Why is writing important to a civilization?
   (c) How would your life be different if you could not read and write?
6. List some reasons for the growth of cities in Sumer.
7. How was life in Sumerian cities different from life in the countryside?
8. Why was the growth of cities important to the growth of civilization?

BABYLONIA

The Environment and Origins of Babylonia

The civilization we call Sumer lasted for over 1000 years. During this time, the Sumerians made many changes in their physical environment that helped develop their civilization. They used the river to turn the desert into farms. They built hundreds of kilometres of canals and ditches. They used clay, mud and straw to make bricks and build cities.

The changes the Sumerians made to their environment helped their civilization to prosper. These changes, however, may also have weakened the cities. The water used for irrigation carried fertile silt to the fields. But it also carried harmful salts. Too much salt kills plants. As more and more water from the rivers was used to irrigate the fields, the soil became saltier and saltier. In time, the land grew nothing at all.

Some historians suggest that, as the fields of southern Mesopotamia became less fertile, the cities there became less powerful. Without adequate food to feed their people, these cities could no longer grow and thrive. Slowly, they began to lose their economic strength as traders and merchants moved to more active areas. Without economic vitality, they lost political power and military strength. New cities, on more fertile lands, grew and became more powerful.

As we see on the map and the time line, between 2350 and 1900 B.C. a succession of **invaders** from the hills and deserts to the east and west of Sumer overran its cities. Some of these invaders plundered the cities, carrying away all the valuable goods. Others remained, taking control of the cities and adapting to the Sumerian way of life. Among the invaders were various peoples from the western deserts, known as Semites.

One group of these Semitic people, known as the Amorites (am'ə rīt's), took over the small town of Babylon, located near the

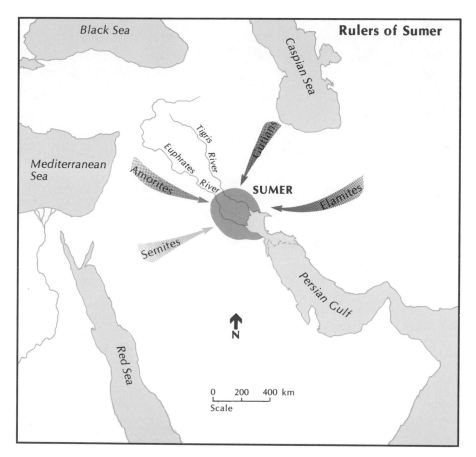

Rulers of Sumer

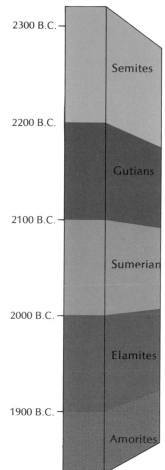

A number of groups wrestled for control of Sumer between 2300 and 1900 B.C.

point where the Tigris and Euphrates flow close together. Babylon had never been an important town and the Amorites set out to change this.

Hammurabi (ham'ù rab'ï), the sixth Amorite king of Babylon, wanted to make it the leading city of southern Mesopotamia. He built new walls to protect the city and new canals and dikes to improve its crops. He had two magnificent palaces built, one for himself and the other to serve as the temple of the city's god, Marduk. By the time he died, Hammurabi had established an empire that covered most of Mesopotamia. This empire became known as Babylonia.

The city of Babylon was surrounded by a huge wall with eight gates. Why was it important that Babylon have strong fortifications?

The Economy of Babylonia

Like that of Sumer, the economy of Babylonia was based mainly on agriculture. In both Sumer and Babylonia, irrigated fields provided food. Sheep provided wool which, when made into cloth, could be used as an item of trade.

Land ownership and business practices in Babylonia, however, did not remain as they had been in Sumer. In Sumer, individuals could only rent the land from the priests, who controlled it on behalf of the gods. Most of the profits from trade went to the temple, because these profits were considered to belong to the gods.

By the time of Hammurabi, individuals in Babylonia owned much of the land around the cities. Artisans and merchants made and sold goods and kept most of their profits, although they did give a portion to the temple and to the king. Some artisans, such as carpenters, potters, spinners and weavers, formed guilds, associations where they worked together and shared business.

The Sumerians had not used money for buying and selling goods. Instead, they used a barter system, with value represented by certain quantities of grain. An amount of wood or metal, for example, could be exchanged for so many sacks of grain.

By the time of the Babylonians, grain was still a widely used medium of exchange inside Mesopotamia. However, a more

The most famous gate into Babylon was the Ishtar Gate, shown in the photo on the left. It was made of enamelled blue bricks. The decoration on a lyre, shown in the picture on the right, also demonstrates the skill of the artisans of Babylonia.

practical system was coming into use. In this system, a unit known as the *shekel* (shek' əl) weighed the same as 180 grains of barley. In turn, a *mina* (mī' nə) was worth 60 *shekels*, and a *talent* was worth 60 *minas*. These units were usually represented by pieces of precious metal, most often silver but sometimes copper or gold.

The *mina* was the most commonly used unit. Merchants who sold their goods in exchange for *minas* would always weigh the pieces of metal very carefully. They had to be sure the *minas* were equal to the value of the goods being sold.

This new system was one of the first uses of money in the world, yet it was still based on grain, a product of the Mesopotamian environment.

As they had been for the Sumerians, the Tigris and Euphrates were important trade routes for the Babylonians. Merchants often sent their goods downriver on boats or rafts. It was difficult for the simple boats of the Sumerians to make the return trip, sailing against the current. Oxen sometimes pulled the boats upriver or along the canals. More often, boats that had floated downriver would be taken apart and the wood sold. Goods shipped upriver were usually carried by donkey caravan.

Cargo was carried downriver in flatbottomed boats made of reeds and covered with skins. Suggest reasons why these materials were used to make the boats.

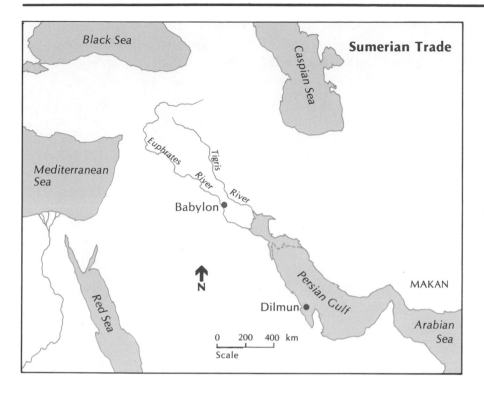

Dilmun was a convenient meeting place for traders. Goods from Babylonia were traded for raw materials from Makan and other distant lands.

Sometimes merchants sailed larger boats down to the rivers' mouths and into the Persian Gulf to reach more distant places. One such place was the port of Dilmun. Archaeologists think that Dilmun was located on what is today the island country of Bahrain (bä rān'), about 150 km south of the Mesopotamian coast, in the Persian Gulf.

Imagine the scene at Bahrain during Hammurabi's reign. A ship from the area known as Makan has just arrived at the dockside. The captain from the ship walks through the town square to the offices of the customs officials. There, they sip date wine and argue about how much must be paid to land the cargo.

Back on the ship, merchants from Babylonia are examining the cargo of copper. When the captain returns, the merchants barter with him for the ship's contents. They have woollen cloth and golden ornaments to trade. Finally, the merchants and the captain agree on an exchange. The copper is unloaded onto the dock.

Over the next week, the Makan ship will load with Mesopotamian goods. The merchants of Babylon will have the copper loaded onto their ship, ready to sail for the ports of the Euphrates.

1. (a) Describe the ways landholding in Babylonia was different from landholding in Sumer.
   (b) Suggest some advantages of each system of landholding.
2. In what ways is the use of *shekels*, *minas* and *talents* better than bartering using grain?

THE BABYLONIAN NUMERICAL SYSTEM AND CALENDAR

Unlike our mathematical system, which is based on multiples of ten, the Mesopotamians used a system based on sixty. All their numbers were expressed as parts of or multiples of sixty. Some parts of the "base-sixty" system still remain in our system: 360 degrees in a circle, sixty seconds in a minute, sixty minutes in an hour. Mesopotamian money also used the base-sixty system.

Babylonian scientists also devised a system for measuring time that is the basis of our modern-day calendar. They studied the cycles of the moon. The number of days between the appearance of two new moons was set as a month. Twelve such cycles made up a year.

The development of the calendar was especially important for farmers. They could plan ahead the times when they would plant, irrigate and harvest. They could predict what would happen in each month of the year.

Law and Government in Babylonia

The kings of the various cities of Babylon were often at war with each other. These wars were harmful to the economy of Babylonia. Men who were out fighting could not tend their farms, dig canals or produce goods in their workshops.

As Hammurabi extended his power throughout Babylonia, he tried to limit the power of the kings in the cities. He wanted them to stop fighting each other. Although he usually allowed the kings to continue ruling their own cities, he forced them to rule in the way he wanted.

To enforce his rule, he collected all the laws of Babylon in a code that would apply everywhere in the land. This system of laws, known as "Hammurabi's Code," is the most extensive law code that we know of from the ancient world. It dates from around 1800 B.C.

Below are some laws from Hammurabi's Code. As you read them, think about these questions:

1. What law applied if a slave was helped to escape? if an escaped slave was caught?
2. What kinds of animals were important in Babylonia? How do you know they were important?
3. For what crimes could someone have a hand cut off? For what crimes could people be put to death?

If a man stole either an ox, a sheep or an ass, or a pig or a boat: if it belonged to the church or state, he shall pay thirty times its value; if it belonged to a private citizen, he shall pay ten times its value. If the thief does not have enough to pay, he shall be put to death.
If a man helps a male or female slave to escape through the city gates, he shall be put to death.
If a man catches a slave in the open and takes him to his owner, the owner of the slave shall pay the man two *shekels* of silver.
If a son has struck his father, they shall cut off his hand.
If a physician performed a major operation with a bronze lancet and has caused the man's death, they shall cut off his hand.
If a veterinarian performs a major operation on an ox or an ass and has saved its life, the owner shall pay one-sixth of a *shekel* of silver. If the veterinarian has caused the animal's death, he shall give the owner one-fourth of its value.

1. Group the facts below under three columns: true only of Sumer; true only of Babylon; true of both Sumer and Babylon. Add two more facts under each column.

   • Some individuals owned land.

   • The economy was based on agriculture.

   • The gods owned all the land.

   • Irrigated fields provided food.

   • *Minas* were used as a unit of money.

   • The Tigris and Euphrates were important trade routes.

   • All profits went to the temple.

2. How had irrigation *harmed* the agriculture of southern Mesopotamia? How did this weaken its cities?
3. How were the Babylonian mathematical system and calendar the same as ours? How were they different?
4. Why did Hammurabi establish his code of laws? How are the laws of the code different from laws which we have today?

ASSYRIA

The Environment and Origins of Assyria

The landscape and climate of northern Mesopotamia are different from those of the south. Unlike the dry, easily flooded plains of southern Mesopotamia, the north is a hilly land. Here, the banks and riverbeds of the Euphrates and Tigris are mostly rock, not sand or clay as in the south. The rivers run faster and rarely flood. Northern winters are cooler and rainfall heavier, especially close to the mountains. The rain encourages trees, grass and other plants to grow more easily in the north than in the south.

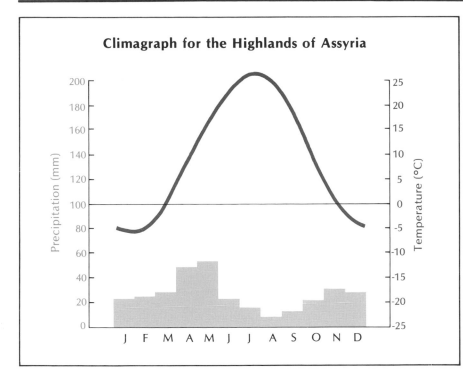

Climagraph for the Highlands of Assyria

Compare the temperatures and rainfall of Assyria with the climate information for Sumer on page 35. What are the differences?

The location of the city of Assur (ä' sür) had made it an important trading centre. On the major east-west routes between Mesopotamia and the surrounding lands, Assur was a major stop for the donkey caravans. These caravans carried tin and textiles from the east and returned with gold, silver and other luxuries from the west.

Partly because it was already an important economic centre, Assur gradually became an important political centre. In Babylon, after Hammurabi died, a number of weak kings occupied the throne. Under them, from about 1300 B.C. on, the Babylonian empire fell apart. As it collapsed, the kings of Assur began to take control of more and more of the area surrounding their city. Through a long succession of kings, wars and conquests, Assur came to dominate all of Mesopotamia. At the height of its power, around 650 B.C., the Assyrian empire included practically all the lands of the eastern Mediterranean, and reached as far as the Nile.

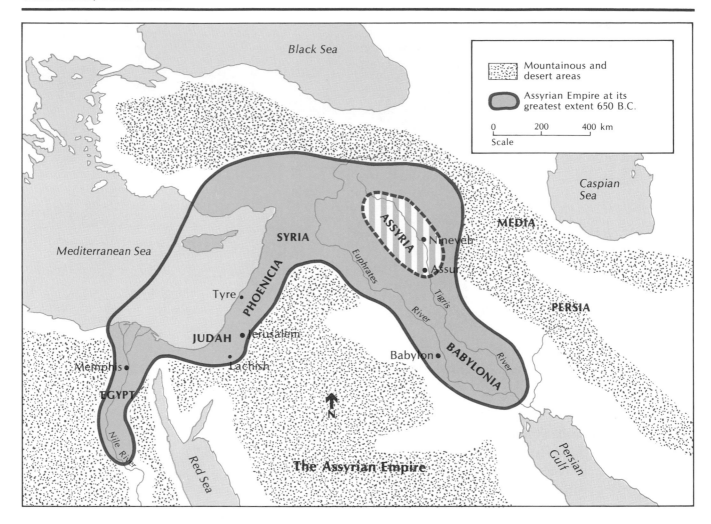

The Assyrian Empire

The Assyrians built the largest empire the world had seen to that time. They were feared for their cruel and heartless acts towards conquered people.

The Economy of Assyria

As the Babylonian empire fell apart, wandering tribes from the east began to take over the grazing lands on the edge of the desert. There were no natural barriers to keep invaders out of these lands. In years when drought struck, these tribes moved closer and closer to Assur, posing a danger to the city. Other tribes from the north sometimes swept down out of the mountains to raid trade caravans, loot towns and overrun farms.

ASSYRIAN PICTURE-CARVINGS

The Assyrian kings wanted to keep records of their accomplishments such as military victories and the construction of new cities and palaces.

One method they used to keep these records was to have the scribes write stories on clay tablets, just as the Sumerians and Babylonians had done. Several kings had many of the ancient tablets copied, and put together enormous libraries of tablets in their palaces.

The Assyrian kings also had artisans carve pictures in huge blocks of stone taken from the hills north of Assur. Some of these stone blocks, up to ten metres long, were placed in the king's palace. Magnificent figures of men, gods and animals were often carved from these stones. Stories of events were also shown through these pictures.

An Assyrian carving showing nobles hunting.

To make the trade routes and farm fields safe, the Assyrian kings decided they would have to control the lands to the east and west. Once they had conquered these lands, they forced the people to pay taxes. The taxes might be in food, animals, precious metals or timber. Each conquered king was expected to send gifts to the king of Assyria. If Assyrians needed anything they could not get through these gifts, they traded what they had for what they wanted.

Although many Assyrians were farmers, many others were soldiers. Some historians estimate that Assyria had more than 200 000 men in its army. Because so many Assyrian men worked as soldiers, and could not do other jobs, the Assyrians had to use prisoners of war to help with the building of canals, palaces, temples and city walls.

Until the time of the Assyrians, most weapons, tools and ornaments had been made of bronze (a mixture of copper and tin). Because both copper and tin were hard to find, weapons and tools made of bronze were expensive. They were particularly expensive in southern Mesopotamia, which had no natural sources of these metals. Usually only the people of the temple and the court could afford metal tools.

Bronze and iron weapons and tools used by Assyrians. What do you think each was used for?

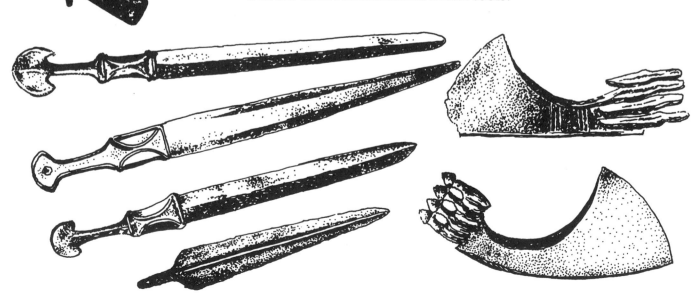

Iron, however, is one of the most common elements on earth. Much harder than tin, copper or bronze, iron can sometimes be found in ore at the surface of the earth; it need not be dug from deep in the ground. About 3000 years ago, people began to learn to use iron to make weapons and tools. The Hittites, who lived in Anatolia, north of Assyria, were the first to learn how to extract or separate iron from rock and to use it. When the Hittites entered Mesopotamia, they brought their skills with them. This new use of the physical environment changed the way of life of the Mesopotamians.

Since iron was readily available, the Assyrians began to find uses for it. Assyrian soldiers carried iron weapons, artisans worked with iron tools and farmers used iron ploughs.

The use of iron also affected the development of the wheel which was invented several thousand years before by the Sumerians. Wheels bound with iron were stronger and more useful than wooden wheels. They were soon used on the new horsedrawn chariots developed by the Assyrians.

1. How did the Assyrians use the people they conquered to increase their own prosperity?
2. Suggest reasons why the Assyrians were quick to use iron instead of bronze.

Government and the Army in Assyria

In some ways, the government of the Assyrian empire was similar to the government of Babylonia. A king, supported by priests, ruled the capital city and controlled the empire. The king and his advisors appointed men to run each part of the empire. He sent governors and officials to enforce the laws and collect taxes and **tribute**.

The Assyrians ruled their empire through fear. They thought that if their subjects were terrified enough, they would not dare to rebel. If a conquered territory did rebel, the army was sent in. The Assyrian kings were the first to have a permanent army made up of professional soldiers who were ready to fight at any time. The Assyrian army became the most powerful and efficient military force the world had ever seen.

When a conquered territory rebelled, the army would be sent in. Sometimes, just the army's arrival was enough to quiet the rebels. If not, the army would burn villages and kill thousands of people, often after torturing them. They sometimes whipped people to death, then stuck their heads on the city walls.

If even these measures did not succeed, the king might order that the subject people must be marched to a distant corner of the empire. Far from their own homes and customs, they would no longer have the courage to fight.

The Assyrian army won most of the battles it waged because it had weapons and techniques superior to those of its enemies. They used battering rams to break down the gates of a city. A wooden framework was mounted on wheels and covered with animal hides. Men were hidden inside and on the platform on top. The men on top shot arrows and spears, while the men inside pushed the ram up to the wall. The pike pole on the front was used to punch a hole in the gates.

The Assyrians used chariots drawn by horses. The charioteers were usually armed with swords and spears and protected by shields. Since no one else used horsedrawn chariots, they were a very effective force for the Assyrians. They moved much more easily and quickly than any other force.

Assyrian soldiers, with their iron weapons and advanced techniques, were able to easily defeat armies from other lands. What protective equipment does this soldier have?

Nineveh, Capital City of an Empire

King Sennacherib (sənak'ərib) ruled Assyria about 2700 years ago. His capital city was Nineveh (nin'ə və). British archaeologists have unearthed much of the ruins of the city and have given us a good idea of what Nineveh looked like and how its people lived.

The walls of Nineveh were thirteen kilometres long, built of mud brick with stone towers at intervals. Two walls and two ditches were arranged alternately, to make entry as difficult as possible for any enemy. The walls were as much as ten metres wide; the gateways were thirty-three metres high. The twenty-seven gates were guarded and supported by stone sphinxes and bulls. The city walls and the canals were constructed by slaves and prisoners of war.

Canals brought water from the hills to Nineveh. To bring the water across a valley, Sennacherib had an **aqueduct** built. This bridge to carry water was 300 m long and twenty-five metres wide; it is the first known aqueduct in the world.

Historians think that about 120 000 people lived within the walls of Nineveh. The richest were the king and the people of his court. They lived either in the magnificent palace or in spacious houses of fire-dried brick, and they dressed in fine cloth of wool, cotton or linen. Plants and seeds from all parts of the empire grew in the royal gardens. One such garden contained garlic, onions, leeks, mint, basil, thyme, saffron, corriander, rue and pistachios. The king owned great herds of sheep, goats, cattle and horses.

The slaves and poor people of Nineveh lived in much the same way as the ordinary people of Sumer had lived centuries before. They dwelt in small houses of mud brick, wore rough woollen clothing and drank date wine, a change from Sumerian barley beer.

Nineveh was capital of an empire for less than a century. Just after it reached its peak, in about 650 B.C., Assyria began to decline. The cruel measures the Assyrians used to keep subject peoples in line made these people hate the Assyrians. Sennacherib's grandsons failed to keep the army as powerful as it had been. Many parts of the empire began to rebel, and the army could not stop their rebellion. Medes from the east and Babylonians from the south jointly attacked Assyria, capturing and burning Nineveh. The Assyrian empire was at an end.

For just a century after the decline of Assyria, Babylon once again ruled Mesopotamia, having rebuilt its empire. Then it too lost power. The era of the great Mesopotamian civilizations came to a close.

King Sennacherib is seated on his throne in the capital city of Nineveh. In 612 B.C., Nineveh was captured by people from Persia.

1. Under the heading "Environment," make two columns in your notebook titled "Southern Mesopotamia" and "Northern Mesopotamia." In each column, write those words and phrases which best describe the landscape, soil, climate and vegetation of these two regions.
2. Which city was the first capital of Assyria? the last?
3. From whom did the Assyrians learn about iron? What uses did they make of iron?
4. Imagine that you are either an Assyrian soldier attacking a city or that you are a soldier defending the city against the Assyrians' attack. Write a page to describe the battle. Use specific details about your weapons, your fight, etc., in your description.
5. In your own words, summarize the reasons why the Mesopotamian empire ended. Make a statement as to how this knowledge can be applied to modern times.

SUMMARY

The Mesopotamian civilizations of Sumer, Babylonia and Assyria lasted for over 2000 years. During this time, the peoples of Mesopotamia used and changed their natural environment, and developed complex systems of economy and government.

The earliest of these civilizations, that of Sumer, was most closely tied to the environment. The Sumerians used irrigation to make their environment suitable for farming. They traded with other peoples to obtain necessities and luxuries their own region did not provide. They developed a system of writing, known as cuneiform, that was probably the first in the world. Religion was important in the government of Sumer. The priests and king, who lived near the ziggurat, home of the city god, interpreted the wishes of the gods.

As the civilization of early Sumer declined, an invading tribe, the Amorites, built up a kingdom centred on the city of Babylon. The Babylonians also depended heavily on the production of food through farming. Under the Amorites, the system of land ownership and profit changed, and private ownership became more important than ownership by the gods. The Babylonians developed a system of mathematics, a calendar and a system of units that could be used as money. Hammurabi, the greatest of the Babylonian kings, collected the laws of the kingdom in a code of law.

As Babylonia declined, the city of Assur in northern Mesopotamia became more powerful. The kings of this region conquered many lands to create the empire of Assyria. With a climate not as hot or dry as that of southern Mesopotamia, the north could produce crops with little or no irrigation. Unlike the south, the northern lands had deposits of ore. The Assyrians became the first Mesopotamian people to use iron extensively. The Assyrian army became the most effective military force the world had seen. We have learned much about Assyria from excavations in such places as Nineveh, the last capital of the Assyrian empire.

The influence of these early Mesopotamian civilizations is still felt. Their developments in writing, mathematics, irrigation, metalworking, tools, trade and transportation have had an impact throughout the world.

The lion was both hunted by nobles and kept by them as a pet. Shamash, god of the sun and of justice, had the lion as his symbol. Lions were also a popular subject for artisans. This lion relief, of glazed brick, is from a Babylonian palace.

Chapter Review: Mesopotamia

NEW WORDS AND IDEAS

1. Write a sentence to explain how each of the following people and places is important to a study of Mesopotamia.
   (a) the Tigris and Euphrates rivers
   (b) Babylon
   (c) Hammurabi
   (d) Hittites.

2. List all the advantages Mesopotamians gained from the Tigris and Euphrates rivers. What disadvantages did the rivers bring?

3. Unscramble the words below and then use them in a sentence:
   CAAEOORCLGYH   PPHIOGRICA
   GGRUTAIZ   PMEEIR
   ZALVIICTIION   CNOOMEY.
   GIIRRONTIA

4. The study of Mesopotamia has been divided into three parts: Sumer, Babylonia and Assyria. Write one or two sentences to describe the economy for each time period.

CHECKING YOUR UNDERSTANDING

5. Complete each of the following sentences:
   (a) Sumer became an important civilization after...
   (b) In order for a region to support a city in ancient times, they first had to...
   (c) The main difference between the government of Sumer and the government of Babylon was...
   (d) Some historians believe the civilization of Sumer was weakened after...
   (e) Both Sumer's and Babylon's economies were based on...
   (f) Money came into use because...
   (g) Hammurabi's most important achievement was...
   (h) It was easy for Assur to become a political centre since...
   (i) The Assyrians conquered other lands to achieve...
   (j) The Assyrians were able to defeat their enemies because they had the advantage of...

6. Choose any three important achievements of the Mesopotamians and explain how each one changed their society.

7. During which of the three civilizations of Mesopotamia would you have preferred to live if you were a farmer? a priest? a soldier?

8. List all the advantages you feel trading with money has over barter.

USING YOUR KNOWLEDGE

9. Civilizations and societies change all the time. Draw a time line, beginning with your year of birth and ending with this year. On it mark some important events that have occurred during the time period. They can be personal events, changes in your community, or world events. When you have finished your time line, write a paragraph about the event you feel has affected your life the most.

10. (a) When the early people of Mesopotamia learned to irrigate their crops they were changing the natural environment to meet their needs. How has the environment in your area been changed to meet people's needs?
    (b) Do you think that all the changes in the environment have been beneficial? Give reasons for your answer.

Chapter 3

Egypt

INTRODUCTION

The Land of Egypt Today

Imagine that you are in a plane flying north over Egypt. Directly below, you see a long green strip, split down the centre by the brown waters of the Nile. On each side of this narrow strip, golden cliffs rise to a brown and red desert. Far to the north, the green strip fans out as the river splits into several channels before it enters the Mediterranean.

The life-giving waters of the Nile create a narrow band of green across the desert. Estimate the width of the valley.

Land your airplane and walk along the valley. You see cities and dams and farms, all centred on the Nile. You see also the massive pyramids and carved lion feet of the Sphinx built 4000 years ago.

The people who built the pyramids were sure that the land of

Egypt would never change. They knew the Nile would always bring life to the farm fields and that the barren lands of the desert would always enclose the green valley. They thought the monuments they created would last forever.

Like the people of Mesopotamia, the Egyptians created a civilization based on a river. This civilization was similar to that of Mesopotamia in some ways, but very different in others.

EVIDENCE OF THE PAST

The ancient Egyptians buried their kings and nobles in tombs made of stone. They placed many everyday objects in these tombs, painted pictures on the tomb walls and carved statues of their kings and gods. Like the Mesopotamians, they developed a system of writing and left many written works.

Thousands of years later, we have opened the tombs and found the treasures. Archaeologists have discovered the bodies of the dead, preserved for centuries in their mummy wrappings. They have been able to translate the writings of Egyptians.

We also have information about the Egyptians that comes to us from other civilizations. The Mesopotamians and other Mediterranean peoples wrote about Egypt. We can consult Hebrew accounts in the Bible and later writings in Greek. From all this evidence, we have been able to put together a picture of the ancient Egyptians and their civilization.

The picture shown here is copied from one found in an Egyptian tomb. By looking at this picture, describe what you think life was like in ancient Egypt.

Pictures found in tombs provide us with important information about everyday life in Ancient Egypt. What can you learn about the Egyptians from this picture?

In this chapter, we will discover some of these similarities and differences. We will look at three different periods of the civilization of Ancient Egypt. These periods are known to us as the Old Kingdom, the Middle Kingdom and the New Kingdom.

The Nile: Basis for a Civilization

The Nile is one of the longest rivers in the world. It has two sources deep in the highlands of central Africa, the White Nile and the Blue Nile, so called because of the color of the water. When flooding, both rivers are muddy-brown because of the soil they are carrying away.

Below Khartoum, where the White Nile and Blue Nile join, the river flows through a desert of granite, sandstone and sand. This desert area is called Nubia. In 1850 km, the Nile tumbles through six series of waterfalls known as cataracts. The First Cataract, the one furthest north, rushes over a ridge of hard red granite. The First Cataract was the southern boundary of ancient Egypt.

Below the cataracts, the river flows slower and more peacefully. It has cut a deep path through soft limestone cliffs to form a valley that stretches north for more than 1000 km and is as wide as twenty kilometres. This land was known as Upper Egypt.

Further north, the cliffs level out and the river enters its delta. In this flat marshy land, the Nile formed many channels. In ancient times, the river had seven mouths on the Mediterranean. The Nile delta was known as Lower Egypt. Although it is the part of Egypt that is furthest north, the delta area was called "Lower Egypt" because it is where the river ends. The area known as "Upper Egypt" lay further south along the Nile.

Like the Euphrates, the Nile picks up tonnes of fertile silts on its trip north. Each spring, heavy rains fall in the highlands of Ethiopia, and swell the waters of the Nile. When these floodwaters reach the valley below the First Cataract, they overflow the river banks and spread silt and much needed water across the valley bottom.

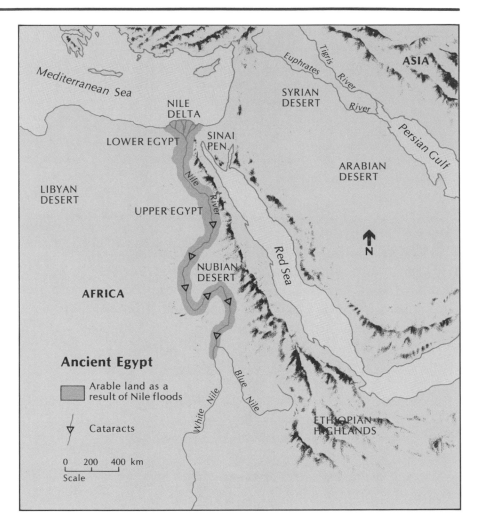

The Nile carries water from its source in the Ethiopian Highlands across the deserts of North Africa. In which direction does it flow?

Unlike the Tigris and Euphrates, the Nile floods every year at the same time. The floodwaters spread evenly, covering most of the valley floor for a month or more.

The Nile Valley slopes toward the Mediterranean at almost three times the slope of the Mesopotamian plain. The flood waters drain away by themselves, leaving behind a new layer of fertile black soil. Because the waters drain and do not evaporate, few harmful salts are left behind.

The ancient Egyptians called the Nile Valley the Black Land. Above it on both sides rose the cliffs that were the beginning of the deserts they called the Red Land. These cliffs are made up of rock and sand that are always dry. Rain rarely falls in Egypt. Areas not touched by the flood remain as dry as dust.

The lack of rain in Egypt has preserved much of what was buried in the tombs of Ancient Egypt that were located along the cliffs. However, little has been found on the valley floor or in the delta because of the moisture in the ground.

On the cliff tops and far beyond, as far as the eye can see, lies a barren desert of rock, dunes and sand that is the Red Land. Sometimes, the desert is broken by the palms of an **oasis**, or by a shallow valley, known as a *wadi*.

Lying between the equator and the Tropic of Capricorn, Egypt is a hot land. Temperatures in the desert can reach 50°C. The valley is cooled a little by winds that often blow upriver, from north to south.

Egyptian artifacts like this wall painting have been well preserved by the dry desert climate.

1. In a few words, explain the relationship between the Nile River and each of the following:
   (a) Central Africa
   (b) Khartoum
   (c) The Black Land
   (d) Lower Egypt.

2. Compare the Nile Valley and the Red Land using these headings: Elevation, Source of Moisture, Vegetation.

THE OLD KINGDOM

Thousands of years ago, the lands to the east and west of the Nile were not desert, as they are today. Enough rain fell to permit **nomads** in the area to gather food, hunt and keep grazing herds. Over the centuries, however, the area became drier and there were long periods of **drought**. The nomads found it more difficult to find food for themselves and their animals. They began to move into the Nile Valley.

At first, these people lived in small villages, hunting, and gardening small plots. Then, their life began to change. They began to improve their methods of farming and produced larger and better crops. They made sun-dried bricks from mud and built brick homes. They learned to work with metal and developed a system of writing. We think these changes probably began with the arrival of people from Mesopotamia, who brought many new ideas with them.

In the period before 3100 B.C., the villages and towns of Upper Egypt gradually became united under one king. Some archaeolo-

PEOPLE CHANGE NATURE

People have changed the physical environment in the thousands of years since the beginning of Egyptian civilization. The construction of the Aswan Dam, near the first cataract, has created one of the biggest changes. This dam regulates the flow of the Nile. Egypt can now release water as it is needed along the banks of the river. For this reason, the flow of water in the Nile today is not like what it was years ago. The chart below, however, shows the height of the water at Wadi Halfa, in Upper Egypt, for 1931-32, before the dam was built. We think it is very similar to the flow in ancient times.

May: 1.2 m
June: 1.2 m
July: from 1.2 to 4.6 m
August: from 4.6 to 8.2 m
September: from 8.2 to 7.6 m
October: from 7.6 to 5.5 m
November: from 5.5 to 3.3 m
December: from 3.3 to 2.6 m
January: from 2.6 to 2.1 m
February: from 2.1 to 1.5 m
March: from 1.5 to 1.2 m
April: 1.2 m

1. When was the water flow highest? When was it lowest? How much difference was there between the highest and the lowest flow?

2. When the water in the river rose, the valley floor was covered with water. When the water level fell, the farm fields emerged. At what time of the year do you think the Egyptians planted their crops? At what time of the year might they have harvested them?

3. Although the Nile was usually a dependable river, in some years little rain fell in the highlands of Ethiopia, the source of the Nile. The flow of the river was then much lower. In some years, the rains were unusually heavy, and the river rose higher than usual. What effects do you think unusually high or low water had on the people of Egypt?

gists think the same thing happened in Lower Egypt. In about 3050 B.C., the king of Upper Egypt took over Lower Egypt, uniting the two areas into one kingdom.

Egypt then entered what many historians think was its finest period. We call this period the Old Kingdom. It lasted from about 2700 B.C. to about 2200 B.C. It was during this time that the pyramids were built.

Egypt: Gift of the Nile

Hecataeus (hek'ə tā us') of Miletus, a Greek traveller who visited Egypt in about 500 B.C. wrote that Egypt was "the gift of the Nile." He saw that Egyptian civilization depended upon the Nile environment.

Every year in Egypt at the same time, the river waters rose and the floods came. This time from mid-June to September was known as *Akhet*, or flood. When the fields were covered with water during *Akhet*, thousands of workers were freed for tasks other than farming. They could then work on construction projects, or devote some time to religion, or develop their skills as artisans.

With the draining of the waters came *Peret*, the sowing season, lasting from October through February. Once the waters subsided, the Egyptian peasants planted their crops. Cultivation was easy in the moist silt. Farmers used simple wooden ploughs, then scattered the seed. Flocks of sheep which they drove across the fields trod the seed into the soil. *Shemu*, the season of harvest, lasted from March to the beginning of June. The farmers harvested their grain with a simple sickle and threshed it by having oxen or other animals trod on it. Egyptian farmers also grew vegetables and some fruits in gardens at the edge of the flood area.

Models showing everyday life were placed in Egyptian tombs. What is this Egyptian farmer doing?

The water, fertile silt and sun of the valley produced good crops and pasture. The farms produced enough food that some Egyptians did not need to work in the fields at all. These people moved to the towns to be near those others who were also freed of farm work; because of this, the towns grew.

The Egyptian Farmers' Year

Once the flood waters of the Nile receded, the farmers began to till the soil.

During the dry growing season, water was drained from the canals onto the fields to irrigate the crops.

Sickles were used to harvest the wheat.

By driving oxen over the wheat, the Egyptians separated the grain from the husks.

Because the Nile's waters flooded the valley, then receded, the Egyptians did not have to work hard at irrigation. They divided their fields into basins separated by high wide banks. They let the water into each basin, then channelled it on to the next basin when the soil in the first basin was wet enough. They also built canals to lead water to areas beyond the reach of the natural flood and dikes to protect their villages.

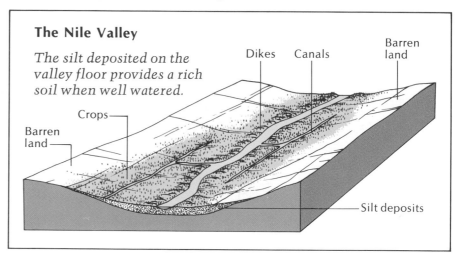

The Nile Valley

The silt deposited on the valley floor provides a rich soil when well watered.

Dikes Canals Barren land

Crops

Barren land

Silt deposits

Some farmers kept cattle, sheep, goats, donkeys and geese. The Egyptians tried, but failed, to domesticate such animals as cranes, gazelles and hyenas. Pictures show us that they also kept monkeys, dogs, and cats. Some cats were trained to retrieve birds killed in hunting expeditions.

The valley and the cliffs produced good farm crops and provided mud and some stone for building. To get gold, copper and semiprecious stones, or limestone, granite and sandstone, the Egyptians had to go to the desert.

Gold was one of the most important products of the desert. It was carried from the highlands to the desert by long-ago rivers. Mining gold in the hot dry climate was a difficult task, done by convicts, slaves and soldiers. In earliest times, gold was separated from the desert sand using water carried by donkey long distances from the Nile. But most of the gold was found below the surface of the earth trapped in a rock called quartz. Workers dug mines into the rock, heated the quartz so that pieces could be broken off the walls, carried the quartz outside, then ground it into fine dust. Then the gold was panned to separate it from the quartz.

The gold dust was heated for five days. When the gold was melted, impurities were separated from the pure gold. It was then formed into rings and shipped by donkey to the valley towns. There, it was weighed and made into beautiful jewellery or used to decorate a king's tomb.

The Egyptians traded with other areas for items which the valley and the desert did not provide. They obtained precious metals, ebony, panther skins and myrrh (a sweet-smelling gum) from Nubia in exchange for barley and wheat, oil, honey and clothing. Egyptian ships sailed to the Red Sea port of Punt for myrrh, ebony and silver. Egyptian papyrus paper was traded on the Mediterranean coast for cedar wood.

1. List ways the Egyptians made use of their physical environment to ensure a food supply.
2. Suggest reasons why the Egyptian civilizations started in the Nile Valley.
3. What did the Egyptians gain from contact with other peoples?

This lion's head, part of the treasure of Tutankhamen's tomb, illustrates the Egyptian artisans' ability to work with gold.

Religion and Government in the Old Kingdom

The centre of each small Egyptian community was the temple of the local god. Priests maintained these temples and accepted gifts from the townspeople. Sometimes priests from different temples argued with each other over which god was the more important and powerful. Let us look at some Egyptian beliefs about their gods.

The Egyptians believed that in the beginning all that existed was Nun, the ocean that covered the world. The first land emerged as a mound from this ocean. From this mound sprang the sungod Re. Also out of the ocean flowed the river god Hapi. Every year, the land appeared again from the floods caused by the

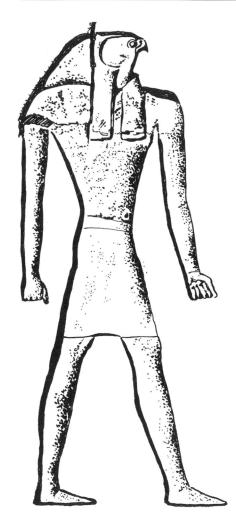

The falcon was the symbol for the Egyptian god of the sky, Horus. The Egyptians often pictured Horus with a human body, but the head of a falcon.

river; every day, as the sun rose then set, Re appeared then disappeared.

Every part of Egyptian religion related to the natural environment that surrounded the Egyptians. The river, the sun, the sky, the stars: all were gods. Horus, the god of the sky, was especially important. Here is the story of Horus:

In the days before people lived on Earth, Osiris, a god-king, was drowned by his evil younger brother, Seth. He tore the body into many pieces and scattered them far and wide. Isis, the wife of Osiris, found most of the pieces and put the body back together again and brought him back to life.

But Osiris could not come back to Earth because his body had been damaged. Instead, he reigned in the underworld. As people died, Osiris judged the way they had lived their lives; the good went to a land of plenty while the evil were devoured by a beast.

Together, Isis and Osiris had a child, Horus who reigned on Earth where he appeared as the king of Egypt. To the Egyptians, their king was therefore not only a man but also a god. Because Horus was both man and god, he could live both on Earth and in the sky.

An Egyptian poem describes the powers of the king:

The skies cloud over, the stars are obscured,
The vaults of heaven shake, the limbs of the earth god tremble,
All is still.
When they behold the king in all his divine power,
The dwellers of heaven serve him.
He roves across the heavens,
He roams through every land,
He, the most powerful, who has might over the mighty,
He the great one, is like a falcon who soars above the falcons
A god is he, older than the oldest.
Thousands serve him, make offerings to him.
His lifespan is eternity.
The borders of his power are infinity.

The king-god of the Old Kingdom wore both the red crown of Lower Egypt and the white crown of Upper Egypt. He owned all the land of Egypt and all its resources. If trade goods were needed, the king organized the expedition that went to get them. King Pepi II of the Sixth Dynasty, for example, sent an expedition deep into the centre of Africa, not only to seek new goods but also to search for the source of the Nile.

The king was in charge of the desert mines and the stone-cutting quarries. Stone could be used only for the buildings of the king and his servants. He could call on anyone to work for him. The farmers of the Old Kingdom usually spent part of their year working for the king. He took part of their crops, using some of it to feed his court and storing the rest to use in a year when the crop failed.

The king had many officials serving him. The most powerful was the *taty*. The *taty* supervised all the details of running the kingdom. Other officials, such as tax collectors, supervisors of farming, judges, and **scribes**, reported to the *taty*.

To supervise each province, or *nome*, the king appointed a *nomarch*. At first, the king appointed a new *nomarch* when the old one died. In time, however, the office became hereditary.

The position of king was also hereditary. But rather than passing from the king to his son, it passed through the king's daughters. The daughter's husband became king. There was often competition over who would marry the king's daughter. It was considered ideal for the king's son to marry the king's daughter, in order to keep the royal blood as pure as possible.

The Egyptians measured time in **dynasties**. As long as the new king was related to the old king, it was considered one dynasty.

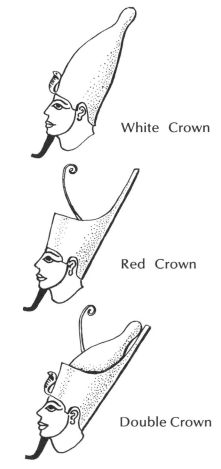

White Crown

Red Crown

Double Crown

During the Old Kingdom, the rulers of Egypt wore a double crown symbolizing the union of Upper and Lower Egypt.

EGYPTIAN CIVILIZATION

Major Divisions of Ancient Egypt

- Upper and Lower Egypt united
- Building of the Great Pyramids
- Reign of Tutankhamen

3000   2000   1000   B.C.   A.D.

2686-2181 Old Kingdom

2133-1786 Middle Kingdom

1567-1085 New Kingdom

OLD KINGDOM AND ITS DYNASTIES

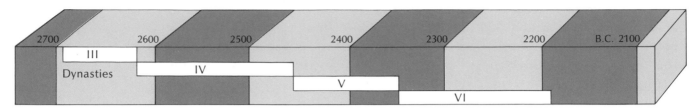

2700   2600   2500   2400   2300   2200   B.C. 2100

III

Dynasties   IV

V

VI

WRITING THE EGYPTIAN WAY

The Mesopotamians used writing mostly as a way to keep track of buying, selling and trading. The Egyptians, however, used writing largely in order to keep records of the dynasties and of the deeds and possessions of the kings.

The Egyptian way of writing was a system of pictograms known as **hieroglyphics** (hī′ər ə glif′ik). In this system, each picture represented a different sound. They wrote with reed pens and ink on paper made from papyrus, a type of bullrush that grows along the Nile.

The papyrus stalks were cut low, just above water level. The lower part of the stem was cut into sections, and the outer skin removed. What remained was cut into strips about half a centimetre thick. The strips were placed side by side, overlapping a little.

A second layer of strips was placed at right angles to the first. Then the strips were pounded with a wooden mallet for more than an hour until they formed a pulpy mass. The papyrus was left to dry, then was pressed in a wooden press or polished with a stone.

The Egyptians used ground charcoal mixed with water for black ink. For red ink, they used ochre, a type of red earth. Their pens were cut from reeds, with the end sharpened to a point to form a nib.

Four Steps in Making Papyrus ▶
1. *Papyrus stems are cut into strips.*
2. *Strips are arranged in layers.*
3. *Covered with a cloth, the strips are pounded into a pulpy sheet.*
4. *Dry sheets are polished with a stone.*

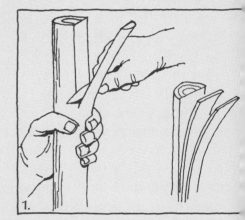

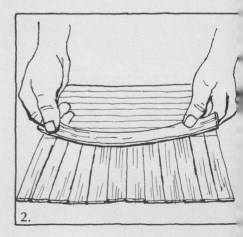

As soon as the new king came from a different family, a new dynasty began. The Old Kingdom was ruled by dynasties three through six.

1. List some of the powers of the Old Kingdom's king-gods.
2. The position of king-gods was hereditary and passed through the kings' daughters.
   (a) Suggest one advantage of this method of changing rulers.
   (b) Suggest other ways of passing leadership of a country from one person to the next.

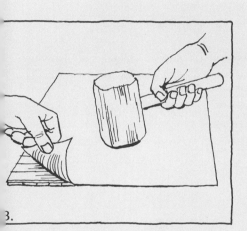

3.

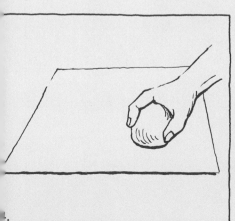

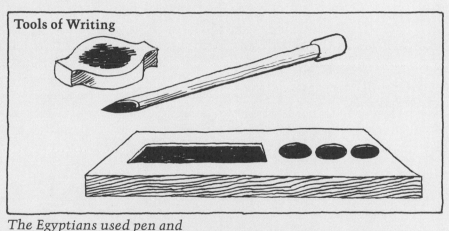

Tools of Writing

The Egyptians used pen and ink to write on the paper, just as we do today.

Weep

Sail upstream

Hill country, desert

Translations of Hieroglyphics

The World of the Living, the World of the Dead

The Egyptians depended heavily on the Nile for transportation. They could sail north with the current. Unlike the Mesopotamians, they could also sail upstream against the current, for the wind that blew from the north filled their sails. Let us join a boat that is carrying wine upstream from the delta, southbound to a noble's large farm at Assiut.

Traders used the Nile to move goods from one city to the next. Notice how all cities are located in the Nile Valley.

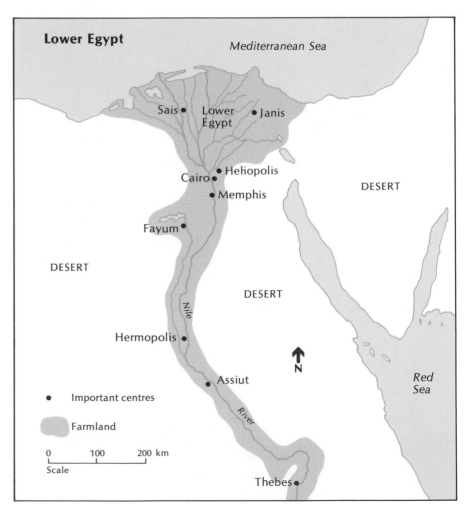

We leave the delta with the boat filled with clay jars of red wine. On either side of us at first are marshes filled with papyrus and reeds; hippos and crocodiles watch as we pass. Cattle graze in pastures. Now our branch of the river joins with another. We sail through wild country with the desert hills far in the background.

The next morning, the landscape has changed again. We sail between high banks with sluices, gates that can be opened to let river water onto the fields at floodtime. Beyond the palm trees that line the banks, men and women, most wearing simple linen loincloths or no clothes at all, work in the fields. Women fill their clay water jars at the river. Children play and shout near the tiny houses made of mud and reed matting. We pass a small town, built above the Nile's waters and surrounded by a dike of branches and mud. Most of the houses here are one room, made of mud bricks baked in the sun.

At noon the next day, we arrive at the noble's estate. His house is also made of dried mud brick, but it has many rooms and open courtyards. It is surrounded by a garden where exotic fruits and vegetables grow. The noble and his wife come to meet the boat.

Once the Egyptians mastered the use of the sail, they were able to travel as quickly upstream as down. Why was this important?

83

Mastaba hall

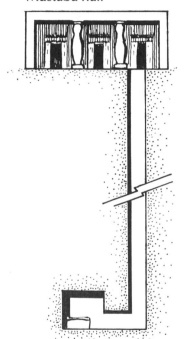

Mummy chamber 12-24 m below

The kings of Egypt had their bodies preserved after death so they could live on in the spirit world with the gods. Tombs were built to house their bodies and worldly goods. What materials were used to build the tombs?

They are dressed in fine linen clothing, and wear sparkling gold jewellery decorated with colored glass.

The wine is unloaded. Some will be drunk tonight, for the noble is hosting a banquet, where he will serve quail, pigeon stew, beef ribs, cakes and caviar, as well as barley bread and beer.

Empty now, the boat is moved to a new mooring. In the morning, workers will load it with barley for the return journey downstream to the delta of the Nile.

The king of Egypt lived even more extravagantly than the nobles did. In fact, the king wanted to continue to enjoy luxury even after he died. Because he was also a god, the king lived in the spirit world with the gods. After his death, he had to be able to return to his body on Earth. To do this, he needed a tomb where his body could be preserved after death, surrounded by the food, clothing and gold he would need whenever his spirit returned to his body.

Before the beginning of the Old Kingdom, the early kings had workers build them tombs that were called *mastabas*. They were flat-topped, slope-sided and made of mud brick.

Early in the Old Kingdom, King Djoser (joz′ər) turned planning for his tomb over to his *taty*, Imhotep. Imhotep created the first pyramid. As far as we know, this was the first stone building in the world.

Some 125 m by 104 m and sixty-one metres high, the Step Pyramid was built from enormous blocks of limestone brought from the cliffs and the desert. The steps in the pyramid were to enable the king to take his place among the star gods.

Two hundred years later, work was underway on the pyramid of King Khurfu. The Egyptians now believed that their king would go to join the sun-god Re as Re made his daily journey by boat across the sky. Khurfu would need a pyramid shaped like a sunburst, so he could climb on the rays of the sun to join Re.

Khurfu's pyramid was made of two million stone blocks, each weighing more than two tonnes. Some blocks were granite, shaped with stone hammers at the quarry where they were cut from the rock. The blocks were cut so precisely that a sheet of paper could not be slipped between them when they were placed

Egypt's oldest pyramid, the Step Pyramid, was built to be King Djoser's tomb.

together. We think that about 4000 people worked at any one time on the pyramids.

The Egyptians did not have iron tools, wheels, levels or computers. Yet the northwest corner of the Great Pyramid is only one centimetre lower than the southeast corner. It is almost exactly square, and its walls run exactly north-south and east-west. It is still the largest stone building on Earth. The Egyptians had to develop many ideas about geometry in order to accomplish such construction.

1. In your notebook, make three columns: (1) Akhet: the flood season; (2) Peret: the sowing season; (3) Shemu: the harvest season. Under each column, write the correct months and activities from this list:

March to early June	Flocks of sheep trod the soil into the earth.
mid-June to September	The fields were flooded.
October to February	The grain was cut with sickle. Oxen trod the grain in order to thresh it. Other work was done while the fields were flooded.

2. Match the names of the gods (on the left) to the part of the environment (on the right) which each one represented.

Re	the underworld
Hapi	the sky
Osiris	the river
Horus	the sun

3. In your own words, explain how the environment of the Nile Valley encouraged the development of writing, architecture, metalworking and religion in Egypt. Think about how the early Egyptians controlled or changed this environment and what they used from this environment.

THE MIDDLE KINGDOM

For 500 years, Egyptians had lived peacefully during the Old Kingdom. But there were signs warning that this peace would not last. The king was losing power to the nomarchs and priests. People fought over who would become king. The environment began to change. In some years around 2200 B.C., the rains did not come and the Nile did not flood. In other years around the same time, heavy rains sent unusually high floods across the valley, destroying dikes, canals and villages. With no strong king to save food for bad years, Egypt faced starvation. The kingdom fell apart into separate provinces. Nomads pushed into the delta area and Nubians raided Upper Egypt.

A writer living in the bad days described what life was like after the collapse of the Old Kingdom:

The wrongdoer is everywhere. A man takes his shield when he goes to plough. A man smites his brother. The robber has riches. He who possessed no property is now a man of wealth. He who had no yoke of oxen is now possessor of a herd. The owners of robes are now in rags. The children of princes are dashed against the walls.

Some princes wanted Egypt to return to the ways of the Old Kingdom. One, Akhtoy III, began to conquer the south and push the invaders back beyond the First Cataract. Then Menthuhotep, successor to Akhtoy, reconquered Lower Egypt. For the second time, all of Egypt came under the rule of one king. This new period, which we call the Middle Kingdom, lasted from about 2050 to about 1800 B.C. It was ruled by the kings of dynasties eleven and twelve.

Little changed between the days of the Old and the Middle Kingdom. The Egyptians saw little reason for change. They thought life had been perfect in the time of the gods, and that the ways of the Old Kingdom were as close as people could get to perfection. In addition, few strangers entered Egypt. For those reasons, the Egyptians adopted few new ideas in the Middle Kingdom.

During the Middle Kingdom, Egypt's artisans continued to create fine pieces of art, like this hippopotamus. How has it been decorated?

The Economy and Government of the Middle Kingdom

The rhythm of the Nile still ruled the economy of the country. Peasants once more worked seeding fields, clearing canals and building dikes. Farming was still the basis of Egyptian civilization.

After the end of the Old Kingdom, trade between Egypt and the rest of the world had almost stopped. The mines had been deserted. The Middle Kingdom kings reopened the trade routes and started up the mines again.

The king still controlled trade and mining in the Middle Kingdom. No merchant class developed to take charge of trade and commerce. But the king no longer had as much power as he had had in the Old Kingdom. The nomarchs and priests would not give up the power they had gained. The king had no large army that could force the nomarchs to give up their power. However, the nomarchs still pledged allegiance to the king and paid taxes to him. They needed peace in the land in order to prosper and live a good life.

The gold that came from Nubia and the deserts made Egypt a rich country. The king wanted to be sure that the mines would always be open. So that the Nubians would not raid Egypt again, Middle Kingdom kings sent troops to build forts and keep order south of the First Cataract.

Trading expeditions were sent south along the Nile and east along Mediterranean shores. Some expeditions went to Punt, on the east coast of Africa. They left from Coptos, on the Nile, and travelled overland by way of the Wadi Hammamat, then by ship to Punt.

Let us join one such expedition. In the middle of Coptos, men are loading donkeys with glass beads, linen and copper ornaments, plus twenty loaves of bread and two containers of water for each man. When the loading is finished, the donkey caravan heads into the desert hills. The sun is hot and the train travels slowly, but not too slowly. Before nightfall, it must reach one of the new wells dug recently by the king's men or there will not be water for the animals.

The next day, the caravan passes by a group of slaves outside one of the king's mines. Men wearing only loincloths and naked women and children toil in the hot sun, their bodies oiled and sweating.

After seven days' travel, the caravan reaches the sparkling waters of the Red Sea. Tied up by the shore with their sails furled

are the ships of the king's fleet. At the shore, the donkeys are unloaded. They will wait here for loads of myrrh, perfume and oils to be brought back by the ships that travel to Punt.

We do not know how these ships got to the Red Sea. Today, they could sail through the Suez Canal, but in ancient times,

Whether brought over land by donkey caravan or by ships sailing the Nile, trade goods brought wealth to Egypt.

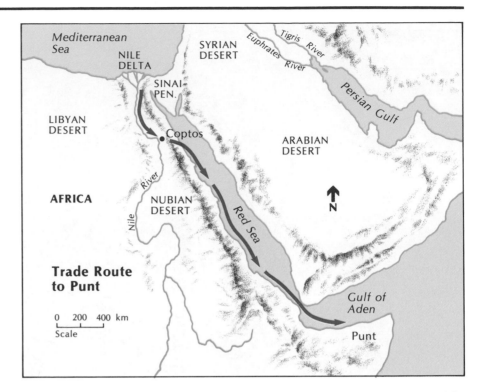

Trade goods from Lower Egypt were shipped up the Nile, across the desert by donkey, and then down the Red Sea to their destination in Punt. Why was this the easiest route?

there was no canal. Some historians suggest the ships were able to sail, unloaded, by way of a branch of the Nile during the flood season. Some say the ships were built on the Red Sea coast.

1. List the factors that contributed to the end of the Old Kingdom.
2. Explain how the kings of the Middle Kingdom brought prosperity back to Egypt.

The World of the Living, the World of the Dead

In the Middle Kingdom, people's beliefs about life after death began to change. The nomarchs and other nobles had gained more power. After the Old Kingdom, they had been able to get copies of the papyrus documents that told the kings how to

RECLAIMING THE FAYUM

Some of the first people to live in the valley of the Nile lived in the Fayum, a low, marshy area to the west of the Nile near the delta. By the early days of the Middle Kingdom, the marsh had shrunk to a fraction of its former size. The channel that led water from the Nile to the Fayum had filled up with silt carried there by the river.

Twelfth Dynasty kings decided to make the Fayum a place where many people could live and farm. They ordered the old channels cleared and new ones dug, and installed barriers and gates to control the water flow. They created a new lake, Lake Moeris (mēr'is), and dug channels from the lake to the land. In this way, they were able to create many thousands of hectares of new farm land.

The Fayum became very important to the Middle Kingdom economy. It provided a new base for the kings, who moved their capital to that area. King Amenenhat III, who ordered most of this work done, was especially proud of the Fayum. He built here large palaces and tombs, with more than 3500 rooms joined by winding corridors. He thought this would make it very difficult for thieves to find the riches buried with the king. He was wrong.

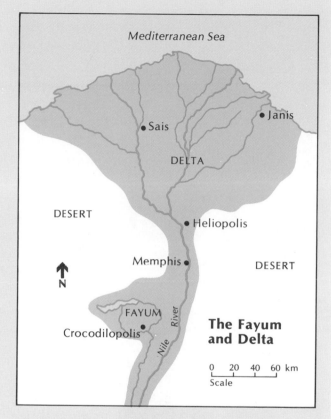

The Fayum and Delta

In time, robbers found the riches and the chambers and palaces were destroyed. We remember them today because of the name the Greeks gave them. They called this place the Labyrinth.

attain a life after death with the gods. They adapted these documents to make a guide for themselves. Some nomarchs and nobles had tombs built, and had food, gold and other riches placed next to their bodies.

Peasants also began to believe that they might live on after death. They would not go to live with gods, but would continue to live in spirit much as they had lived in body: farming, eating,

An Egyptian scribe at work.

Women busy making cloth in a weaving shop.

drinking. Since they could not afford to build tombs, they were usually buried in the desert.

Middle Kingdom kings and nobles built their tombs underground in order to foil the kind of robbers who had emptied Old Kingdom tombs after the fall of the Old Kingdom. They built ornate temples and gardens on top of the tombs. Often, they used stones from Old Kingdom pyramids and tombs.

Because the sun sets in the west, the Egyptians believed that the west was the land of the dead. All tombs and cemeteries were on the west side of the river. Many people were afraid to wander here after dark, because the dark belonged to the dead.

The tombs of the Middle Kingdom have provided much information about the world of the living. Some kings and nobles had placed in their tombs clay models of many activities that took place in daily life. These models show men making bread and beer and planting seeds, and show women making linen cloth and cooking meals. Ships sail and soldiers march.

1. What changes in the physical environment happened near the end of the Old Kingdom? How did these changes affect the life of the Egyptians?
2. What differences were there in government between the Old and Middle Kingdom? in religion?

Papyrus boats were used by fishermen on the Nile.

THE NEW KINGDOM

We are not sure why the Middle Kingdom collapsed. We know only that the kings were unable to resist invaders who swept in from the north and east.

Up until then, the Egyptians had been lucky. Egypt had been strong when Sumer, Babylon, and other areas had been strong. Armies from these areas had not challenged the Old and Middle Kingdoms. The natural boundaries of the Mediterranean, the desert and the cataracts of the Nile had protected Egypt from full-scale invasion.

By the time the Middle Kingdom collapsed, things had changed. A people from the east, the Kassites, pushed nomads, whom we know as the Hyskos, from their traditional lands just east of Egypt. The Hyskos swept down on the Nile delta, looking for new lands. They must have looked terrifying to the Egyptians. Their armies were led by men riding in wheeled chariots, pulled by horses. The Egyptians had no horses and used the wheel very little. As far as we know, the delta Egyptians did not even put up a fight, but let the Hyskos take over easily.

The Hyskos ruled Lower Egypt for more than 200 years, but did not invade Upper Egypt. It remained under the rule of priests who took over when the Middle Kingdom collapsed and established a new dynasty of kings.

Explain why horsedrawn chariots gave the Hyskos, a people from the east, a military advantage over Lower Egypt.

The Rise and Fall of the New Kingdom

With the arrival of the Hyskos, people from outside Egypt had conquered part of the Nile kingdom for the first time. For centuries, the Egyptians had believed that no enemy could cross the mountains, deserts and seas that guarded the borders of Egypt. The Hyskos proved them wrong.

Changes in technology overcame the natural barriers ending Egypt's traditional isolation. New ships sailed the Mediterranean and chariots strengthened invading armies. The kings of Upper Egypt realized that Egypt needed to change. It had to have a strong army and use new technology to drive out the invaders.

So the Egyptians adopted the horsedrawn chariot and expanded their armies.

In about 1567 B.C., King Ahmose, from Upper Egypt, and his army drove the Hyskos out of the delta. He reunified all of Egypt under the rule of the Eighteenth Dynasty, to begin what we know as the New Kingdom. Then he marched his armies south along the Nile and recaptured parts of Nubia. Amenhotep, a later king of the same dynasty, took over all of Nubia, then marched east across the Sinai Peninsula and conquered the land of Canaan. A later king moved into Syria, taking his troops as far as the upper Euphrates.

Because Egypt is so dry, Egyptian soldiers had never seen rain. Having never left Egypt before, they believed all rivers flowed from south to north. They called the rain "Nile falling from the sky." Their description of the Euphrates was "the river that in flowing north flows south."

Nomads lived along the Mediterranean coast and beside the chain of oases that bordered Egypt to the west. They often raided Egyptian villages in the time between the Middle and New Kingdoms, seeking plunder. Amenhotep decided to end this threat by moving Egyptian settlers into the oases and along the coast. He drove the nomads further west, increasing the distance between them and the Nile. This made it more difficult and less profitable for the nomads to raid Egypt.

The three dynasties of the New Kingdom ruled the empire for about 350 years. Toward the end of the Twentieth Dynasty, the Egyptians began to lose control of their empire. Kilometre by kilometre, they were forced to fall back toward the Nile. Even here, they were not safe. Mycenaeans (mī′sə nē′ən), known to the Egyptians as the People from the Sea, swept down upon the delta in about 1100 B.C. Libyans and Nubians swept into Egypt from the deserts. In 671 B.C., the Assyrians expanded their empire into Egypt. Then, in turn, the Babylonians, the Greeks, the Persians and the Romans each ruled Egypt.

The New Kingdom was the last great age of an independent Egypt in the ancient world. There are many possible answers to the question of why Egypt fell. The Egyptians did not want to

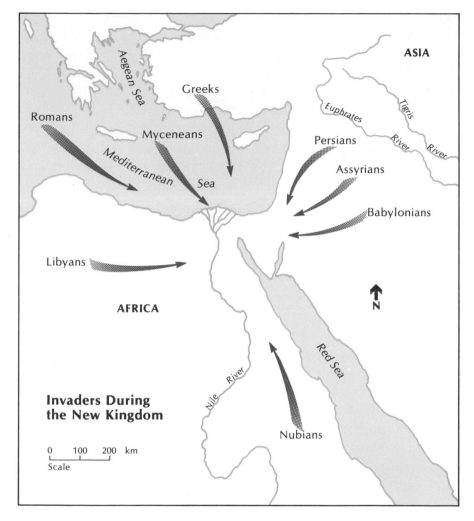

Invaders During the New Kingdom

0   100   200 km
Scale

Because of its wealth, Egypt was invaded by a number of attackers from many different lands. Describe the routes these invaders took.

fight outside their own borders or to change the way they lived. Other peoples with stronger and fiercer armies wanted the riches of Egypt, especially its gold.

1. List the factors that contributed to the end of the Middle Kingdom.
2. How did changes in technology help the Egyptians regain control of their country and begin the New Kingdom?
3. Suggest reasons why Egyptians attacked the people around the Euphrates River.

The Economy and Government of the New Kingdom

The New Kingdom brought many changes to the economy of Egypt. The kings of the Old and Middle Kingdom had sponsored some trading expeditions. Under the New Kingdom, Egypt received many more goods from distant areas. Some was loot taken by conquering soldiers. Some goods were demanded by Egyptian kings as tribute, payment made by conquered rulers. Cedar, horses, chariots, cattle, grain, elephant tusks, silver, precious stones, myrrh, baboons, ebony and ostrich plumes all came home to Egypt.

The armies also brought home prisoners. These prisoners became slaves who were set to work in the fields and mines, replacing men who had been taken into the army. But Egyptians did not really want to be soldiers invading new lands. They thought they would not have a life after death if they died in a foreign land. For this reason, the kings of Egypt took many foreign soldiers into their armies.

Although agriculture still depended on the regular rise and fall of the Nile, change did come to the fields. Many of these changes were the result of ideas that arrived with invaders or came from conquered lands. Many of these changes made life easier for average people. Stronger, larger ploughs with metal parts replaced the old, simple wooden plough. Curved metal sickles replaced sickles with cutting edges made of flint. A fat-tailed woolly sheep, like those we raise now, replaced an earlier type with twisted horizontal horns. Wheat largely replaced barley as the main crop. Wheat makes better flour and thus better bread than barley.

Under the New Kingdom, the king regained the absolute power he had had in the Old Kingdom. He even got a new name: Pharaoh (fer'ō), meaning "He of the Great House." The pharaoh's job was much larger now. He had an empire to govern and an army of more than 20 000 men to run. The pharaoh now had two *tatys*, one for the Upper Kingdom and one for the Lower King-

HATSHEPSUT, QUEEN OF EGYPT

The Egyptian rules said that only a man could be king. Only one woman ever set aside this custom. Hatshepsut (hät shehp'sut), daughter of the Pharaoh Thutmose, governed as pharaoh for twenty years.

Hatshepsut was able to take over power because Thutmose III, son of the pharaoh, was too young to rule when his father died. At first she reigned for the young boy, then she proclaimed herself pharaoh. She even wore the ceremonial beard pharaohs wore on court occasions.

She ruled well. Among her successes was the first expedition to Punt in several centuries. However, Thutmose III did not appreciate her control of his empire. When she finally died,

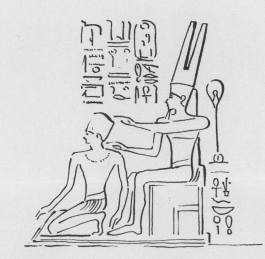

and he became pharaoh at last, he had all the drawings of Hatshepsut removed from her monuments.

dom. He had thousands of civil servants who reported to these *tatys*. They took a census (an official count) of cattle every two years, measured grain produced, raised men for the pharaoh's building projects, looked after the courts, collected taxes and kept records.

The pharaoh did not run his empire personally, but usually let the rulers of the conquered areas stay in command. He simply sent tax collectors and other administrators to the various parts of the empire. These officials were supposed to make sure the rulers sent regular taxes and tribute to the pharaoh.

1. Below are listed items the Egyptians received from other lands, either as loot or tribute. Suggest at least one use for each item:

cedar	cattle	silver	baboons
horses	grain	precious stones	ebony
chariots	elephant tusks	ostrich plumes	myrrh

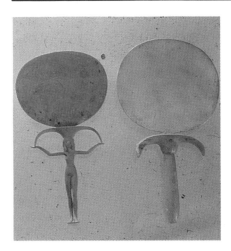

Hand mirrors of the ancient Egyptians.

Man's kilt   Woman's dress

Nobleman's   Priest's robes
costume

Clothing Styles

2. What problems might arise as a result of having large numbers of foreign soldiers in Egyptian armies?
3. Explain how each of the following benefited average people in the New Kingdom: metal ploughs, metal sickles, woolly sheep.

The World of the Living, the World of the Dead

Few of the changes in the New Kingdom affected the everyday life of the peasants. But there were some changes for the nobility. By the time of the New Kingdom, dress, hairstyles and make-up were all much fancier than they had been in previous dynasties.

A New Kingdom pharaoh might appear in a pleated, ornate, embroidered robe covered with tiny glass beads. These clothes, however, were still made of white linen. His sandals might be decorated with gold.

Egyptian women had always worn make-up. The first eye make-up was probably an ointment worn to help prevent eye disease. New Kingdom make-up might include green and dark grey eye shadow, and rouge and lipstick made from red ochre. A well-dressed New Kingdom noblewoman might wear a sheer linen robe covered with tiny pleats, tied with a brightly embroidered sash.

Both men and women oiled their bodies to keep their skin from drying in the hot dry climate. Myrrh and other scented oils were the most popular. New Kingdom jewellery was heavy and highly ornamented, made of gold, with semiprecious stones and glass beads.

Just as they took care of their bodies in life, the Egyptians wanted to be sure that their bodies would be preserved after death. Without a body, death would be final. New Kingdom Egyptians perfected the process of preserving bodies, known as mummification.

We think the Egyptians got the idea of mummification by seeing what happened to bodies buried in the hot, dry sands of the desert. These sands preserved the bodies almost perfectly.

But when bodies were hidden away in tombs, they decayed. Mummification was an artificial process of drying the body.

Kings and nobles underwent the most thorough and expensive mummification. Priests made cuts in the body and removed all the internal organs except the heart. They used forceps (a type of tweezers) to draw the brains out through one nostril. Then the body was covered with *natron*, a type of salt, and the organs put in jars and covered with *natron*. They were left to dry for several weeks.

Next, the organs were put back into the body. The priests stuffed the body with straw to restore its shape, painted the face with cosmetics and added artificial hair and false eyes if they thought it necessary. The body was then wrapped in bandages, with many layers around each body part.

Finally the mummy was placed in the tomb. A king or noble would be placed with his favorite tools and riches, needed for use in the next world. Noblewomen would be surrounded by fine clothing, jewellery and tools. Sheets of papyrus, with instructions telling the dead person how to answer the questions of the gods, were often placed in the tomb.

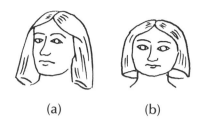

(a)   (b)

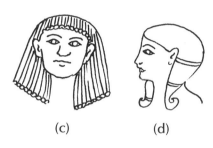

(c)   (d)

1. In your notebook, make three columns. Label them (1) Only Before the New Kingdom; (2) Only During the New Kingdom; (3) During the Old, Middle and New Kingdoms. Under each column, write the sentences below that belong.
   (a) Metalworkers used mostly copper.
   (b) Metalworkers used mostly bronze.
   (c) Wheat was the main crop.
   (d) Barley was the main crop.
   (e) The women wore eye make-up.
   (f) Agriculture was the basis of Egyptian civilization.
   (g) Ploughs with metal parts were widely used.
2. Identify and explain the forces that brought an end to Egypt's isolation.
3. How did their relationship with the environment influence the temples and tombs of the Egyptians?

(e)   (f)

Hair Styles
Old Kingdom
(a) man   (b) woman
Middle Kingdom
(c) man   (d) woman
New Kingdom
(e) man   (f) woman

TOMBS AND TEMPLES OF THE NEW KINGDOM

Thieves looted many of the above-ground tombs of Old Kingdom kings. New Kingdom pharaohs wanted to be sure they would rest undisturbed. They selected an area near Thebes, on the west bank of the river, for underground tombs to be built. These were huge, much larger than the underground tombs of the Middle Kingdom, with many rooms and passages built of stone. The builders and architects tried to hide the room containing the pharaoh or the noble and its treasures so that thieves could not discover it.

They were not successful. By the twentieth century A.D., almost every New Kingdom tomb had been looted. In 1922, however, British archaeologist Howard Carter found an untouched tomb. It was the tomb of Tutankhamen, a relatively unimportant king's son of the Eighteenth Dynasty. The treasures of this tomb were many and fabulous. They have travelled to museums around the world, enabling people in other countries to see some of the riches of Ancient Egypt. The picture on this page shows some of the treasures of Tutankhamen's tomb.

In the New Kingdom, temples to the gods were usually larger than tombs for the kings. The giant temples were modelled on the landscape of the Nile Valley. The pillars of the hall were set up like reeds and carved to look like papyrus or lotus. The temple shrine suggested a lowland where barley grew, and the tomb shrine represented an upland area where wheat grew. The shape of the temple resembled a valley where the flood would come, and the tomb was in the shape of a mound, like the islands of silt that emerged from the flood.

The beaten gold mask of King Tutankhamen.

Entrance to the Tomb of
Ramses VI

The largest of Egypt's temple
halls is found at Karnak. Some of
the columns in this hall measure
over twelve metres high and
eight metres around. How do
you suppose these columns were
built?

SUMMARY

The Nile Valley provided an environment suitable for the development of civilization. The growth of this civilization was speeded by ideas from Mesopotamia. The civilization was based on the environment of the Nile, but used elements from the deserts that surrounded the river valley.

Once unified, Egypt was ruled by a god-king who, the Egyptians believed, lived on after death. Over time, the king's power grew, then declined, then grew again.

The Egyptians based their beliefs on the environment around them. Their pyramids, tombs, temples and other buildings united the earthly world and the spiritual world. For the Egyptians, death was not final, but a step to a new life in the next world.

In the Old and Middle Kingdoms, the Egyptians were able to live a life that changed little over the centuries. In the New Kingdom, however, technology and new contacts with outside people forced the Egyptians to make many changes in their way of life.

The developing civilizations of Ancient Egypt produced magnificent monuments, fine art and other achievements that have not been equalled since.

The life-giving waters of the Nile have supported hundreds of generations of Egyptians.

Chapter Review: Egypt

NEW WORDS AND IDEAS

1. Use a dictionary to write a definition for each of the words listed below. Give an example of how each term is used in your study of Egypt.
   (a) artisan
   (b) cataracts
   (c) delta
   (d) dynasty
   (e) mummification
   (f) domesticate.

2. Copy the following sentences into your notebook and fill in each blank with the correct word(s):
   (a) The source of the Nile River is located in the _____ .
   (b) Egyptian kings of the _____ Kingdom were the first to build pyramids for their tombs.
   (c) Egyptian kings in the New Kingdom began to call themselves _____ .
   (d) The _____ were the people who introduced the horsedrawn chariot to the Egyptians.
   (e) Egyptian _____ kept records of daily life in Egypt by writing on sheets of paper made from _____ .

CHECKING YOUR UNDERSTANDING

3. Sketch a picture to show the difference between the Red Land and the Black Land of Ancient Egypt.

4. List the trade goods exchanged between the Egyptians and their trading partners.

5. Using the headings, the *pharaoh*, the *taty*, the *nomarch*, and other officials, write a description of the government of Ancient Egypt.

6. (a) How were the clothing, tools, buildings, and food of Egypt different from ours?
   (b) How were they the same?
   (c) Suggest ways in which the climate, vegetation, or landforms of Egypt were responsible for these differences and similarities between our culture and Egypt's.

7. The study of Egypt has been divided into three parts: the Old Kingdom, the Middle Kingdom, and the New Kingdom. Choose one or two events for each time period and explain how each one changed Egypt.

8. Explain how Egyptian beliefs were tied to their environment. Think about the powers of their gods, and the Egyptian beliefs about the afterlife to help you write your answer.

USING YOUR KNOWLEDGE

9. Tombs like Tutankhamen's help us understand the culture of the ancient Egyptians. The following items were found in Tutankhamen's tomb:
   (a) a gameboard
   (b) a trumpet made of copper and brass
   (c) a leopard-skin cloak.
   What can each of these objects tell us about the Egyptian way of life?

Chapter 4

Greece

INTRODUCTION

One of the most famous stories of ancient times, the myth of the Minotaur, is still popular today. It goes like this:

Columns like these found at Olympia, stand as evidence of the beauty of Greek architecture.

Pasiphae, the wife of King Minos of Crete, fell in love with a god of Crete, a god in the form of a bull. She gave birth to a half-bull, half-human creature known as the Minotaur. To house this vicious creature, King Minos ordered a long and winding series of tunnels to be built. At the centre of this, the Labyrinth, the Minotaur lived.

The true son of Minos was killed in a war with King Aegeus of Athens. As revenge, Minos forced Aegeus to send him, every few years, seven young men and seven young women. Minos then had these unfortunate youths slain and thrown into the Labyrinth as a sacrifice to the Minotaur. Eventually the son of King Aegeus, named Theseus, became one of the youths who was to be sacrificed.

Theseus was determined that he would live. He told his father to wait for his ship to return from Crete. If Aegeus saw a white sail, he would know Theseus was still alive. A black sail would mean Theseus was dead.

While in Crete awaiting his death, Theseus and Ariadne, the daughter of King Minos, fell in love. She gave Theseus a sword and a ball of string, whereupon Theseus went into the Labyrinth alone.

Unravelling the string as he went, Theseus made his way to the middle of the Labyrinth. There he found and slew the Minotaur. He simply followed the string to find his way back out.

Theseus took Ariadne and sailed for Athens. As the ship approached, the sailors mistakenly put up a black sail. Seeing this, Aegeus thought his son was dead and threw himself into the sea.

Theseus defeated the Minotaur and so freed Athens from paying tribute to King Minos of Crete. What makes the story of the Minotaur a good legend?

Even today, we call this sea the Aegean, after the name of this mythical king. In the lands around the Aegean, the Greeks built one of history's most remarkable civilizations. They wrote hundreds of stories, poems and plays about their gods, heroes, and the important people, places, and events of their day. This literature is a chief source of information about life in ancient Greece. Monuments like the *Parthenon*, in Athens, tell us about ancient Greek art and architecture. Designs on Greek pottery tell us about everyday life. Archaeological discoveries of the past century have also added to our knowledge of ancient Greece.

But the Greeks are important to us for more than just their stories and legends. Many of the ways we do things—from government, to art, to military methods—are based on ideas developed by people in Greece. Their ideas are alive today.

105

GREEK CIVILIZATION

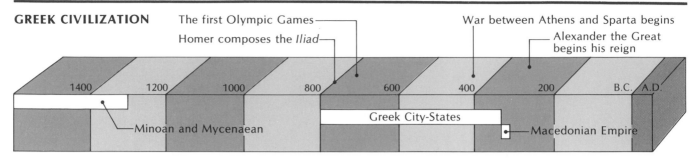

The first Olympic Games
Homer composes the *Iliad*
War between Athens and Sparta begins
Alexander the Great begins his reign

1400 1200 1000 800 600 400 200 B.C. A.D.

Minoan and Mycenaean

Greek City-States

Macedonian Empire

In this chapter, we will look at three major periods of Greek civilization. First, we will learn about the earliest civilizations, Crete and Mycenae (mī sē′ nē). We have only the barest knowledge of this time. Next, we will study "Classical Greece," a time dominated by the cities of Athens and Sparta. It was during the classical period that many of the ideas that shape our society were formed. Finally, we will look at Alexander the Great and the Macedonian (mas ədō′ nē ə) empire.

This map shows ancient Greece was composed of separate city-states separated by seas and rugged mountains. What water bodies were important to the Greeks?

Ancient Greece

MACEDON

Mt. Olympus △

Corcyra

Troy

Aegean Sea

PERSIAN EMPIRE

Delphi

Thebes

Ionian Sea

Corinth

Athens

Olympia

Mycenae

Miletus

Sparta

N

• Major cities

■ Important shrines and oracles

0   100   200 km

Scale

Knossos

CRETE

CRETE AND MYCENAE

The Earliest Greeks: Legend and Fact

The *Iliad*, a long story-poem by a Greek named Homer, tells of the Trojan War; a war between the Greeks and a rival city across the Aegean Sea, called Troy. This poem is read and enjoyed by people today, just as it was in ancient Greece.

THE LEGEND OF TROY

Troy was a rich and powerful city on the east coast of the Aegean Sea, in what is now Turkey. Priam was king of Troy, and his son was Paris.

On a visit to the Greek city of Sparta, Paris fell in love with Helen, the wife of Menelaus, king of Sparta. She was known as the most beautiful woman in the world. Paris kidnapped Helen and took her back to Troy.

Menelaus was enraged at this kidnapping of his wife and started a war on Troy. He enlisted the help of his brother, Agamemnon, king of nearby Mycenae, the most powerful of the Greek cities.

For many years the Greek soldiers tried to conquer Troy. But the great walls of the city could not be surmounted. The Greeks decided to play a trick.

Outside the walls of Troy, the Greek soldiers built a huge hollow wooden horse, in which a few of their number hid. The Greek leaders then told the Trojans that they were giving up the war and that the horse was an offering to the goddess Athena. They pretended to sail back to Greece.

Believing that the horse would bring them good luck, the Trojans hauled it inside the walls. The Greek soldiers inside the horse quietly crept out and opened the city gates while the Trojan soldiers slept.

The Greek armies waiting outside rushed in and overwhelmed the Trojans. They then burned the city down and took Helen back to Greece.

The Trojan Horse

In the nineteenth century most historians believed that the *Iliad* was not the story of a real event, but a story based on myths and legends. Heinrich Schliemann (shlē' män), a German businessman-turned-archaeologist, believed differently. As a boy, he had read the *Iliad*. He remained fascinated by the story throughout his adult life, convinced that it had really happened.

In 1870, Schliemann began to dig at a site in present-day Turkey, the area where Greek tradition claimed Troy had been. Near the village of Hissarlik, he found a mound of earth that matched the location of Troy as described in the *Iliad*.

As layer after layer of earth was removed, the ruins of not only one, but nine, cities were uncovered. Each city had been built on top of the ruins of an earlier one. At the seventh level, Schliemann found the remains of a city wealthy and old enough to have been Homer's Troy.

He now went in search of the Greeks who had conquered this city. The site he chose was the ruined city of Mycenae, one of the Greek cities mentioned by Homer.

In November 1876 Schliemann sent telegrams to *The Times* (London) and to the president of Greece, announcing he had found the grave of a warrior-king, buried with his bronze weapons and a golden funeral mask. "I have gazed upon the face of Agamemnon," the telegram read. Schliemann believed he had uncovered the grave of one of the Greek heroes of the Trojan War.

Schliemann also uncovered evidence that an early Greek civilization, wealthy enough to send an army to defeat Troy, had existed in 1200 B.C. Schliemann named this early Greek civilization Mycenaean, after the city of Mycenae.

A quarter-century after Schliemann's discovery at Mycenae, a British archaeologist, Arthur Evans, began work at a site called Knossos (nos' əs), on the island of Crete. Tradition claimed a civilization even earlier than that of Mycenae had existed here. Evans' excavation revealed a palace with small rooms and winding corridors. This palace reminded Evans of the Labyrinth, home of the mythical Minotaur. Believing the palace of Knossos could be the source of this myth, Evans named the civilization he

This fresco, uncovered during excavations at the Palace of Knossos, has been called "The Peaceful Prince." There are no names or titles written on the fresco. Why then do you think archaeologists believe this young man is a prince?

Above right: An example of Linear B writing. What information might have been recorded on clay tablets such as this?

Above left: Excavations at Knossos have uncovered artifacts that suggest a flourishing civilization existed on the island of Crete around 1400 B.C.

had excavated "Minoan."

From Knossos came the first evidence that these early Greeks had a written language. Three different styles of written language, all on clay tablets, were identified. Only the latest form, called Linear B, has been deciphered. These tablets have been dated from 1400-1200 B.C. This form of writing has been used as evidence to show that the Mycenaeans and the Minoans were the ancestors of modern day Greece.

1. In one or two paragraphs, summarize The Legend of Troy found on page 107. In writing your summary, answer the five important questions: Who?, What?, When?, Where?, and Why?
2. Heinrich Schliemann believed there was some truth to the story of the Trojan War. How did Schliemann convince other historians and archaeologists that he was right?
3. Why did Arthur Evans name the civilization he discovered on the island of Crete Minoan?
4. What evidence is there to show that the Minoan and Mycenaean civilizations were early Greek civilizations?

Origins and Environment of the Earliest Greeks

Farming communities have existed in mainland Greece since 6000 B.C. We do not know where these early farmers came from. The most accepted theory is that they migrated south from the land around the Black Sea. Crete's earliest settlers were also farmers. They had arrived by 4000 B.C., sailing across the Aegean Sea. Where their journey began no one knows for sure. By about 2000 B.C., the people of Crete had developed the civilization we call Minoan. About four centuries later, mainland Greeks of the Peloponnesian (pel'ə pə nē" shen) Peninsula had established the civilization we refer to as Mycenaean.

Let us look at the geographic features shared by both the Minoan and Mycenaean civilizations.

The river Peneios is one of Greece's few permanent rivers. Why would early Greeks have chosen to settle here, in the Thessalian Plain?

CLIMATE OF ATHENS

Climate statistics for a place usually include the average monthly temperature and the monthly precipitation. Average monthly temperatures are calculated in this way: (a) Record the highest and lowest temperatures each day; (b) Find the average of the two temperatures for each day; (c) Add the average daily temperatures for the month and divide by the number of days. The monthly precipitation figure is the total of all precipitation that falls during the month.

Normally climate statistics are averaged over a number of years. This evens out the effects of unusual weather conditions, such as a dry spring or warm winter.

Use the climate statistics for Athens, Greece, to answer these qustions.

1. Which months of the year are the warmest? the coldest?

2. Which season of the year gets the greatest amount of precipitation?

3. Using the climate statistics, give evidence to show Athens is in the northern hemisphere.

	Temperature (°C)	Precipitation (mm)
Jan.	10	62
Feb.	10	37
Mar.	12	37
Apr.	16	23
May	20	23
June	25	14
July	28	6
Aug.	28	7
Sept.	24	15
Oct.	20	51
Nov.	15	56
Dec.	11	71

Both are mountainous areas with narrow valleys, few fertile plains and few rivers. The climate is mild in winter and hot in summer. Most of Greece's rainfall occurs from October to March. This gives the region a long growing season, although it is dry during the summer months.

The higher slopes of the mountains once covered with forests provided timber and wild game. The lower slopes did not produce pastures rich enough for cattle, so goats and sheep were raised. The goats' milk was used to make a fine cheese and the wool of the sheep was spun and woven into cloth.

Grain was grown on the fertile plains, but olives and grapes became the most important crop. They were not only used as food, but were also turned into other products. Olives were pressed and their oils served for cooking, as lamp fuel and even

In "bull-leaping," a young man or woman would seize the horns of a charging bull. As the animal heaved the athlete into the air, he or she would try to do a somersault and land as gracefully as possible. "Bull-leaping" may have been as much a religious ceremony as a sport. The many pictures of bulls on Cretan pottery suggest that the bull was an object of worship. How does this help us to understand how the myth of the Minotaur developed?

as soap. Grapes were turned into wine. Both wine and olive oil became trade items for these early Greeks. Clay was found in great quantities throughout Greece and could be made into jars, cooking utensils, figurines, vases and writing tablets. Beautiful examples of the potter's craft have been found throughout Greece and the eastern Mediterranean.

Crete is an island, with many fine natural harbors. Its location in the middle of the Aegean (see map page 106) helped the Minoans gain control of sea trade routes. The resulting contact with other Mediterranean communities, such as Egypt, helped Minoan civilization develop. Historians think that the Minoans had a strong navy that successfully held off invasions for centuries. They think this because the palaces and towns that have been uncovered have few walls and guard towers.

The Minoans have left us with a picture of a people whose

rulers lived in comfort. Their drawings and frescoes (murals) show dancing, athletics, and festivals. "Bull-leaping" seems to have been a particularly important form of entertainment.

The Mycenaeans seem to have been more interested than the Minoans in war. Their grave sites reveal many weapons and pieces of armor. Mycenaean pottery recreates scenes of hunting and soldiers preparing for war. Unlike those of the Minoans, the Mycenaean palace walls are heavily fortified. Historians suggest the Mycenaeans developed a strong army as protection against raids from northern tribes or rival kingdoms of the Aegean.

Mycenaean architecture and pottery from before 1400 B.C. is less developed than the Minoan. After 1400 B.C., Mycenaean craftsmanship develops; Mycenaean palaces adopt much of the technology already known to the Minoans. The Mycenaeans became a powerful trading civilization around 1400 B.C. It was about this time that the Minoan power in the Aegean was decreasing.

Why Minoan civilization suddenly declined after 1400 B.C. is not known for sure. Mycenaean civilization began to disappear after 1200 B.C. Historians do have some suggestions, or **theories**, as to why. The next section looks at some of these theories.

1. Assume you are a farmer planning to settle near Athens. List the advantages and disadvantages of the Greek environment from a farmer's point of view.
2. Environments can both encourage and discourage the growth of civilizations. Sometimes an aspect of the environment can do both; a river benefits an area by bringing water but harms the community when it floods. Give one advantage and one disadvantage of each of the following:
   (a) climate of Greece
   (b) landscape of Greece
   (c) clay soils of Greece.
3. List the ways the Greeks used olives and grapes.
4. Why do archaeologists believe the Mycenaeans were more warlike than the Minoans?

The Fall of Crete and Mycenae

There are three theories that try to explain the fall of Crete.

One theory claims the eruption of a volcano on a nearby island ended Minoan civilization. Winds could have carried volcanic ash to Crete. The poisonous ash would have caused the soil of Crete to lose its fertility, forcing its people to migrate to other areas. A second theory argues that the Minoans' palaces and towns were destroyed during a war. This war might even have been between the Minoans and the Mycenaeans. The final theory suggests that the Minoans continued to live at Knossos after 1400 B.C. but that their trade and naval power in the Aegean had weakened. Slowly the Minoans began to adopt the way of life of other Aegean peoples, such as the Mycenaeans.

The fall of Mycenae remains as much a mystery as the fall of Crete. Two theories have been suggested.

The first is that the climate of Greece may have undergone a shift in rainfall patterns, resulting in a two hundred year cycle of long- and short-term droughts. This drought would have resulted in low crop yields, in turn, causing food shortages. The people of Mycenae would have been forced to move to more fertile valleys and plains. The second theory holds that a tribe of nomadic warriors from north of Greece, called the Dorians, destroyed Mycenae. Since they were not interested in settling the area, the Dorians might have decided to loot and destroy the Mycenaean cities and palaces.

With continued work on the excavations of early Greek communities, we may one day be able to put the pieces of the puzzle together. Until then, you must judge for yourself which theory best explains the decline of the Minoan and Mycenaean civilizations.

1. Write a sentence to identify each of the following:

    a. Heinrich Schliemann
    b. Arthur Evans
    c. The *Iliad*
    d. Linear B.

The legacy of the ancient Greeks to the modern world includes these architectural remains. The carving on this marble section of an ancient Greek temple illustrates not only the artisan's skill but the Greek love of simplicity and beauty.

2. In your notebook, match the names of the figures from Greek stories in the left column with their descriptions on the right.

   1. Menelaus
   2. Agamemnon
   3. Homer
   4. Aegeus
   5. Helen
   6. Theseus
   7. Minotaur
   8. Ariadne
   9. Minos

   a. half-man, half-bull creature
   b. king of Crete
   c. daughter of the king of Crete
   d. king of Athens
   e. kidnapped and taken to Troy
   f. king of Sparta
   g. escapes from the labyrinth
   h. king of Mycenae
   i. Greek poet.

3. Compare the Minoan and Mycenaean civilizations in a chart using these headings: location, the physical environment, time period, military strength, artistic achievements.

4. Evidence about the early Greeks has been obtained from stories and legends, pictures on pottery, the remains of buildings, writing on tablets, and so on. What evidence will scientists use 2000 years from now to learn about our civilization? Make a list.

CLASSICAL GREECE

The Origins and Environment of Classical Greece

We know very little about the civilization of Greece from 1200 to 800 B.C. These people left no written records. The only evidence of their civilization we have is a few fragments of pottery.

Beginning around 800 B.C., a new civilization began to develop in Greece. Historians have evidence to show that these later Greeks and the people of the earlier Greek civilizations all share a common ancestry.

Both the early Greeks and the later Greeks lived in the same environment. They grew the same crops, raised the same livestock, and used the same resources to build homes and to manufacture tools and utensils. Both took advantage of Greece's natural harbors to develop trade.

There were some differences. Iron had come into widespread use by 800 B.C. The later Greeks used more marble in their architecture and began to make sculptures out of it. The written language had developed into a style that closely resembles modern-day Greek.

A	B	Γ	Δ	E	Z	H	θ	I	K	Λ	M
a	b	g	d	e	z	ē	th	i	k	l	m

N	Ξ	O	π	P	Σ	T	Υ	φ	X	Ψ	Ω
n	x(ks)	o	p	r	s	t	u,y	ph	kh,ch	ps	o

Written accounts from the time after 800 B.C. show us that, by then, the Greeks had developed an alphabet used throughout the area of the Aegean Sea. This alphabet had been adapted from the language of the Phoenicians (fə nish' ən), a people from the eastern shore of the Mediterranean. For many centuries, Phoenician traders had sailed all the lands of the Mediterranean. Which Greek letters most closely resemble those of our own alphabet?

The political organization of Greece was linked to conditions of the environment. As we have seen, Greece was, then as now, a very mountainous country with few major rivers. Travel between different parts of the country was difficult. Therefore, the communities of one area tended to be isolated from those of another.

Some of these communities developed into what is called a *polis*. We usually translate this term as "city-state." Each city-state had its own form of government, laws and money. The city-state included the surrounding farmland. Farm products were an important part of the Greek economy. The city-states sometimes traded with and went to war against each other.

Some city-states, such as Corinth, Eretria, Thebes, Athens and Sparta, grew up from communities that had existed for centuries. As they grew, the local environment sometimes became

GREEK GODS AND ORACLES

Around 750 B.C., a poet named Hesiod wrote a history of the Greek gods. He counted twelve major gods and a number of minor ones. Among the major gods, most of whom lived atop Mount Olympus, were Zeus, Poseidon, Athena and Apollo. Each god represented an aspect of the Greek environment.

As the most powerful god, Zeus controlled the skies: the rain, wind, lightning and thunder. Poseidon had unsuccessfully battled with his brother Zeus for control of the sky. He moved to a palace under the Aegean Sea and became the god of the oceans. Athena, daughter of Zeus, was the goddess of wisdom. She taught human beings how to tame horses and how to make pottery. Apollo, son of Zeus, was the god of the sun and of light. He was also the god of the Oracle of Delphi, the most important of the more than 250 oracles (advice-givers) in Greece.

Delphi was a sacred place. Kings and wealthy people from all over the Mediterranean would come to have their fortunes told by the Oracle of Delphi. The Greeks believed that the temple of the Oracle marked the centre of the world.

Before entering the temple, the person seeking Apollo's advice sacrificed a goat to him. Once inside, the questioner waited on one side of a curtain while, on the other side, a priestess sat above a well of volcanic rock. The priestess breathed deeply of the fumes emerging from the well. Dizzy from the fumes, she then began to talk in a strange, almost hysterical way. Priests beside her wrote down what she was saying. The priests then interpreted the message to whomever was seeking Apollo's advice.

People did not always understand the message of the Oracle. King Croesus (krē" səs) of Lydia, a kingdom on the eastern Aegean shore, visited Delphi in 549 B.C. He wanted to know whether he should go to war against Cyrus, king of Persia. The Oracle told Croesus that, if he went to war, a kingdom would be destroyed. Croesus took this to mean that he would destroy the kingdom of Cyrus, so he went to war against Persia. Unfortunately for Croesus, it was his own kingdom that was destroyed.

The goddess Athena is holding an owl in her right hand. What do you think the owl represents?

unable to support an increasing population. The small pastures and thin, rocky soil of Greece did not produce a great deal of food. As a result, some Greek families had to leave their home city-states and set up life elsewhere.

From about 700 B.C. to 500 B.C., groups of Greek people established new homes, or **colonies**, throughout Europe and Asia. They would make the journey carrying a flame and a bottle of earth from the old home to the new. Among the many such colonies established were Syracuse, on the island of Sicily; Cyrene, on the north coast of Africa; Massilia, the site of present-day Marseilles, France; and Olbia, on the north coast of the Black Sea. From these colonies, the mainland city-states got grain and timber. In return, they sent out oil, pottery and wine.

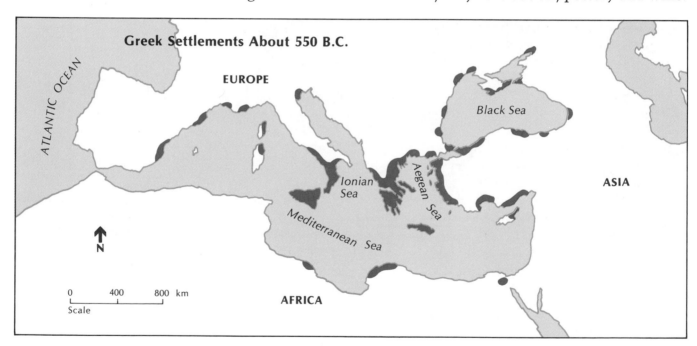

Greek Settlements About 550 B.C.

The early Greeks settled along the coasts of the Black Sea and the Mediterranean Sea. Why did they not establish settlements inland?

By about 500 B.C., two city-states had become particularly powerful: Athens and Sparta. Let us take a closer look at these two.

1. What benefit did the ancient Greeks receive from the indented coastline of Greece?

2. What is a Greek *polis*? How was the development of the *polis* a result of the Greek environment?
3. List the differences between the Minoan and Mycenaean civilizations, and the Greek civilization that began to appear around 800 B.C.

Athens and Sparta: Allies and Enemies

Around 500 B.C., the Greeks were divided into more than a hundred independent city-states. Most of the lands to the east of the Aegean Sea, however, had come under the rule of one king, Cyrus of Persia. Several Greek city-states of Asia Minor had also come under Persian control.

In 499 B.C., one of these Asia Minor city-states, Miletus, rebelled. Although Athens and Eretria sent ships and soldiers to help Miletus, the Persians were able to crush the rebels. To teach the Greeks a lesson, the Persians burned down both Miletus and Eretria. They then attempted an invasion of Athens.

Though greatly outnumbered, the Athenians beat back the Persians. But this attack made them realize that the Greek city-states must unite against Persia.

Some of the city-states decided to avoid war and to surrender to Persia. Thirty others, however, decided to form an alliance against Persia. Both Athens and Sparta were members of this alliance. For two years, the Greek allies did battle with Persia. Despite two Persian invasions of Athens, the war ended in 479 B.C. in victory for the Greek allies.

For the next half-century, the Greek city-states lived mostly in peace. Under the leadership of Athens, a number of them formed what is called the Delian League. (Delos, a small Greek island, was where the League's members first met.) The Delian League was not only a military alliance, but a commercial one. Since Athens was its most powerful member, most of the League's profits from trade and most of its taxes went to Athens, in return for Athenian protection.

Sparta never became a member of the Delian League. Sparta

set up its own alliance, known as the Peloponnesian League. It was so called because all of its members were on the Peloponnesian Peninsula.

In 431 B.C., war broke out between Athens and Sparta. The immediate cause was a quarrel between Corinth, which was one of Sparta's allies, and Athens. Sparta used the quarrel as an excuse to attack Athens. Year after year, the war dragged on, neither side able to defeat the other. While the Spartan and Athenian armies were equally matched, Sparta could not match Athens' navy.

In 404 B.C., Sparta struck a deal with the old enemy, Persia. In exchange for gold, Sparta gave up to Persia the Greek city-states it controlled in Asia Minor. The gold was spent to strengthen its navy. Finally, Sparta was able to defeat the navy of Athens.

Sparta then blocked off Athens, stopping the ships that brought the city's food supply. Rather than starve, Athens surrendered. Sparta had defeated the enemy that, earlier in the century, had been its ally.

1. In your notebook, rewrite the following events so that they are in their proper historical order:

   (a) Sparta defeats Athens.

   (b) Delian League is formed.

   (c) Combined force of Greeks defeat Persia.

   (d) Peloponnesian League is formed.

   (e) Sparta strengthens its navy.

   (f) Sparta sells control of city-states in Asia Minor to Persia.

   (g) Miletus rebels against Persia.

   (h) Greek city-states form an alliance to defeat the Persians.

   (i) Athens defeats Persian forces trying to capture the city.

   (j) War between Sparta and Athens begins.

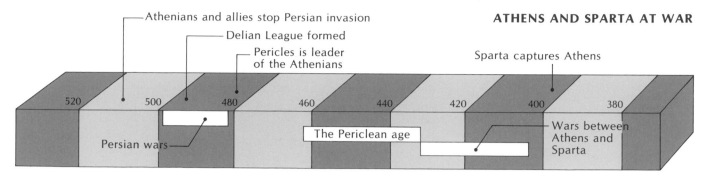

Athenians and allies stop Persian invasion
Delian League formed
Pericles is leader of the Athenians
Sparta captures Athens

520 500 480 460 440 420 400 380

Persian wars
The Periclean age
Wars between Athens and Sparta

Government and Society in Athens

During the fifth and fourth centuries B.C., Greece, and Athens in particular, produced a series of philosophers, poets, playwrights and scientists whose work has had a tremendous influence on our whole outlook on life.

The politics of fifth century B.C. Athens has also had a great influence on our way of life. Many historians feel that Athens was the world's first example of a **democracy.** The term "democracy" comes from Greek words meaning "rule by the people." In other governments of ancient times, kings, priests or other powerful individuals made all the decisions about laws, taxes, and wars. The situation was different in Athens.

The environment of Athens, suggest some historians, played a role in encouraging democracy. Like much of Greece, Athens enjoyed a pleasantly warm climate practically all year round. People spent a great deal of time outdoors; walking, talking, working and playing under the blue Aegean sky. Because they were not shut off indoors by themselves, Athenians were constantly involved in public life. Most of their business and sports were carried on in open-air places where large groups of people could gather easily and comfortably. Consequently, the feeling of community was strong in Athens. Its **citizens** felt that public affairs were their own responsibility, not just the responsibility of their leaders.

In the Athens of the mid-fifth century B.C., all adult male citizens could play a role in the city's government. Every month, any man could come and speak his mind before the Council. The Council's 500 members served a term of one year, at the end of

SOCRATES

A few years after the city's defeat by Sparta, the leaders of Athens put on trial one of the city's best-known men, Socrates.

Socrates had served both as a soldier and as a member of the Council, Athens' governing body. But he did not always agree with the city's leaders. Some of Socrates' friends had criticized the way the Council had conducted the war against Sparta.

Socrates was a familiar figure in the streets of Athens. A good-natured fellow, he was always chatting with both friends and strangers in the *agora*, or marketplace, of Athens. His conversations always led to questions about the purpose of life. Socrates never gave firm answers to such questions. Instead, he encouraged people to seek their own answers. Indeed, he had sometimes been heard making fun of the gods.

Many members of the Council felt that Socrates' conversations were a bad example to the young people of Athens. Some blamed Socrates' teachings for the loss of the war to Sparta.

By a vote of a **majority** of the Council's members at his trial, Socrates was found guilty of corrupting the young people of Athens. He chose death over exile from Athens. Even as he drank the glass of poison hemlock handed him by the weeping executioner, Socrates was still making jokes.

1. Imagine you are a citizen of Athens. Tomorrow, Socrates will appear before the Council charged with corrupting the youth of the city. Any citizen may give their point of view during the trial. Write a brief speech in defence of Socrates. Remember you want to persuade others to support your position.

which the members were chosen anew by lottery. Any adult male citizen of Athens could have his name put into the lottery.

From the Council's members various Committees, usually made up of ten members, were again chosen by lottery. These Committees supervised public affairs such as tax collecting, street cleaning and policing.

PERICLES

Pericles was a Council member who was elected to the Military Committee almost every year from 461 B.C. to his death in 429. So influential was he that the Athens of his time is sometimes called "The Periclean Age." It was Pericles who ordered the Parthenon, burnt during the Persian invasions, to be rebuilt.

Pericles also had built a pair of walls, 6 km long and 500 m across, from the edge of Athens to its port of Piraeus. As long as Athens' navy controlled the port, the walls would ensure the safe passage of goods between Piraeus and Athens.

Pericles encouraged a greater use of the natural environment surrounding Athens. He had workers mine more marble and silver in the nearby mountains. Clay was dug from the Plains of Attica. The craftspeople of Athens turned the marble into statues, the silver into tools and weapons, and the clay into vases. These goods served both in the households of Athens and as exports to other Greek city-states.

Pericles was Athens leading statesman for thirty years. He brought about political reforms that allowed any citizen of Athens to hold public office.

The only Committee chosen by election, rather than by lottery, was the one responsible for military affairs. The Athenians felt that the military leadership of the city had to be trusted to experienced soldiers. The most famous such soldier was Pericles.

When we say that Athens was a "democracy," we do not mean that all its people had a role in government. Women, slaves and

Athenian homes usually included a weaving room where the woman of the household turned wool into cloth.

foreigners could not speak before the Council, be members of it, or vote.

When they were fifteen years old, Athenian girls were considered ready for marriage. Marriages were arranged by their fathers. Most Athenian women spent their day managing the household. Many were also highly skilled potters and weavers.

Most slaves in Athens were prisoners of war, the children of slaves, or poor outsiders who had come to the city to find work. Some of these slaves had extremely difficult lives as workers in the silver mines outside of the city. The majority of slaves were household servants. They cooked, cared for the children and cleaned house. Slaves also worked at trades. A few even ran their own shops. Their masters received royalties from the items sold. Since most Athenian farms were small, Athenian farmers tended to work their land with little or no help from slaves. Some slaves were paid small wages. If they saved up enough money, they could sometimes buy their freedom.

Historians estimate that as much as 40 percent of the people in the Athens area were slaves. In many ways it was their work, and that of the women, that allowed Athenian men to spend their lives discussing philosophy and taking part in politics.

1. (a) How did the climate and physical landscape of Greece encourage a sense of community?
   (b) Does the natural environment of your area encourage a feeling of community? Explain your answer.
2. Describe the government of Athens. Be sure to include the length of term, method of selection, and duties of each division.
3. Athenians believed their government was a true democracy because all citizens could take part.
   (a) Do you agree with the Athenian's belief that their government was a true democracy? Explain.
   (b) How is our definition of a citizen different from the Athenian's?

Daily Life in Athens

Imagine you are the guest of an Athenian family. It is a summer day sometime around the year 436 B.C.

As the first light of dawn streams in through your window, you awake. You stand up from the rug of woven rushes that is your bed and shake the sheet under which you have been sleeping. You wrap this sheet around you as a cloak, called a *chiton.* Other than a pair of sandals, it is all you need to wear.

As in all the rooms of the house, your windows are small and high on the walls of clay brick. Athens gets very hot in the summer, and such windows help keep the house shady and cool.

With the family, you share a simple breakfast of wheat or barley bread, dipped in wine or olive oil.

It is the time of the Olympic Games, and they proudly tell you of their cousin. He is travelling to the town of Olympia over on the Peloponnesian Peninsula. At the Olympic Games there, he will take part in the Pentathlon.

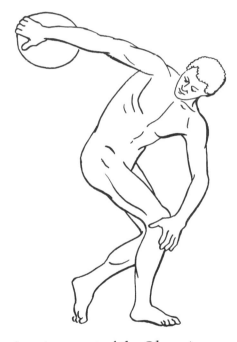

A major event of the Olympic Games in ancient Greece was the Pentathlon. In order to win, an athlete had to prove his skill in five events: leaping, foot racing, wrestling, discus throwing, and casting the javelin. What is the modern-day equivalent to the Pentathlon?

125

After breakfast you plan to tour the city of Athens. You begin by walking towards the *agora*, or market square.

Once on the street, you notice young boys carrying wax-coated tablets. They are on their way to school. Many have slaves to help them. There are no girls headed for school. They will remain at home to be taught by educated slaves.

Public fountains were built over natural springs. Women would come here each day to collect water for their households.

A few women walk past with large clay jars resting on their heads. Not all Athenian homes have their own well. These women are on their way to the *agora's* public fountain. At the fountain the women will have a chance to socialize as well as to collect the family's water supply.

Once you reach the *agora*, you are amazed at the variety of shops and stalls. Here are merchants and artisans not only from Athens, but from all over Greece and even from lands across the Aegean. However, not everyone in the market is there to sell or buy goods. This early in the morning there are also groups of men, some free and some slaves, who are waiting to be hired as laborers.

In the section of the market where the bankers are set up, you listen in while a shipping merchant tries to arrange insurance for his new ship. Tomorrow, it will sail from Piraeus to collect a cargo of grain in Egypt. The merchant wants to protect his investment in case the ship is sunk at sea. It is not only storms at sea that he is worried about; he is also afraid of piracy.

Nearby, you hear one of the elders retelling the story of Solon and the olive tree.

The old one relates how, more than 100 years ago, the hills around Athens had been heavily forested. But too many trees had been cut down to build ships or to burn for fuel. Without trees to hold the earth into place, heavy winter rains washed away the topsoil. Farms had suffered.

The old one goes on to tell how Solon, the city's leading citizen back then, urged Athenians to replant the hills with olive trees. But the deep roots of the olive trees had drawn up all the moisture from the soil and failed to hold it together. Since then, Athenian farms have not been as productive. Athens has had to import most of its grain for over a century now.

By now you are hungry. You search the market for cheese, figs and bread for your lunch. You notice that men are doing most of the shopping. Some have brought slaves with them to carry the purchases. When you ask why there are so few women, an Athenian explains that the women are busy at home, managing the household. There is little time for most of them to do the shopping. Their job will be the storage and preparation of the food once it has been brought home.

While you are eating lunch you spot some children playing a game of knucklebones. You take a turn, tossing the shin-bones of a sheep in the air and catching the bones on the back of your hand.

A procession of a dozen white oxen passes by. You remember that, in a few days, the festival of the goddess Athena will take place. The oxen will be driven up the hill of the *Acropolis*, followed by throngs of people. At the *Parthenon*, the oxen will be slain as a sacrifice to Athena. If she is pleased, prosperity and peace will continue in Athens.

You walk leisurely around the rest of the *agora*. You pass merchants selling textiles, ribbons, cooking pots, lamps and tools. At a potters stand you buy a small terra cotta figurine of an owl. At the bookseller's stall you envy a man's purchase of a copy of Homer's *Iliad*. You would like to see more, but you are tired and dirty from your long walk.

You return home to treat yourself to a bath. You splash yourself with water from a huge basin and rub olive oil over yourself. Gently, you scrape the oil and dirt off with a dull knife. Since it is such a hot afternoon, you return to your mat for a nap, already eager for tonight's special meal.

Since you are a guest, tonight's supper will not be the usual fare of fresh or smoked fish. Athens is close to the sea, so its people eat a great deal of fish. Tonight, however, the meal will consist of real delicacies: cutlet of eel, squid, boiled pig's feet and thrush-birds in a coating of honey.

In mid-afternoon, you decide to visit the *Acropolis*. Your first stop is the open-air theatre. The stone benches of the theatre are arranged in a semicircle with the rear seats higher than the front, much like the construction of a modern stadium. The actors

Every year Athens held a drama contest to honor Dionysus, the god of wine. Notice how all the spectators in this theatre have a clear view of the actors.

The fortified walls of the Acropolis *were built to protect the Athenians. Today it is the beauty of the* Parthenon *that attracts people to the* Acropolis.

perform on a raised platform, so that the people seated in the back rows will have a clear view. Last spring your father had come to Athens for their drama festival. His favorite play had been *Antigone* (an tig″ ə nē′), by the Athenian citizen Sophocles.

Finally you go to the *Parthenon*, Temple of Athena. Here you leave the figurine of an owl that you had bought. The owl is Athena's symbol. It is your offering to her. If she is pleased, perhaps one day she will allow you to return to her city of Athens.

1. List the activities that took place in Athen's *agora*.
2. The *Acropolis* is one of Greece's most famous ancient sites. Using the picture on page 129 as a guide, write a description of the *Acropolis*, as it appeared in 436 B.C.
3. It is the view of some historians that the work of the women and the slaves made it possible for the men of Athens to spend so much of their time running the city. Draw two columns, one labelled "women" and one labelled "slaves." List the jobs each was responsible for in 436 B.C.

Government, Society and Daily Life in Sparta

Had you lived in fifth-century B.C. Sparta, rather than Athens, things would have been very different for you.

Sparta's natural environment was unlike that of Athens. **Landlocked** on the barren hills of the Peloponnesian Peninsula Sparta did not have a port, as did Athens. It could not trade as easily with other communities of the Mediterranean.

Yet despite its isolation and harsh environment, Sparta defeated Athens in the Peloponnesian Wars (see page 120). We have seen how the citizens of Athens put their energy into art, philosophy, drama and business as well as into the military. The citizens of Sparta, however, put all of their energy into the military.

It had not always been that way. Some historians feel that in earlier times, around 700 B.C., Sparta was superior to Athens in its art and culture. Spartans were making fine ivory carvings and beautiful pottery. Spartan song-writing and poetry flourished.

Then, in 640 B.C., the *helots*, or peasants, of Sparta and the surrounding area rebelled. Many *helot* families had farmed in the area for generations. They resented having to give up part of their crops to the Spartan army. It took twenty years before Sparta's army finally crushed the rebellion. Determined never to be threatened again, Sparta began to direct its whole way of life to one goal: the creation of a strong army.

The Location of Sparta

While the Athens of 500 B.C. had already established itself as a democracy, Sparta was ruled by two kings. One king was in charge of military affairs, the other in charge of religion. The leading members of the army chose from their ranks a Council of twenty-eight men. Along with the two kings, these men formed a group known as The Thirty Elders. The members of this group held power for life, and made all political decisions in Sparta.

Whereas sons of citizens in Athens entered school at age seven, boys in Sparta of that age went to a military camp. They remained there until they were twenty and were considered adults. They then went into the regular army. The boys were taught to read and do figures but physical fitness and the use of weapons were the most important part of their education. Their training aimed to make them tough and able soldiers, whose first duty would be to their comrades and to the state, rather than to themselves. Though girls lived at home, they too were taught running and wrestling. Spartan girls had to be strong to be worthy future wives and mothers of Spartan soldiers.

Like the men, the boys slept in harsh barracks and ate mostly "black broth," a none-too-tasty soup of pork stock, vinegar and salt. The portions of food given the boys were small to encourage them to steal. Stealing was not seen as dishonest. In Sparta, everything belonged to the state. But, getting caught showed lack of skill. If caught, boys were punished.

A story is told about the toughness of one such Spartan boy. He had stolen a fox and hid it under his cloak. When stopped and questioned by an adult soldier, he silently let the fox gnaw at his stomach, rather than confess.

Though men could marry after the age of twenty, they had to live with the army until age thirty. Some soldiers were able to return for a while to their farms. Yet they remained part of the army, and had to be prepared, at a moment's notice, to go to battle.

Therefore, it was mostly the wives of Spartan soldiers who supervised the farms. They often directed the physical labor of the *helots*, who made up about two-thirds of the population of Sparta and the surrounding lands. The necessary craftwork and

A Spartan Warrior

trading was carried out by the *perioeci* (pēr″ ē ō′ cē), a group of non-citizens despised by the Spartan warriors.

After the Peloponnesian Wars, Sparta's military strength in Greece did not last for long. Worn out from the wars, Sparta had trouble controlling the other Greek city-states, many of which rebelled against the harsh Spartan rule.

By 371 B.C., only three decades after its defeat of Athens, Sparta had lost its position as Greece's leading military power. This leadership then passed to the city-state of Thebes, which held it for barely a decade.

Meanwhile, as the exhausted city-states of Greece continued to quarrel among themselves, a new power was rising to the north of them: Macedonia.

1. In your notebook match the names on the left to their correct descriptions on the right.

   1. Pericles   a. condemned to death in Athens
   2. Miletus   b. city-state of mainland Greece
   3. Socrates   c. temple of Athens
   4. Delphi   d. area of northern Greece
   5. Sophocles   e. Greek god of the sea
   6. Macedonia   f. Athenian political and military leader
   7. Poseidon   g. Greek city in Asia Minor
   8. Thebes   h. Greek colony of western
   9. Massilia   Mediterranean
   10. *Parthenon*   i. famous Greek oracle
                  j. author of *Antigone*.

2. List four of the major Greek gods and write down what aspect of the environment each one represented.

3. Why did some Greek city-states found colonies?

4. How did Solon try to improve farming conditions in Athens? Why did he fail?

5. Make a chart to compare Athens and Sparta. Include topics such as education, government, and the military. Which place would you have preferred to live in? Why?

THE MACEDONIAN EMPIRE

The Origins and Environment of Macedonia

The origin of the people of Macedonia is unknown. Macedonia appears to have been overrun by the same Dorian tribes who swept into much of southern Greece. For centuries, these tribes fought among themselves, with various warrior-kings in turn taking power from each other.

Like the southern Greeks, the Macedonians found themselves at war with Persia in the decades around 500 B.C. Although occupied by the Persian army for a few years, Macedonia had fought off the Persians by 479 B.C.

By this time, the territory known as Macedonia consisted of the lands stretching in a rough semicircle around the northwest arm of the Thermaic Gulf. Pella, the major city of the region, served as its capital. Yet, unlike Athens, Macedonia had not established itself as a maritime power. The coastal areas of Macedonia were very shallow and swampy, therefore, unfit for harbors. Malaria-carrying mosquitoes bred in the swamps, making much of the coastal land unhealthy for settlement.

Because of their environment, the Macedonians lived mostly inland. They were not sea traders and colonizers, like the Greeks of the southern Aegean. Many Macedonian people lived as groups of wandering shepherds, following their flocks of sheep. No fig or olive trees grew here. The cooler climate of Macedonia was unsuitable for both these important crops. However, grain could be grown.

Macedonia was rich in forests. By the time of the Peloponnesian Wars, much of southern Greece had become deforested. Macedonia became the nearest source of wood for the city-states. Macedonian traders sold sturdy oak timber for shipbuilding both to Athens and to Sparta.

Macedonia became an important source of gold during the time of Philip, who ruled Macedonia from 359 to 336 B.C. Continuous war among the southern Greeks had financially exhausted the city-states. As the closest gold-producing region,

A Macedonian gold coin issued during the reign of Philip. One side shows the head of Apollo, the other shows a two-horse chariot, or "biga." Macedonian money like this became so common throughout Greece around 300 B.C. that all gold coins came to be called "Philips."

Macedonia became their chief provider of gold. In return Macedonia received olive oil and figs.

Philip was the first Macedonian ruler to unify all of northern Greece under his command and to rule it from the city of Pella. For centuries, Macedonia had lain between the **barbarian** tribes of the north and the city-states to the south. Both sets of neighbors had influenced Macedonia. Because of the constant threat of attack from the north, Macedonia built a strong army. The common ancestry of the people of Macedonia and the people of southern Greece gave them similar languages. They both worshipped the same gods. The Macedonians saw themselves as fellow Greeks.

Philip admired the civilization of southern Greece. As a youth, he had lived for a few years in the city-states of Thebes. As king, he wanted to arrange Macedonia's military and cultural life on the model of southern Greece.

But Philip not only wanted to imitate southern Greece. He wanted to rule it. He believed that system of city-states caused Greeks to quarrel and to make war among themselves. Instead, he wanted all Greeks to join forces against the barbarians to the north and the Persians to the east. He believed that Greek civilization needed unity, under his leadership.

During the twenty-three years of his rule, Philip managed to conquer much of mainland Greece. His military success was in large part due to methods, especially the "phalanx," which he had learned from the southern Greeks. The weakness of the city-states after decades of war among themselves also contributed to Philip's success. In 338 B.C., the combined forces of Athens and Thebes were defeated by Philip's army at the battle of Chaeronea (kėr ən ē" ə). Philip was now master of Greece.

Only two years after Chaeronea, Philip was murdered at his daughter's wedding by a traitor in his bodyguard. He was succeeded by his son, Alexander.

WHAT DOES "BARBARIAN" MEAN?

To the north of Macedonia were wandering warrior tribes whom the Greeks considered uncivilized peoples. Their languages made no sense to the Greeks, who mocked their speech, saying it was a lot of rough sounds like "bar-bar-bar." Hence the Greeks came to call these tribes "barbarians." The Romans also later used this word as a name for the foreigners who lived outside of their empire.

1. Compare the environments of southern Greece and Macedonia using these headings: location, climate, crops, resources, problems.

THE PHALANX

The phalanx was a formation of soldiers armed with spears four metres long. In rows sixteen deep, the soldiers marched, the front rows with spears pointed forward and the rear rows with spears pointed upright. Often three phalanxes would trap an enemy—the middle phalanx stood its ground while the left and right phalanxes closed in on either side. Cavalry and shield-bearers supported the phalanxes.

Although we have no eyewitness accounts of the battle of Chaeronea, some historians think that the phalanxes probably played an important role in Philip's victory.

A phalanx section was made up of 256 men. A full phalanx included several thousand men. Why was the phalanx an effective fighting technique?

2. Describe Philip's plan for the future of Macedonia and the Greek city-states.
3. Suppose you are a Macedonian. Write a reply to an Athenian's charge that you do not have the right to call yourself a Greek. Base your reply on facts, not opinions.

Alexander the Great

A story is told about Alexander at the age of ten. His father bought a magnificent wild black stallion. The skilled stablemen of Philip's court could not tame the horse. Philip promised Alexander the horse if Alexander could tame him. The young Alexander succeeded. In wonder at his son's effort, Philip said to him, "When you grow up, you will have to find a bigger kingdom. Macedonia will not be enough for you."

135

Alexander proved the truth of his father's words beyond what Philip could have ever imagined. In a mere thirteen years, Alexander would establish the largest empire the world had ever seen.

As a boy in the court of Macedonia at Pella, Alexander was taught by the great philosopher Aristotle. He learned about the ancient legends and always carried with him a copy of Homer's *Iliad.* Alexander wanted to relive the glories of Agamemnon and the other heroes of the distant Greek past.

As a teenager, Alexander served in his father's army. Although only fifteen he commanded the cavalry of Chaeronea.

At the age of twenty, Alexander succeeded his murdered father. Three years later, Thebes rebelled against Macedonia. Alexander tried to negotiate peace with the rebels. When they refused, he had the city burned down. He did, however, spare the home of Pindar, a Thebian poet whom Alexander greatly admired. Throughout Greece, people now stood in awe of this young soldier.

Alexander's next step was to plan an attack on Persia. As a boy, he had learned of the wars between Greece and Persia. He knew that Macedonia had been ruled for a time by the Persians. Now, he was determined that, under his leadership, Greece would rule Persia.

With an army drawn from both Macedonia and the southern city-states, Alexander set forth. His first great victory against the Persians was at Issus, in Asia Minor, in 333 B.C. He fought against an army commanded by King Darius of Persia. The Persian army was three times the size of his own, yet he won handily, although Darius escaped.

Alexander then marched down the coast of Asia Minor, taking other major cities such as Tyre. When he swept into Egypt, the Egyptians did not even attempt to resist. Alexander had himself crowned pharaoh at Memphis, then moved up again through Asia Minor.

Marching into Mesopotamia, he met King Darius again at Gaugamela, just north of the old Assyrian capital of Nineveh. Once more, Alexander defeated the army of Darius; again, Darius escaped. But shortly afterward, Darius was murdered by

The ruins of Persepolis, destroyed by Alexander the Great during his march to Asia. Why did Alexander destroy the city?

some of his own soldiers. It is said that when the Macedonian army found the body of Darius, Alexander lay his own cloak over it, out of respect for his enemy. He had the assassins of Darius tracked down and executed.

Alexander continued eastward, capturing first the city of Babylon, then Susa and finally Persepolis, Persia's capital. Here, tradition says, Alexander discovered a vast treasure—so vast that it is supposed to have taken 20 000 mules and 5000 camels to carry it from the city. It was also at Persepolis that Alexander finally declared himself ruler of Persia.

Alexander decided to rest awhile in the city. While dining late one night, one of his guests—Thais, a woman from Athens—

offered Alexander a challenge. She reminded the group that when the Persians had attacked Athens a century and a half earlier, the Persians had burned the city. She dared Alexander to avenge this long-standing insult to her home. Alexander picked up a torch and set fire to the palace. Soon the whole city of Persepolis burned to the ground. Later, however, Alexander was to regret the destruction of the city.

Alexander was now master of Greece, Egypt, and Persia. But he did not stop. He knew of the fabulous kingdoms that lay beyond the Hindu Kush Mountains.

Alexander led his troops through the scorching plateaus of central Asia, over the Hindu Kush Mountains, and down into the Punjab region of the Indus Valley. Since leaving Pella, Alexander's army had marched over 17 000 km. It now stood at the edge of the mighty Maghada kingdom.

The Macedonian army found itself in an environment as unfamiliar as it was uncomfortable. The troops had survived the searing heat of the Asian plateau as well as the cold and danger of the Hindu Kush Mountains. But conditions in the Punjab were even worse.

It was the season of the **monsoons**, a season of violent and constant rain. The rivers were flooding, rising as much as a metre a day. The rains soaked the army's food and supplies, rusted its weapons, and mildewed the leather uniforms and saddles. Poisonous cobras slithered into the Macedonian tents.

As well, many soldiers had been on the campaign, away from home, for eight years or more. Alexander's generals insisted their exhausted troops would fare badly against the elephants and fierce warriors of the Maghadan army. The horses of the Macedonian cavalry had been terrified during their first encounters with the elephants in the Punjab.

Alexander's generals begged him to go no further. They told him that the monsoon-swollen Beas River was too dangerous to cross. Reluctantly, Alexander heeded the warnings of his generals. The army headed back. They marched southward to the coast of the Arabian Sea, along the coast, then back through Mesopotamia.

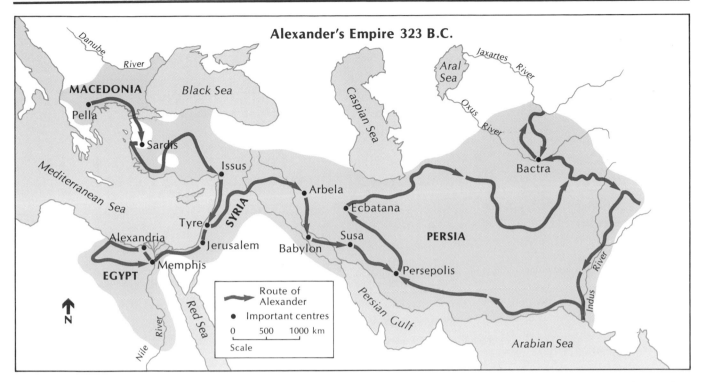

Alexander's Empire 323 B.C.

Alexander was never to return to Macedonia. He reached Babylon in 324 B.C. and immediately began to organize his new empire. Alexander also began to learn about the geography and culture of these new lands. In Babylon, he stopped and took a boat into the Euphrates marshes, where he wanted to inspect an irrigation canal. It seems that he picked up an infection while there, likely malaria.

As news of his sickness spread, thousands of soldiers insisted on seeing their commander. A second door had to be knocked into Alexander's sick room so that the great lines of troops could all file past silently, paying their last respects. Alexander died at the age of thirty-two, having established the greatest empire the world had ever known.

1. Use the map and an atlas to answer the following questions:
    (a) List the modern-day nations that make up the area conquered by Alexander.

List in order the cities Alexander conquered as he established his empire.

Below are two different opinions of Alexander.

...He did have the intention of uniting the peoples of his empire in fellowship and concord... he prayed for a partnership...between Macedonian and Persian... not partnership in rule only, but true unity between them...he was the pioneer of one of the supreme revolutions in the world's outlook, the first man known to us who contemplated...the unity of mankind.

...he was vain and conceited, and sometimes very cruel and violent. He thought of himself almost as a god. In fits of anger or whims of the moment he killed some of his best friends, and destroyed great cities...He left nothing solid behind him... Like a meteor in the sky he came and went, and left little of himself behind except a memory.

1. How could you resolve the differences between these two views?
2. Which view do you support? Give reasons for your opinion.

(b) Use the map's scale to measure the greatest length and width of the empire.

(c) What means of transportation did Alexander use during his journey? What means of transportation could you use to make the same journey today?

2. List the reasons that finally caused Alexander to end his journey of conquest.

The End of the Macedonian Empire

After Alexander's death, the empire fell apart as quickly as Alexander had built it.

The western portion of the empire continued to be ruled from Pella, with Alexander's half brother in charge. Ptolemy (tol' ə mē), one of Alexander's most able generals, took charge of Egypt. He founded a dynasty that would last for two centuries. Most of the remainder of the empire, centred in Babylon, went to Seleucus (sel yü' kəs), another general.

In all three of these areas, constant fighting went on, as one general or noble took power from another. Alexander's empire, which had stretched from Macedonia to India, was soon only a memory. Yet during his short life, Alexander had left the marks of Greek culture throughout Asia and northern Africa. These marks would stay.

He had founded more than a dozen new cities, naming most of them "Alexandria." The most famous of these cities is now Cairo, the capital of Egypt.

Under the Persians, Asia had experienced few cultural or scientific advances. Alexander's conquests spread Greek knowledge of architecture, drama, sports and mathematics, throughout his empire. Greek became a second language for many educated non-Greeks throughout Europe, North Africa, and Asia. It continued as such right on into Roman times.

Not all historians hold the same opinion of Alexander. Some historians feel that Alexander was only a power-mad soldier. Others feel, however, that he wanted to unite the Greek and Persian peoples. We do know that Alexander invited some groups of conquered Persians into his army. He arranged the marriages of 10 000 soldiers in the Greek army to Persian women. In fact, one of his wives was a daughter of Darius. He welcomed the leaders of conquered peoples into his presence, becoming friends with some of them. He gave government positions to non-Greeks. He wanted his empire to be one people.

Whatever we think of Alexander, it is certain that he is one of the most remarkable people in all of history.

1. Write a short sentence to explain or identify each of the following:

   1. Phalanx
   2. Darius
   3. Thais
   4. Punjab
   5. Chaeronea
   6. Pella
   7. Susa
   8. Cairo.

2. Give two reasons why Philip was able to conquer most of mainland Greece.
3. Imagine you are a soldier in Alexander's army. After many years, you are at the Beas River, as Alexander argues with his generals whether to press on. In a journal, write a couple of paragraphs to describe the experiences you have had, and whether you want to continue.

SUMMARY

For a long time, our knowledge of the earliest Greek civilizations was based on myths and legends. From archaeological discoveries of the past century and a half, we now think that parts of these myths and legends may have been true.

The earliest Greeks relied heavily on sea travel. They traded the resources of their environment with other Mediterranean peoples. The early Greeks kept mostly sheep and goats. Olives and grapes were their most important crop.

Historians can only guess about why the civilizations of Crete and Mycenae went into decline.

After 800 B.C., a new form of civilization grew up in Greece. This civilization featured a common Greek language, a common religion, but separate city-states. The separate city-states, relatively isolated from each other in the mountainous Greek environment, founded many colonies in other lands around the Mediterranean.

The two most important city-states, Athens and Sparta, were at first allies against Persia during the fifth century B.C. Athens and Sparta later fought each other, a time known as the Peloponnesian Wars. Sparta finally won.

During the fifth century B.C., Athens developed into what many historians feel was the world's first democracy. Historians have suggested that the climate of Athens played a role in this development.

Unlike Athens, Sparta's whole way of life was based upon the military. Despite its victory in the Peloponnesian Wars, Sparta had lost its military leadership of Greece by the middle of the fourth century B.C.

About this same time, Macedonia arose as an important political and military power. Situated between the barbarian lands to the north and the city-states to the south, Macedonia was influenced by both sets of its neighbors.

For centuries, Macedonian shepherd people took advantage of their mountain environment in order to raise livestock. Macedonian resources of timber and gold were important to the city-states of the south.

Under Philip, an admirer of Greek civilization, Macedonia conquered much of Greece. His son, Alexander, went on to conquer an empire that included Egypt and Persia. When Alexander tried to extend his empire into India, conditions of the local environment forced him to turn back.

While Alexander's empire fell apart after his death, the marks of Greek civilization did stay in the lands he had conquered.

Chapter Review: Greece

NEW WORDS AND IDEAS

1. Write one or two sentences to explain why each of the following is important to a study of Greece.
   (a) the *Iliad*
   (b) city-states
   (c) Greek colonies
   (d) the war between Athens and Sparta
   (e) Alexander the Great

2. Under each classification below there is one item that does not belong. Copy the classifications into your notebook, leaving out the incorrect item. Try and add one item to each category.
   (a) *Colonies of the Greek city-states:*
       Syracuse   Massilia
       Olbia   Alexandria
   (b) *Uses for olives:*
       oil   wine   soap   food
   (c) *Greek city-states:*
       Athens Sparta Macedonia Thebes
   (d) *Greek gods:*
       Athena Socrates Zeus Poseidon

3. Copy the following statements into your notebook. After each one, write whether it is true or false. Rewrite each false statement, so that it is true.
   (a) A volcanic eruption on an island may have ended the Minoan civilization.
   (b) Only citizens of Athens could take part in their government.
   (c) Persia successfully captured Athens in 404 B.C.
   (d) Sparta belonged to the Delian League.
   (e) All historians agree that Alexander of Macedonia was a great man.

CHECKING YOUR UNDERSTANDING

4. Marble, silver, gold and clay are some resources that were available to the ancient Greeks.
   (a) Explain how they used each of these resources.
   (b) Describe at least two other ways the ancient Greeks used their environment.

5. Explain how each of the following people tried to change the Greek way of life:
   (a) Socrates   (c) Solon
   (b) Pericles   (d) Philip of Macedonia.

6. How did women and slaves contribute to Athens' way of life?

7. Explain why Sparta built a strong army.

8. During the Greek war against Persia, Sparta and Athens were allies. However, this friendship did not last. Why did Athens and Sparta become rivals?

9. Draw a time line showing the important events from the time when Philip of Macedonia became king until the death of his son, Alexander the Great.

USING YOUR KNOWLEDGE

10. Imagine that you are a tourist guide in ancient Greece. Design and write a tourist brochure describing Greece and suggesting places of interest that people should visit.

11. Transportation was a problem in ancient Greece. The Greek hills and mountains made it difficult for people to travel overland. They turned instead to the sea and water transportation. What transportation problems exist in your area? How might these problems be solved?

Chapter 5

Rome

INTRODUCTION

Imagine yourself on a whirlwind tour of Europe. After landing at London, England, you are whisked 500 km by bus to see the remains of a wall that once divided England from Scotland. It is more than 1800 years old. You return to the airport to get another plane. By the next day, you are staring at the magnificent stone columns of an outdoor theatre in Arles, France. Into the air you go again, this time to Spain, where you view an aqueduct built of thousands of carefully shaped stones. Although parts of it are 2000 years old, it still brings water to the people of Segovia.

Roman ruins, such as this wall in Britain, are found throughout Europe and northern Africa. This wall is named after the emperor who ordered it built. Do you know his name?

Evidence of Roman engineering is still standing. This aqueduct at Segovia, Spain, was built around 100 A.D. and yet it still carries water.

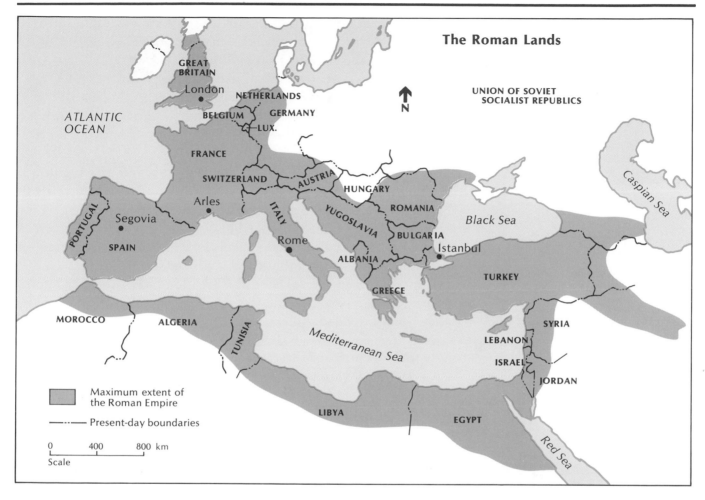

The Roman Lands

UNION OF SOVIET
SOCIALIST REPUBLICS

GREAT
BRITAIN

London

NETHERLANDS

*ATLANTIC
OCEAN*

BELGIUM   GERMANY

LUX.

FRANCE

SWITZERLAND   AUSTRIA

HUNGARY

PORTUGAL   ITALY   YUGOSLAVIA   ROMANIA   *Black Sea*

Segovia   Rome   BULGARIA

SPAIN   ALBANIA   Istanbul

Caspian Sea

Arles

GREECE   TURKEY

MOROCCO   ALGERIA   SYRIA

TUNISIA   *Mediterranean Sea*   LEBANON

ISRAEL

JORDAN

Maximum extent of
the Roman Empire

Present-day boundaries

LIBYA   EGYPT

Red Sea

0   400   800 km

Scale

Next, you travel to a museum in North Africa. There, you see tiny squares of colored stone that tell a story in mosaic of a hunt for snarling lions and leopards. You then journey by plane and car to Yugoslavia, where you walk the uneven paving stones of an ancient road. You head east, to Constantinople (now called Istanbul), to see statues and books that have lasted 1500 years.

Finally your plane touches down in Rome, Italy. All around you are the buildings and the ruins of buildings that existed long before our time. In the Colosseum, lions roared and **gladiators** duelled. At the Forum, people talked and traded. Tall arches celebrated an emperor's triumph in war.

This map shows those parts of present-day countries that were once within the Roman Empire. From humble beginnings on the Italian Peninsula, the Romans eventually controlled all the lands around the Mediterranean Sea.

You have travelled more than 7000 km, through Europe, Africa and Asia. Everything that was just described was built by the people of the ancient Roman Empire.

What you have seen is not all that links us with ancient Rome. Many of the words you have just read began as Latin words, spoken by the Romans. Our alphabet, apartment buildings, roads, laws and methods of war all owe something to the Romans.

Many sources tell us about the Romans and their empire. Buildings, paintings and sculptures in many countries portray the life of the Romans and the people in their empire. We have accounts by the Greeks, the Hebrews and the early Christians describing Roman life. We have modern archaeological research from historians, geographers and geologists.

Most importantly, we have the words of the Romans themselves. Roman historians described every event of the empire in great detail. Roman poets wrote about life and love. Other Roman writers dealt with the subjects of religion, morality and daily life.

For almost a thousand years, Rome dominated what is now Europe. At its height, the Roman Empire stretched from the Euphrates to the Irish Sea. In this chapter, we will look at the growth and the decline of Roman civilization.

First, we will look at the period from about 800 to about 100 B.C., a time known as the Roman Republic. We will then study the period until about 150 A.D., centuries often referred to as the Golden Age of Rome. Finally, we will learn about the three centuries up to about 450 A.D., during which time the Roman Empire gradually fell apart.

ROMAN CIVILIZATION

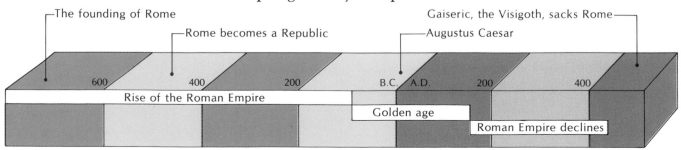

The founding of Rome

Rome becomes a Republic

Augustus Caesar

Gaiseric, the Visigoth, sacks Rome

600 400 200 B.C. A.D. 200 400

Rise of the Roman Empire

Golden age

Roman Empire declines

THE ROMAN REPUBLIC

The Environment of Rome

The peninsula of Italy sticks out like a high-heeled boot into the centre of the Mediterranean Sea. The Adriatic Sea lies along the east coast of the boot; the Tyrrhenian (tī rē' nē ən) Sea borders the west coast. Halfway between the toe and the top of the boot, the River Tiber enters the Tyrrhenian Sea.

Although it has now been drained, for centuries the area at the mouth of the Tiber was marshy. The river here is wide and flat. About twenty-seven kilometres above the river mouth, the river cuts a path through rock. This is where the marsh ends and the Tiber River Valley begins. Here, above the south bank of the river, seven hills stand in a rough semicircle. One of these hills, the Palatine, looks out over the Tiber. It was at this site that the city of Rome was founded.

This was the lowest point on the river that could be bridged; southwest of this point, the marshes made it very difficult to cross the river. Routes lead from this point to the coast and then north and along the river valley, through mountain passes to the east, all the way to the Adriatic coast. Other routes go along the Tyrrhenian coast to the south and beside the river west to the salt flats at the river mouth.

Travel in Italy is not easy. More than three-quarters of the peninsula is mountains or hills. Only one-quarter is occupied by valleys or plains. The plain of Campania, lying to the south of the site of Rome, is the largest in southern Italy.

The mountains above Rome are volcanic. For many centuries, these mountains spread lava down the hillsides and valleys of the area. This lava helped form the soil of the region around Rome. A fertile soil, it encouraged the growth of forests of oak and pine.

This area has a Mediterranean climate of long warm summers and mild winters. The average temperature in Rome in July is 26°C; the average winter temperature is 7°C. About 800 mm of rain falls each year, much of it in short, violent rainstorms in winter.

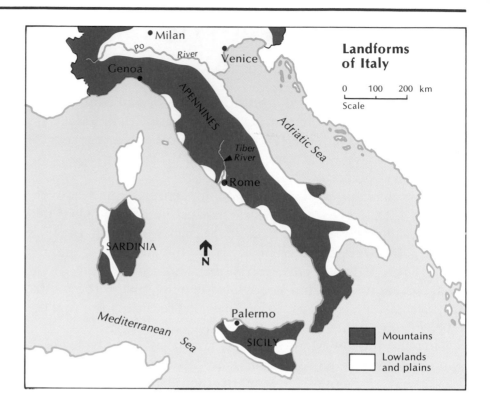

The physical environment of Italy is dominated by the Apennines, a mountain range running along the length of the peninsula. What advantages and disadvantages do you see in Rome's location?

The Italian Peninsula lies in the centre of the Mediterranean, halfway between east and west. Attached to the northern shore of the sea, it reaches almost to the southern shore and Africa. It provides a link between Europe and Africa. Ships can easily sail along the coast of Italy and Sicily to make the 150 km trip across to the African shore. Ships can also travel along the coastline from the Black Sea to the Adriatic and then to the Italian coast, or sail along the North African or French and Spanish coastlines.

At the northern end, or top, of the boot, rise the Alps Mountains. These mountains form a barrier between the Italian Peninsula and the rest of Europe.

1. What physical characteristics made the site of Rome a good place to begin a settlement?
2. Explain how Italy's location on the Mediterranean Sea was an advantage to early traders and travellers.

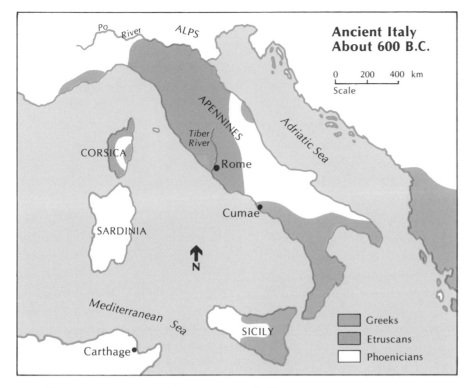

Ancient Italy About 600 B.C.

0   200   400 km
Scale

Greeks
Etruscans
Phoenicians

Before about 600 B.C. the Greeks, Etruscans and Phoenicians competed for control of the lands of ancient Italy. Which group controlled the site of Rome?

Early Rome and its Neighbors

The first people to live in a village on the hills of Rome arrived around 750 B.C. These people were farmers who probably came to the area from the south and east. They settled on the hills, out of the way of the floods that coursed down the Tiber during the winter rains. For about two centuries, they lived a simple life of raising crops, herding animals and making simple tools of bronze and iron.

There were many other similar villages on the Italian Peninsula. There were also Greek settlements to the south, such as Cumae (kyü'mē), founded in the eighth century B.C. To the north lived a people we know as the Etruscans, who had come to Italy from somewhere to the east in about 1400 B.C. These groups all had great influence on the development of Rome.

The Etruscans are the mystery people of the ancient world. No one has ever been able to decipher the Etruscan language, so our knowledge of the Etruscans is limited. We do know that they established cities north of the Tiber. They used bronze and iron to make tools and weapons, painted pictures, and wrote books. In about 600 B.C., the Etruscans conquered Rome and other nearby villages. An Etruscan king took over the villages.

During this time, Rome grew and became a city. By changing the physical environment, the Etruscans created a new base for the growth of Rome. Many people moved to Rome after one of the Etruscan kings had a marshy area drained near the river between two hills. To do this, he had an enormous ditch dug that became known as the *Cloaca Maxima*, the Great Sewer. The drained area was named the Forum. It became the heart of Rome, a place where people gathered to talk, trade, govern and worship. In time, the Forum contained shops, government buildings, temples and open spaces.

At first, the Romans did not oppose the Etruscan kings. In about 500 B.C., however, the Romans rose up and threw out the Etruscan king. Roman historians writing centuries later say this rebellion happened because the king ruled badly.

Free of the Etruscans, the Romans set up a form of government we know as the Roman **Republic**. "Republic" is a word we use to describe a government where representatives are elected by the citizens. These representatives make decisions on everyone's behalf. The Romans decided they must control more of the Italian Peninsula in order to make sure that no other group tried to take over Rome. They also wanted to drive the Greeks out of the areas to the south and to take over the plain of Campania. They needed this rich farming area so that they could feed Rome's growing population.

By 194 B.C., the Romans controlled the former Greek settlement of Cumae. But the Greeks left their influence. The Romans adapted the Greek alphabet and learned Greek methods of making buildings of stone and brick. They also borrowed Greek ideas in religion, art and government.

From 500 to 300 B.C., Rome was almost constantly at war. By 300 B.C., the city already controlled most of the Italian Peninsula. But Carthage, a region in North Africa, ruled areas of

Little is known about the Etruscan people. What we do know of them comes from sources such as this picture of an Etruscan playing a double pipe. What does this scene tell you about these early people of Rome?

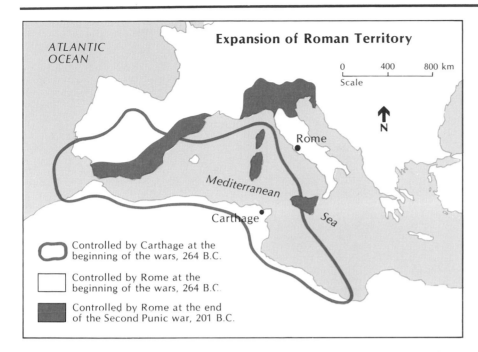

Expansion of Roman Territory

0   400   800 km
Scale

N

ATLANTIC OCEAN

Rome

Mediterranean

Sea

Carthage

○ Controlled by Carthage at the beginning of the wars, 264 B.C.

□ Controlled by Rome at the beginning of the wars, 264 B.C.

■ Controlled by Rome at the end of the Second Punic war, 201 B.C.

Before the Punic Wars, Carthage and Rome competed for control of the Mediterranean. When the wars were over, only Rome remained as a powerful force.

Sardinia and Sicily. These islands were not far from the Italian mainland. Romans worried that this growing power would soon threaten their control of Italy. They also looked enviously at the rich farm fields of North Africa and the wealth they knew Carthage possessed. They decided to go to war against Carthage.

The three wars between Rome and Carthage are called the Punic Wars. They almost destroyed Rome. The great Carthaginian general Hannibal marched his army and his elephants across the Alps, then penetrated almost to the heart of Rome. But he could not capture the city itself. After winning many victories in the countryside of Rome and Campania, he was finally defeated. The Roman army chased him back to Carthage, defeated him and destroyed the city of Carthage. This victory gave Rome control of North Africa and of Carthage's provinces in Spain.

Over the next century, the Roman Republic continued to fight wars and take over more territory. Macedonia and Greece became Roman provinces. Pergamum, part of present-day eastern Turkey, became the province of Asia Minor, the first Roman possession in Asia. As such, it gave Rome access to the mineral

HANNIBAL'S MARCH

Hannibal's troops went by ship to what is now Spain, where they conquered much of the southern and eastern part of the peninsula. They marched north through Spain, then east along the coast of present-day France. Since the coast route into Italy was guarded by Roman troops, Hannibal led his men north, then east along a tributary of the Rhone River. Fighting local tribes as they went, they reached the Alps. They crossed the mountains by way of a snowy pass, then descended into the plains of northern Italy. The march from Spain to Italy took five months.

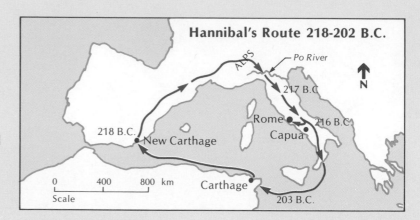

Hannibal's journey across Europe and through the Alps is one of the most heroic stories in military history. However, even supported by Gauls from the Po Valley, Hannibal was unable to conquer Rome.

and agricultural wealth of Asia. Southern Gaul (the southern half of present-day France) was conquered, completing Roman control of southern Europe.

In the 400 years between the expulsion of the Etruscans and 100 B.C., Rome had expanded from a city on the hills of the Tiber into a power that controlled the Mediterranean and the lands that surrounded it.

1. The early Romans borrowed many ideas from other peoples. Give an example to show this statement to be true.
2. Describe the improvement that needed to be made to the physical environment of Rome before it could grow into a large settlement.

The Economy in the Early Days of the Republic

In the early days of Rome, the economy was based on small family farms in the hills around the city. Each family grew enough crops and raised enough animals to support itself, with some left over to sell to town dwellers.

As the city expanded, its people needed more and more farmland. Level farmland near Rome was very limited. Once the trees there were cut down on hilly land, rains quickly washed away topsoil and nutrients. Through its wars in Italy, Rome acquired enough good farmland in the south to provide grain for the city. When Rome defeated Carthage, it got control of a land that was ideal for the growing of grain.

The republic needed this land to reward its armies. Romans believed that land was the only important form of wealth, and that farming and soldiering were the only honorable occupations. The soldier-farmer worked the land, went to fight when called, then returned to the land again. Often, soldiers were resettled in conquered lands outside of Italy and given some of this land to farm. Local residents were less likely to revolt with a part of the Roman army nearby.

Some of the soldiers grew rich from the gold and silver of captured cities. Some of this wealth was sent home to Rome, as tribute, or forced payments, for public projects. Over time, some Roman soldiers were able to buy a great deal of farmland. By about 200 B.C., most farms were large, unlike the small family farms of 400 years earlier. People who still owned small farms could not compete with the large farms worked by slaves. Many left their farms and went to the city to find work.

Most of the goods needed in Rome came up the River Tiber. Ships sailed from Campania to the port of Ostia, at the Tiber mouth, carrying grain, wine, olive oil and timber. Other ships brought grain from North Africa. The cargoes were then transferred to ships called **lighters** or to barges that could proceed upriver.

RUNNING A FARM

Cato was an important figure in the Roman government until his death in 149 B.C. He wrote many books of advice for rich Romans. One, titled *De Agri Cultura*, was for farmers. Here are some of his suggestions:

A successful farmer will want a vineyard, an irrigated garden to provide vegetables for the city market, willows for making baskets, an olive grove, a meadow for fodder, some grain, trees for stakes, an orchard, some oaks to provide acorns for your pigs. You can sell olive oil, vegetables, meat, leather and wool.

The other products will support the running of the farm.

The vineyard should be about twenty-five hectares in size, and will require sixteen slaves. The olive grove should be about sixty-five hectares in size. Thirteen slaves will be needed here, with free contract labor hired in the harvest season.

Cato's recommended farm included the three products most necessary to Romans: grain, usually wheat (for bread and gruel); olives (for oil); and grapes (for wine).

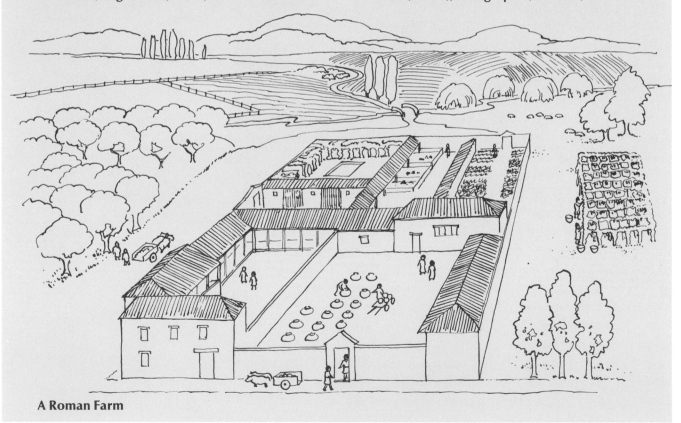

A Roman Farm

The environment of Rome did not produce a great deal of grain. As the population grew, the need to buy grain from other peoples increased. Ships were built with broad and deep holds so they could carry large quantities of grain. How did this encourage trade in other products?

The barges were towed upriver by oxen or by slaves who walked beside the river on towpaths, hauling on ropes attached to the barges. When the barges arrived at Rome, they were unloaded at the quays (kē) at Rome Tiberside and stored in warehouses. In 193 B.C., a large concrete market was built here in order to handle the goods arriving by river.

The Romans had no great supply of natural products to trade for these goods. Instead, they used money made from precious metals captured in war. Sometimes they even used the coins from these places as Roman money. In this way, Rome's foreign wars and colonies paid for imported food and luxuries for the wealthier citizens.

1. List the ways the conquered lands benefited Rome.

Government in the Republic

In the days before the Etruscans, before 600 B.C., each village chief had been advised by the heads of the families in the village. These people were known as *patres*, the Latin word for fathers. These early settlers of Rome became known as *patricians*. The rest of the residents of Rome were known as *plebeians*, from the Latin word *plebs*, or common people.

After the Romans expelled the Etruscans in about 500 B.C., they set up a republican form of government. Because they did not want to hand power to one man, they decided to have two elected rulers known as *consuls*. From their own group, the *patricians* elected the *consuls* for a one-year term, with each *consul* ruling for a month at a time at home. If they were at war, each commanded the army on alternate days.

Sometimes, the system of consulship broke down. In times of trouble, the *consuls* could appoint a single person to rule as dictator for a maximum term of six months. Dictators were usually appointed when Rome was threatened by invasion and decisions had to be made quickly. As soon as the threat was over, the dictators had to give up power.

The *consuls* appointed assistants, known as *quaestors* (kwes' tər). Later, these officals, too, were elected by the *patricians*. Their job was to look after the finances of the Roman Republic. As Rome expanded, more officials were needed to look after the business of government. A system of official appointments was worked out, from the least to the most important.

Early in the republic, *patricians* held almost all power in Rome. Each group of *patricians* had one vote in the election for *consul*. Only they could vote for *consuls* and only their assembly, known as the senate, could decide on laws. The senate also advised the *consuls*.

The *plebeians*, or common people, were not pleased with this system. They demanded to be represented. They said that unless they had their way, they would leave Rome and found a city of their own. At one point, they laid down their arms and refused to defend the city against an advancing enemy until they were given more power. The *patricians* backed down and new government offices were created to represent the *plebeians*.

The *plebeians* also demanded and got a council of their own, known as the *concilium plebs*. Over time, decisions made by this group were binding on all citizens of Rome. Once this happened, the distinction between the *patricians* and the *plebeians* was wiped away.

1. What rules made sure that no single person ruled Rome?
2. Draw a diagram to show the relationship between *patricians*, *plebeians*, *consuls* and *quaestors*.
3. How could individuals or groups get more power in Rome?

Romans at War, Romans in Peacetime

War was a major part of life in the first 300 years of the republic. At first, the Romans copied the methods of fighting of the Greeks and other ancient peoples. The phalanx (see page 135) was one such method.

By about 300 B.C., the Romans had developed a new method of warfare. They arranged their men in **legions** of about 4300, with 3000 heavily armed men; 1000 more mobile, lightly armed men; and about 300 men on horseback, known as *equites* (ek' wə tēz'), from the Latin word "*equus*," meaning horse.

The legions were divided into groups, or "maniples" of 300 men each. On the battlefield, the maniples took up positions like the squares on a checkerboard. The first two lines of the checkerboard were armed with short heavy swords and short throwing spears. The third line had long spears. This arrangement made it easier to advance, and safer to retreat. When the first line retreated the second held fast, converting the checkerboard into a phalanx.

Unlike the solid phalanx, which could move well only on level ground, the maniples were well suited to the hilly environment of the peninsula. The maniples could move easily around and over hills, fighting and regrouping as necessary.

In the early days, soldiers were not paid. They had to have enough property and money to support themselves during the long campaigns. In about the fourth century B.C., the Romans decided to allow men without property to join their army. Soldiers would now be paid. Many peasants were now able to join the army and serve in campaigns without worrying about the farm at home. Some of these campaigns kept men away from their homes and farms for as long as seven years.

This Roman soldier is in full uniform. List the ways in which his uniform protects him during a battle.

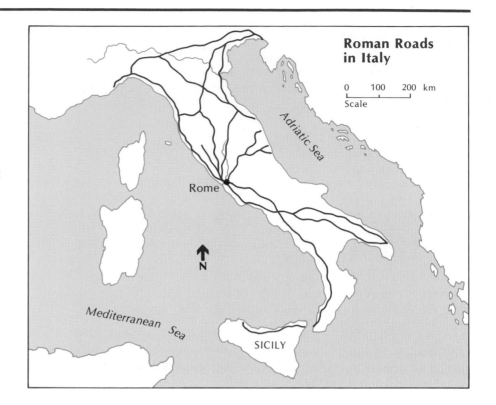

Roman Roads in Italy

Roman roads were designed to move goods into Rome and so focus on this city like the spokes of a wheel. They also allowed soldiers to move quickly throughout the countryside. Why was a road connection to the Adriatic Sea important?

In order to move their armies around quickly, the Romans built an excellent road system throughout Italy. They dug a road bed up to one metre deep, and filled it with crushed stone. On the top of this they laid stones, fitted carefully so that they could take the weight of loaded wagons. The Roman roads were so well made that some of them are still in use today, 2000 years or more after they were built.

1. What advantages did good roads give the Romans?
2. Draw and label a cross-section of a Roman road.

Although they fought well on land, the early Romans did not have ships and could not fight at sea. To fight Carthage, they had to develop a navy. They had no idea how to build ships until, during the first Punic War, they came upon a Carthaginian ship that had been beached upon the Italian shore. They learned so quickly from it that they were able to make 100 warships in sixty days. They even made improvements, inventing a grappling hook that could be lowered from their ship to an enemy ship. Roman soldiers used the hook to climb aboard the enemy ship.

When Roman soldiers won a war and returned home, they marched in a triumphal procession through Rome. Let us march with one of these processions.

We enter by one of the stone city gates. Already, the people line the sides of the street, cheering us on. Most of the poorer people are dressed in simple woollen tunics. We can tell who the richer people are, for they wear togas, long lengths of woollen cloth draped around them and over their shoulders.

We march past the elaborate stone homes of some of the senators and other *patricians* as we make our way further into the city. We enter the crowded streets near the Forum. On both sides of the street are apartment buildings that rise three to five storeys. They are ramshackle wooden and sun-dried brick buildings–we see why fire can be a problem in Rome. Hundreds of people live in these buildings. They, too, cheer us as we pass.

The streets are noisy, narrow and dirty. Even though there is a law forbidding carts and other commercial traffic in the daytime, hundreds of people still push and shove their way along the road. We continue on our way to the Forum, past the temple of Jupiter, the sky god. We stop here to honor Jupiter: he has brought us good fortune in this latest battle. Other shrines on this hill, the Capitoline, are dedicated to Jupiter's wife, Juno, the goddess who looks after women.

When the parade is over, we tag along with one of the officers to his home. His wife and daughters have prepared a feast for his return. We enter and recline on couches in the dining room, where we are handed basins of water to wash our hands and large napkins to dry them. From a table in the centre we take our food: fish, game birds, roast pork and roast lamb. There is a salad seasoned with garum, a sauce made from fish, salt and herbs. The basins of water come in handy, for there are no knives or forks.

Half-lying down, we eat, taking frequent draughts of wine mixed with water. Sometimes, a daughter feeds her father,

The army was able to win new territory for Rome by using superior military strategies.

selecting for him the best foods. By the end of the meal, we agree that the slave who is the cook has done a good job.

As we relax after dinner, we notice the shrines of household gods in the room beyond the dining room. These are the gods who protect and help this family. If everything is done according to their ritual, in the proper manner, good fortune will bless the household.

1. Match the items from column A with their correct descriptions in column B.

A	B
1. Cumae	a. Carthaginian general
2. *Cloaca Maxima*	b. Italian river
3. Sicily	c. Roman author and politician
4. Cato	d. Greek settlement in Italy
5. Hannibal	e. the Great Sewer
6. Juno	f. assistant to the *consuls*
7. Maniple	g. military formation
8. Tiber	h. Roman goddess
9. Palatine	i. one of the Seven Hills of Rome
10. *Quaestor*	j. island south of Italy

2. Why could the physical environment around Rome not supply enough food for Rome? What did the Romans do to overcome this shortage of food?

3. In your own words, describe how the economy of Rome changed during the republic.

4. Why did the Romans decide to change to a republican form of government? Describe this system of government. In your description, explain the role of the *consuls*, the dictators, the senate, and the *concilium plebs*.

5. Why was the Roman method of fighting better adapted to the physical environment of Italy than the Greek phalanx system?

THE GOLDEN AGE OF ROME

Rome and Its Empire: Expansion and Change

The expansion of Rome brought many changes to and problems for the Romans. Some problems came from the far reaches of the provinces. In 113 B.C., northern peoples called the Cimbri poured into Gaul, looking for land where they could settle. The Cimbri and their allies marched as far as the borders of Italy. They were thrown back only after a series of fierce battles that frightened the people of Rome.

Another army threatened the eastern border of the empire. There, Mithradates, king of Pontus, was taking over land for an empire of his own. When he tried to conquer one of Rome's allies, Roman soldiers marched against him. The Romans won; this victory and others in the east extended Rome's possessions further into Asia.

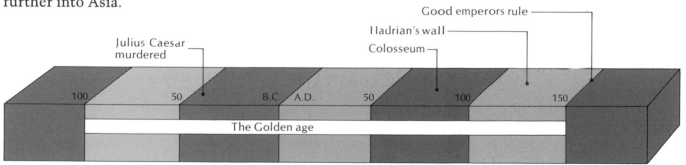

Other problems were closer to home. The Italians living outside of Rome were angry. They felt they should have the same privileges as Roman citizens. Romans could vote for their government and paid no taxes. When Rome refused to give the Italians Roman citizenship, they rebelled and threatened to attack Rome. Because they needed their armies to fight enemies in Asia, the Romans offered all Italians Roman citizenship.

In Rome itself, the republican system was having difficulties. Several *consuls* were assassinated as others tried to take the position by force. Slaves rebelled against the severe treatment they received from their masters. Roman governors in the provinces made enormous fortunes, robbing the people and imposing huge taxes on them. The governors then kept the money for themselves, buying up more and more land in Italy. Without land, poor people had difficulty getting enough to eat. Rich people who wanted to keep the system as it was fought with reformers who wanted life made easier for the rest of the people.

In 81 B.C., Sulla, a popular army general declared himself dictator and killed many of his enemies. One man who gained power during this time was Gaius Julius Caesar. He was sent to govern Gaul. When he returned, he and two others took over the government, declaring they would rule as a *triumvirate*. This word means "a group of three."

Caesar then had himself elected *consul* and headed back to Gaul to subdue the tribes who had risen up against the Romans. Triumphant, he returned to Rome to find the city was torn by civil war among the different groups that wanted power. Tired of the fighting, the Roman senate and people declared Caesar **dictator** for life.

Caesar was killed a few months later, stabbed by jealous rivals. After another fifteen years of fighting, the Romans accepted Octavian, a nephew of Julius Caesar, as their leader. He was called Augustus, the Great One, and his rule began the Roman Empire.

1. The republic was being attacked from both outside and within. Give evidence to show this statement to be true.
2. Explain why Roman citizenship would be important to Italians.
3. Make a list of the qualities you would hope to find in a person made dictator for life.

The Economy: Slaves, Traders and Citizens

As the Romans conquered new territory, more and more people and goods moved between the many areas of the empire and Rome. Thousands of slaves were shipped to Italy. Taxes and goods in the form of tribute were also sent to Rome. Farm products and manufactured goods were traded from Italy to the provinces. Soldiers, traders and government administrators went from Rome to other parts of the empire. This movement of goods and people to and from Rome shaped the economy of the Roman Empire.

By the time of Augustus, more than a quarter of the people living in Italy were slaves from other parts of the empire. Slavery played a large role in the economy of Italy. Slaves built roads, monuments and other public works. Many worked the large farming estates in Italy. Some slaves were well-educated people who worked as doctors, dentists, writers and civil servants.

Since slaves and freedmen (former slaves who had bought or been given their freedom) were available to do much of the work, many citizens found themselves with little to do. There were few small farms left in Italy. Most of the farm families had moved to Rome looking for work. City officials found it necessary to give out free grain in order to keep the people from starvation. By the time of Augustus, free grain was being distributed to almost 200 000 unemployed workers in the city.

There were limits to the amount of grain and other food that could be produced in Italy; more and more food came from outside the peninsula. When Augustus came to power, more than three-quarters of Rome's food came from Sicily, North Africa and Egypt. The Roman government needed money to pay for this food. Since Roman citizens paid no taxes, tribute and taxes from the rest of the empire had to be used for the food.

As the empire expanded, the Romans made it easier for areas of it to trade with Rome and with one another. As soon as a new province was added to the empire, slaves, peasants and freedmen were set to work building roads to connect this area to Rome. Traders, merchants, and soldiers moved along these new roads. With control of the Mediterranean, the Roman navy was able to capture or kill most of the pirates who had robbed ships on the sea, thus making the Mediterranean safe for traders' ships.

Wine, oil and pottery were the most important goods sent from Italy to the rest of the empire. Far more goods came from

Blacksmiths

Carpenter

Potter

Roman Slaves at Work

163

IMPROVEMENTS TO THE ENVIRONMENT; BUILDING THE AQUEDUCTS

As the empire grew, so did the cities. One of the greatest needs in the cities was for a good water supply.

Throughout the empire, aqueducts were built to transport water from the river to the homes. The best path from the water source to the city was laid out by a surveyor, usually an officer of the Roman army. Water was collected in a basin near the water source. Mountain springs were the best source, since the water could then be drawn by gravity down from the mountain to the city.

The water travelled through channels often many kilometres long, made of stone or of pipes of pottery or lead. To keep gravity at work, the aqueduct had to travel through or around hills and be supported above low ground on high stone arches.

Slave labor was often used for these aqueducts. In 33 B.C., Agrippa, a public official, used slaves to have a new aqueduct built and other aqueducts repaired in Rome. Along the aqueduct, the slaves built several hundred basins and fountains. They adorned it all with statues and marble columns.

Building an Aqueduct

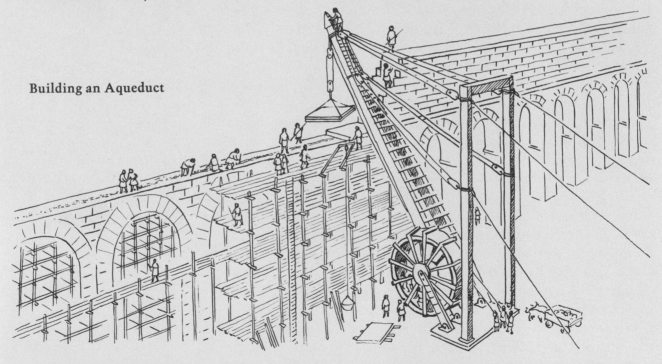

Using only the simplest machines, like the pulley and crane pictured here, Romans were able to build structures that have lasted for over 2000 years.

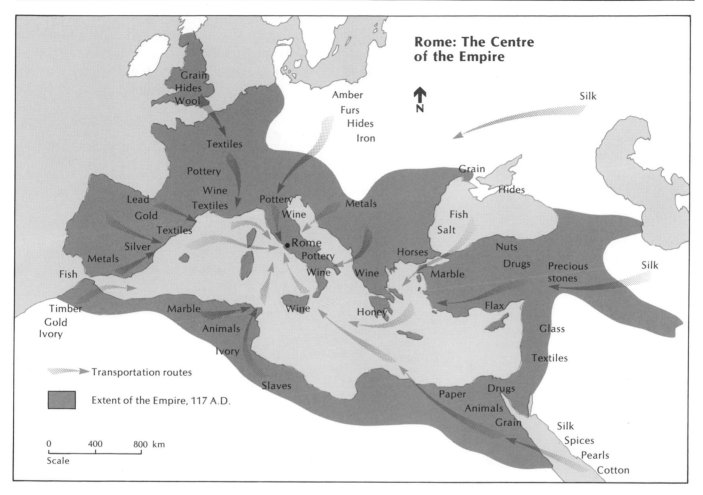

Rome: The Centre of the Empire

N

Grain
Hides
Wool

Amber
Furs
Hides
Iron

Silk

Textiles

Pottery

Wine
Textiles

Pottery
Wine

Metals

Grain

Hides

Lead
Gold

Fish
Salt

Textiles

Silver

Metals

Pottery
Wine

Rome
Pottery
Wine

Horses

Wine

Marble

Nuts

Drugs

Precious
stones

Silk

Fish

Flax

Timber
Gold
Ivory

Marble

Wine

Honey

Glass

Animals

Textiles

Ivory

Drugs
Paper
Animals
Grain

Slaves

Silk
Spices
Pearls
Cotton

Transportation routes

Extent of the Empire, 117 A.D.

0   400   800 km
Scale

the provinces to Rome: grain from Sicily and Africa, metals from Spain and Britain, papyrus from Egypt and textiles from Asia. Trade routes were also developed to places outside the empire. Romans bought pepper and jewels from Aden, silk from China and amber from the lands around the Baltic Sea.

At first, Rome tried to make sure that goods such as pottery, wine and oil were not produced in the provinces. In this way, Roman goods could be sure of a market there. But by the second century A.D., most of the provinces produced enough food, cloth, building materials, pottery, glass and other basic goods to supply their own needs.

Goods from the empire, and beyond, were transported to Rome. The Romans had trade ties to Africa for ivory and gold, to India for spices, and to China for silk.

Life in the other cities of Italy and in the cities of the provinces was in many ways similar to life in Rome. The people of the provinces tried to copy Rome, for they thought of it as the centre of the civilized world. They often modelled their towns on Rome, imitated Roman architecture and clothing, and spoke Latin.

1. (a) Where did the slaves used by the Romans come from?

   (b) Explain how slaves were important to the economy of the empire.

   (c) Give one example of how slaves were harmful to the empire.

2. Give reasons why the Romans were concerned about trade with the empire.

3. What did the Romans do to encourage trade?

Imperial Government

During the republic, power was held by a number of people. With the coming of Augustus, the empire entered a period of rule by individuals. These rulers were known as *Princeps*, the First Citizen. In time, they also became known as emperors. The emperors were the commander-in-chief of the army and the head of the priesthood. In this way, they controlled government, the army and religion.

The senate and people's assembly continued to exist for many years. The senate was supposed to suggest and approve the choice of emperor. It also advised the emperor and looked after much of the routine administration. Although the senate had the right to pass laws, it rarely disagreed with the emperor. If members of the senate did not like the emperor, however, they might try to have him killed and replaced.

The Romans had different ways of ruling different parts of their empire. City states in Italy, such as Campania, continued to

A Roman Consul

After the Romans expelled the Etruscan king, his powers were shared by two consuls. Their responsibilities included commanding the Roman Army and advising the Senate.

look after their own affairs. As citizens of Rome, the men of these city states were expected to provide soldiers and money for Rome's armies.

Governors from Rome ruled the provinces outside Italy. Augustus divided the provinces into two types: he was responsible for the more warlike ones, such as Syria, Spain and the provinces on the Rhine. He let the senate appoint governors for the more peaceful ones, such as Greece and Africa.

The job of emperor was very insecure. Of the first twelve emperors, seven died violently by poison, stabbing, or suicide. In the years after Augustus, several emperors were violent, insane, or both. The emperor Nero, for example, spent much of his time playing the violin, acting in plays and appearing as a charioteer. He had both his mother and his wife killed, finally fleeing from Rome and killing himself.

The second century A.D. brought a succession known as the "good emperors," many of whom were born outside Italy. Hadrian, from Spain, is the best-known of them. He travelled throughout the empire to make sure that each province was well-run and safe from invaders. In Britain, he ordered built a long stone wall near the Tyne River, still known as "Hadrian's Wall," to separate the Roman province from the land of the Celtic tribes to the north.

The good emperors developed a larger civil service and separated the governing of the empire into military and civil affairs. Hadrian created special departments to control such things as correspondence, justice, taxes and records.

1. What would the change to emperors mean for the people in the Senate and people's assembly?

2. Compare the leadership of Rome before and after Augustus using these headings: Leaders, Senate responsibilities, People who had power, How leaders were chosen.

3. Suggest reasons why the job of emperor was insecure following the rule of Augustus.

Life in Rome: Bread and Circuses

Rome had changed since the early days of the republic. The first buildings of wood, dried mud and straw had been replaced by thousands of homes, shops and public buildings. The finest were built of marble; Caesar Augustus boasted he had found a city of brick and turned it into a city of marble. Most buildings were made of stone found near Rome, or of cement made from a volcanic sand also found near the city. We are not sure if the Romans invented cement, but they were the first people to use it widely.

Life for the poor people of the city revolved around "bread and circuses." One day a month, the emperor's employees stood at the Gate of Minucius in the city walls, distributing free grain that the poor could make into bread. Many more times a month, poor and rich alike flocked to the Circus Maximus, one of the main Roman arenas, for the games and celebrations that were a feature of Roman life.

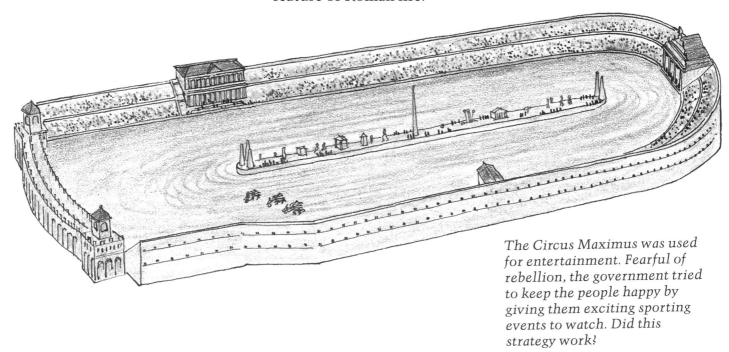

The Circus Maximus was used for entertainment. Fearful of rebellion, the government tried to keep the people happy by giving them exciting sporting events to watch. Did this strategy work?

Let us follow the crowd to one of these celebrations, the first day of the games held every year from July 20-30 to celebrate the victories of Julius Caesar.

The crowd streams into the Circus Maximus early, so people can get good seats on the hillside that overlooks the playing field. The Circus Maximus is built to take advantage of the environment: the area where the contestants gather is between the Palatine and Avantine hills. The marshy ground in this valley acts as a cushion for the many falls the gladiators will take.

For several hundred years the spectators have crowded the hillsides. Just a few years ago, Caesar had tiers or platforms carved out so up to 150 000 spectators could sit at their ease and watch the games. Nobles sit nearer the bottom of the hill, in boxes with comfortable seats.

Emperor Caesar Augustus enters the royal box and the games begin. First comes a chariot race. A trumpet sounds. The race official throws down a white handkerchief. Wheels spin and dust flies as the four-horse chariots gather speed. They cut as close as they can to the turning posts as they race around the oval track. One crashes, and the charioteer slashes the reins with his dagger to keep from being dragged to his death.

One of the four chariots carrying the blue colors completes the seven laps first. The crowd supporting blue cheers and whistles. But the reds, whites and greens will have their chance: there will be eleven more races before the day is out. Meanwhile, acrobats tumble into the arena, leaping from horse to horse in frantic motion.

Today is dedicated to chariot racing, but tomorrow there will be a battle to the death between slaves and elephants and lions. You can hear the lions roar in the distance even now. Later in the week, gladiators will fight each other; unless Caesar shows mercy to the loser, only the winner will live, to go on to another fight. It is said that Augustus plans a show that will pit 10 000 gladiators against one another. Perhaps this week too there will be hippopotamuses splashing in the moat that keeps the wild animals from the spectators. If we get bored with all this, we can wander down to the theatre, where actors present dramatic plays

Chariot racing was one of the popular sports held in the Circus Maximus. Which of today's sporting events do you think is like the chariot racing of Roman times?

for the crowds. Both the games and the plays will continue to sunrise the next morning.

1. Write a sentence to identify or explain each of the following:

   a. the Cimbri   e. Campania
   b. Sulla   f. Hadrian
   c. Aqueducts   g. Mithradates
   d. *Princeps*   h. Octavian.

2. In your notebook, make a chart to show the differences between the Roman Republic and the days of Augustus. Use these headings: Government, Economy, City of Rome, Everyday Life.

3. How did the presence of so many slaves affect life in Rome? Describe the effects both on rich people and on poor people.

4. Suggest some ways in which the extension of roads into the provinces might have changed the life of the people living there.

THE BREAK-UP OF THE EMPIRE

Invasions and Plagues

By the time of Hadrian, who was emperor from 117 to 138 A.D., the Romans had an empire that stretched from Britain to the middle of Asia. Yet they wanted to expand it in order to bring in more taxes and tribute and to push back any tribes that threatened the peace of the empire. But the larger the empire became, the more problems it brought to the Romans. It became more and more difficult and expensive to control regions far from Rome.

In the years after 200 A.D., provinces such as Gaul and Britain declared their independence from Rome. Tribes to the north of the empire threatened Roman provinces. As the attacks continued, the emperors realized that it was very difficult to direct defence from a capital that was so far from the borders. They moved parts of their government to such cities as Augusta Treverorum in Gaul, so they could keep these provinces under control.

THE DECLINE OF ROME

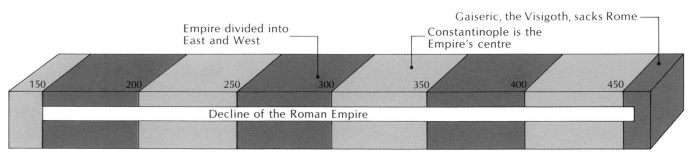

Empire divided into East and West

Gaiseric, the Visigoth, sacks Rome

Constantinople is the Empire's centre

150　200　250　300　350　400　450

Decline of the Roman Empire

In the second and third centuries A.D., plagues spread into Italy. Although we do not know exactly which diseases these were, we think they were smallpox and bubonic plague. Some of the germs were brought back by Roman soldiers fighting in the eastern part of the empire and by travellers who passed through Egypt and Asia. The plagues killed many people and greatly reduced the population of Rome, Italy and the western provinces.

In time, the Romans realized that it was more trouble than it was worth to defend some parts of the empire, so they decided to give up some of their northern lands, withdrawing behind the Rhine and the Danube rivers. These natural borders made it easier to fight off enemy attacks.

Recognizing that the empire was too large to manage, Diocletian divided it into two, the east and west empires. Each was further divided into two prefectures, with their own ruler.

They also realized that the empire had become too large to be ruled successfully by one man. In 286 A.D., Diocletian (dī ək lē shən) divided the empire in two, ruling the eastern half himself and giving the western half to Maximian, a friend. Later, Diocletian divided the empire into four, with a ruler for each.

The eastern provinces of the empire in time became richer and

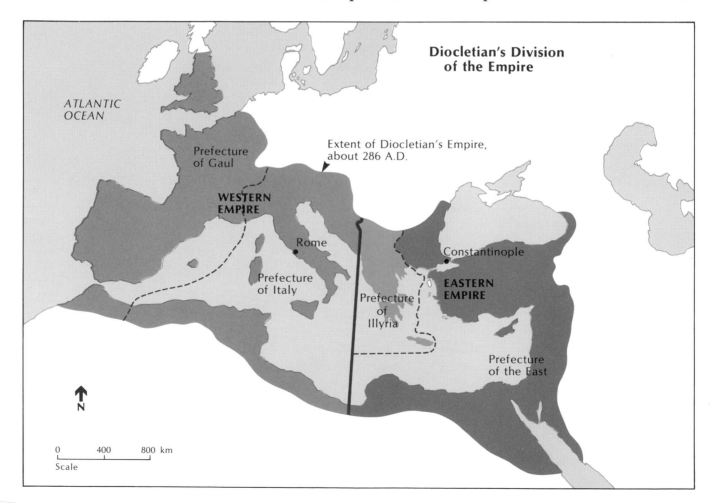

Diocletian's Division of the Empire

ATLANTIC OCEAN

Prefecture of Gaul

Extent of Diocletian's Empire, about 286 A.D.

WESTERN EMPIRE

Rome

Prefecture of Italy

Prefecture of Illyria

Constantinople

EASTERN EMPIRE

Prefecture of the East

N

0   400   800 km

Scale

more important than the western ones. In 324 A.D., the emperor Constantine began work on Constantinople, a new capital in the east, to replace Rome as the centre of the empire. He modelled the new city exactly on Rome, with gates, roads and buildings just as they were in Rome. Although residents of Rome retained their privileges–no taxation, free grain–Rome itself became less and less important in the empire.

Fifty years later, the western empire was threatened again. Huns, Visigoths, Ostrogoths and Vandals crossed the borders of the empire and began to conquer land. These barbarians challenged Roman troops again and again. In 455 A.D., Gaiseric (gī sər ik), the Visigoth, reached and sacked Rome. The Visigoths established an empire of their own, including North Africa and Spain. The western Roman Empire was at an end.

Despite attacks and rebellions in the eastern provinces, the eastern empire survived. For another 1000 years, a Roman emperor ruled the eastern empire from Constantinople.

1. What actions did the Roman leaders take to try to stop the empire from declining?
2. Make a list of some of the problems a leader might have had because the empire was too large.

The Changing Environment, the Changing Economy

The years after the good emperors also brought many changes to the environment and the economy of the Roman Empire. These changes contributed to the downfall of the western empire.

The early Romans had relied on the environment near Rome, and then on the fields of southern Italy, to provide them with the raw materials for food, shelter and clothing. As the population of Rome grew, the Romans took advantage of the many different types of environment in the empire. They obtained grain from Sardinia, North Africa and Egypt; wine from Gaul and Spain; olives and olive oil from the Mediterranean coast. They found new sources of gold in Egypt and Spain, and brought stone from Greece. Fine woollen cloth was imported from Asia. These imports in some ways made life more comfortable for Romans. However, they also made Romans more and more dependent on the resources of environments far from Rome.

As time went on, Rome needed more and more soldiers to defend the borders of the empire. The emperor Diocletian doubled the size of the army and expanded the civil service. He took many people from their farms to fight in the army. As a result, food production dropped, especially in the western empire.

The provinces could not provide enough soldiers and farmers. The emperors even began recruiting people from outside the empire to serve in the army and to work the farm fields. These recruits learned about Roman methods of fighting and about the riches of the Roman provinces. When they returned home, they took what they had learned and sometimes used it against the Romans.

The growing cost of defence was a great burden on the empire. Money had to be found to feed, clothe and arm the soldiers. Many of the gold mines in the empire were exhausted, and there were no new supplies of silver. To meet the high cost of the armies, emperors began making coins of less valuable metal. The value of the coins fell and goods began to cost more and more. After a time, the emperors did not have enough money to support the armies. They told the provinces where the soldiers were based that they would have to feed and clothe the army.

To move soldiers and trade products, the Romans had expanded their road system. More roads made it simpler for them to travel, but they also made it easier for the people who wanted to take over parts of the empire. Enemy armies could advance on Rome along Roman roads.

Agriculture underwent changes. Owners of large farms had to have workers to work their fields. But, as the empire stopped growing, there were no new sources of slaves. Plagues killed off many freemen who might have worked the farms. Landowners began to rent out some of their fields, usually the worst and most distant ones, to tenant farmers. At first, these tenants paid rent with part of their crops and by part-time work in the owner's fields. By the end of the fourth century, however, the tenants were forced to give most of their crops to the owner and to work full-time for him. They were also forbidden to leave the land to look for jobs elsewhere.

The system of tenant farming was not as efficient as farming with slaves had been. A single large farm worked by slaves was usually more productive than a collection of small farms worked by tenants.

In Italy, changes in the environment also made the land less productive. Once trees were stripped from hilly land to be used as building materials, rains washed much of the good soil down the hills and into the sea. As crops were planted on the level lands year after year, the land produced less and less. Italy became increasingly dependent on the other provinces for its food supply. It became poorer and the other provinces became richer.

As the population of the western empire fell, it became difficult to find enough people to construct buildings and fortifications. The emperors decided that the members of craft guilds (societies) would be responsible for this construction. They also forced people to assist without pay in the building of roads and fortifications. To be sure that enough grain reached Rome to feed the people, they made the shipping guilds responsible for transport of the grain.

Emperors began to impose very heavy taxes on the provinces. If an official could not collect enough money from the people, he had to pay the taxes himself. To make sure that the taxes were paid, the emperors forced all people of a certain class to take their turn as provincial officials.

Changes were also happening in the way in which emperors were chosen. The most powerful group in the empire was now the army. Different groups within the army often agreed to support a man for emperor if he would promise to pay them large sums of money. When their choice became emperor, he usually had to raise this money through taxes. If rival groups in the army were unhappy with the choice of emperor, they might overthrow or kill him, putting another man in his place. In one year, seven different people ruled as emperor or co-emperor; six of them were murdered.

Tenant farmers paid rent to landowners with either money, crops or animals. In what ways were the landowners unfair to the farmers?

1. Summarize in point form the ways in which the leaders of the Roman Empire attempted to deal with these problems: defence, food supply, public administration.
2. Describe how the life of average people in the Roman Empire changed as it went into decline.
3. Give several reasons why farming became less and less productive during the fall of the empire.
4. Explain why the system of tenant farming is not very efficient.

ROMAN LAW

Roman emperors and their civil servants set up regulations to help govern the empire. These regulations became part of Roman law, which had been developing since the beginnings of the Roman Republic.

Under the republic, Romans had used the Twelve Tables as their laws. According to the tables, no one could put himself beyond the law. While we take such a notion for granted, there had been times when a Roman senator could try to say that laws did not apply to him.

Hadrian had the laws written down again in the second century A.D., bringing them up to date and setting down rules that applied across the empire. When laws are written down in this way, we can refer to them as a **code**. Under Hadrian's code, the emperor, not court officials, was the source of the law. The emperor made the laws, and the courts enforced them.

The last and greatest codification of Roman law was ordered by the eastern emperor Justinian in the sixth century A.D. Over the centuries since Rome was founded, various lawyers had written so much law that it took Justinian's advisors fifty volumes just to compile the summaries. Like the previous codes, Justinian's stressed the importance of the individual, and of fair application of the law.

Some of the laws in Justinian's Code were written by his wife, Theodora. Theodora ruled with her husband, and was thought by many people to be more intelligent and powerful than Justinian. She was especially interested in women's rights, and wrote laws that protected these rights, such as one that gave more help to women in divorce cases.

Many people think that Roman law was Rome's greatest contribution to the building of western civilization.

Religion and the Rise of Christianity

As the Roman Empire expanded, Romans came to know new gods and new religions. They adopted the god Isis from Egypt, and the goddess Cybele from Asia Minor. They took up the worship of the Persian god Mithras. Astrology, developed in Babylonia, became very popular. Emperors and *plebeians* alike studied their horoscopes and made decisions based on what they thought the stars foretold. The system of the zodiac that is still popular today dates from these early times.

In the first and second century A.D., another new religion began. For more than two thousand years, a group of people known as Jews or Hebrews had lived around the eastern Mediterranean. They worshipped only one god and said he was the only god that existed. Most Jews lived in Judea, an area that became a province of Rome in 6 A.D.

It was about 4 B.C., historians now believe, that a Jew named Jesus was born. After life as a village carpenter in the town of Nazareth, he left at the age of thirty and began to preach in the area around the Sea of Galilee. During his three years of preaching, he urged his followers to help him prepare for the Kingdom of God. Some people interpreted his preaching to mean that Jesus claimed to be the King of the Jews, and therefore a rival to the power of the Roman Empire. Since only the emperor could appoint kings, they had Jesus arrested, tried and found guilty of treason. He was sentenced to death by crucifixion, a common method of execution in the Roman Empire.

After Jesus' crucifixion, his followers said that he had risen again, and that he was the son of God. Paul of Tarsus, a Roman citizen who had converted to these beliefs, travelled through his home province of Asia Minor and through Syria to preach and to write. To history, he has become known as St. Paul. The early growth of the new religion, which came to be known as Christianity, was largely his doing.

At first, the Romans did not worry much about the Christians. Although Christianity was illegal because it denied that the emperor was a god, it was tolerated as long as Christians prayed

NUMBERING THE YEARS

A.D. is the symbol for *anno Domini* which means since Christ was born. This system of numbering the years was not used until about 1582 when Pope Gregory developed the system for Roman Catholic countries. Many other countries in the world adopted it as well.

Actual historical records dating the birth and life of Christ are incomplete. The scholars responsible for determining the precise year of Christ's birth had to work from records which used a Roman calendar. They identified a particular year and started numbering forward (A.D.) and backward (B.C.) from there. It was only later that inaccuracies in the calender were uncovered. It is now generally felt that Christ was born around the year 4 B.C.

for the health of the emperor. But, as more people converted to Christianity, emperors began to see the religion as a threat to their power. Some emperors decided that Christians must be executed. When Rome began losing battles to the barbarians, some emperors blamed the losses on the Romans' loss of belief in their old gods. They made it a crime not to believe in the old gods.

In the fourth century A.D., Constantine, who was ruler of the eastern empire, marched on Rome, eventually taking over all the western empire. Constantine claimed to have had a dream in which he was told to mark his soldiers' shields with the Christian cross. He felt that his success was due to his following the message of the dream, and so came to adopt the Christian god as his own.

In 313 A.D., Constantine passed the Edict of Toleration. In this proclamation, he gave freedom of religion to everyone in the empire. Later in that century, emperors declared that Christianity was the official religion of both the eastern and western empires. In less than 400 years, this new religion had spread from a small group of followers to take in many people across the empire.

1. Suggest some reasons why a group of people would begin to worship new gods.
2. The emperors felt threatened by Christianity and eventually outlawed it. What else could they have done to deal with their "problem"?

Life in Rome and in the Provinces

Rome in the third century A.D. was very different from the Rome we saw in the early days of the republic. Now, Rome contained almost a million people, many of them immigrants from the four corners of the empire. Let us follow one of these people, a wealthy trader from northern Gaul, on his daily rounds.

Breakfast is first, bread and fruit, followed by several hours talking to other traders about shipments. Then our trader walks to the baths of Caracalla, in the centre of the city.

The average Roman had no bathtub at home. Instead, he or she went to the public baths. They were not a place just to get clean. They were a way of life for anyone who could afford the entry fee.

Our trader walks along a pathway through the majestic gardens that surround the baths. He passes by the shops where his wife and her friends are looking at the silks and perfumes that have travelled here from China. He heads straight for the sports ground, where he plays a type of tennis for a while. Through the

The bath houses of Rome were more than places to wash. Here a Roman could take part in athletics, study, eat, swim or just meet with friends. Would all Romans have been able to enjoy bath houses?

hedges, he can hear women on another sportsground, rolling hoops and playing handball. He looks at the wrestlers, but does not feel like joining them today.

Not satisfied with the sweat he has worked up at sports, he enters the sweatroom, a dry, heated room. Then he moves on to the hot bath, relaxing in the hot water. He takes a metal tool and scrapes the dirt off his skin; a slow cooldown and a quick plunge into the cold pool follow. After the bath, he chats with his friends, then visits the library to read a report on crop yields he hears has just arrived. Later in the day, he joins his wife and friends in their spacious home for dinner.

He is luckier than the poorer people, who spend their evenings in the dirty, noisy crowded apartment buildings that rise above the narrow Roman streets.

After spending some time in Rome, our trader and his wife head home to Augusta Treverorum, now called Trier, near the Rhine River. Like most provincial capitals, Trier has been modelled on Rome. The trader and his wife pass into the city through the Porta Nigra, a handsomely-carved stone gate set into the wall that surrounds the city. Their horsedrawn carriage takes them past the royal palace, the baths and apartments. They also pass the Forum, an amphitheatre, shops and apartment buildings before they reach their stone house.

The next day, the trader's wife goes by carriage to meet some friends for lunch. Her route takes her past small workshops. She stops at one to examine the fine woollen cloth, and to buy a robe for sale in the small shop beside the workshop. Above the shop lives the family that makes the cloth. In other shops, she can see metalworkers making jewellery and tools, woodworkers crafting furniture and barrels, potters and glassmakers making containers and stoneworkers making the millstones to grind grain. She does not stop at any of these; whatever she needs, her servants can buy for her. She stops at the university, where she will meet her son, who is studying law.

The trader also visits the wool shops today, for fine woollen cloth from Trier is in demand in Rome. He also goes to the shops of artists who lay the mosaics, picture-stories told in arrange-

The Greengrocer

The Blacksmith

The illustrations on this page and the next were taken from carvings on Roman monuments.

ments of tiny pieces of colored stone.

In another part of the city, on the river, shipwrights make the ships that sail the Rhine. In the fields around the city, farmers and their slaves and tenants produce wine and honey. They also grow wheat and other cereals and raise animals for the local market.

1. Make a chart with columns for the Roman Republic, the early Roman Empire and the late Roman Empire. List the headings: Environment, Government, Religion, Economy. Fill in the chart to show the differences between each stage.
2. Make a list of the things that you think contributed to the decline of the western empire and the survival of the eastern empire.
3. Look again at the map on page 172. Notice the sections that made up the Roman Empire in the third century A.D. What countries cover these sections now?

The Butcher

SUMMARY

The first people to settle on the hills of Rome arrived around 750 B.C. Among their neighbors were the Etruscans, a people of the northern peninsula who ruled Rome for about two centuries. After rule by the Etruscans, the Romans set up a form of government known as a republic. By about 300 B.C., the Roman Republic controlled most of the Italian Peninsula. Over the next two centuries, the Romans went on to conquer most of the lands of the Mediterranean.

The economy of early Rome was based on small family farms. As Roman power grew, much of the farmland fell into the hands of wealthy soldiers and citizens. The Romans used the River Tiber and the Mediterranean as trade routes, using coins made from the precious metals of conquered lands.

The government of the republic was made up of *consuls*, dictators, *quaestors* and a senate of *patricians*. In the later days of the republic, the *plebeians* also gained a role in government.

Much of the republic's military success was due to a formation

The Cobbler

known as the "maniple." Rome's excellent network of roads made it easy to move armies around quickly.

In the "Golden Age" of Rome, from about 100 B.C. to almost 150 A.D., the republic became an empire. Early in this period, Romans had to fight off peoples to the north and to the east, and as well to satisfy the other peoples of the Italian Peninsula. The republican government had its problems as *consuls* and governors fought amongst themselves. Eventually Octavian, son of Julius Caesar, became *Princeps*, or leading citizen, and in practice became emperor.

Slavery was of great importance to the economy of the republic and the empire. The growing population of Rome came to rely more and more heavily on goods from other parts of the empire.

Under the imperial system, Rome was divided into provinces, ruled by various governors appointed by the emperor. The emperor's job was very insecure; many emperors died violent deaths. Yet some, such as Hadrian, did much to improve the defence and administration of the empire.

"Bread and Circuses" were a feature of life in Rome. The poor people of the city were given free grain, while both rich and poor enjoyed the chariot races, gladiator duels and other spectacles of the Circus Maximus.

During the three centuries following 150 A.D., the empire gradually fell apart. Plagues and barbarian invasions were factors in this break-up. The Romans attempted to improve defence of the empire by dividing it up into two, and later four, sections.

The expense of maintaining the army and Rome's growing dependence on imported goods also weakened the empire, as did the system of tenant farming.

In the early centuries A.D., a new religion, Christianity, emerged. Its early followers were often persecuted. But within four centuries it had spread throughout the Mediterranean and become the official religion of the empire.

Life in the provincial capitals was often modelled on life in Rome. Augusta Treverorum, on the Rhine River, was one such capital.

Chapter Review: Rome

NEW WORDS AND IDEAS

1. Explain the jobs done by each of these positions in Rome:
   patricians consuls princeps equites

2. Name the seas that border the Italian Peninsula.

3. (a) Name the three major rivers of the Roman Empire.
   (b) Explain why they were important.

4. For each of the people listed below, write one or two sentences describing their contributions to Roman civilization:
   Theodore   Constantine
   Hadrian   Cato

CHECKING YOUR UNDERSTANDING

5. Explain how the environment of the Italian Peninsula encouraged the Romans to conquer other places.

6. Suggest two or three reasons for Rome's success in building an empire. Write a paragraph titled, "Reasons for the Success of the Roman Empire."

7. Compare agriculture in Rome during its three time periods: the Republic, the Golden Age, Rome's decline. Use the headings: size of farms, ownership, laborers and crop yield.

8. What special privileges were given to the citizens of Rome? Do you think this system was fair? Give reasons for your opinion.

9. (a) List the goods the Romans received through trade, and state where each item came from.
   (b) Explain why trade was important to the Romans.
   (c) What did the Romans offer in return for the goods they needed?

10. (a) Reread the section on Roman law found on page 176. What were the Twelve Tables?
    (b) How did the Twelve Tables help control the power of the emperor?
    (c) How did Hadrian change the law of Rome? How did Justinian change the law?

11. List four causes for the fall of Rome. Which one do you think is the most important? Give reasons for your choice.

USING YOUR KNOWLEDGE

12. The Romans learned from the people they conquered; they borrowed ideas about engineering from the Etruscans, and the arts from the Greeks. Canada is a country made up of many different peoples. Make a list of things that are a part of your everyday life that came from cultures other than that of your parents. Think about things like food, entertainment, and clothing to get you started.

13. (a) The Romans were famous builders. Their aqueducts and roads are two examples of Roman engineering that still remain. What structures found in your area do you think will still be standing one hundred years from now? a thousand years from now?
    (b) What will the people in the future learn about our way of life from these structures?

UNIT 2

OTHER ANCIENT CIVILIZATIONS

INTRODUCTION

From our study of early civilizations, we can see that they have something in common. Mesopotamia, Egypt, Greece and Rome all developed in similar stages.

In the first stage, farming techniques improved, food supplies increased and populations grew. As agriculture spread across Asia, North Africa and Europe, the human population multiplied many times. During this stage, sometimes called "The Agricultural Revolution," the physical environment was modified so that the needs of people were better met.

In the next stage, people began to live in large, highly organized groups. First villages grew, then cities. In and around these cities, some people farmed while others worked as artisans, tradespeople, or soldiers, controlled by the ruling families. The development of these governments marked the beginning of **states.** This stage of adaption to the human environment of cities is sometimes called "The Urban Revolution."

In the final stage, these states spread their influence far and wide. By trade and by war, they absorbed other states and became

The Inca people learned to adapt to the Andean environment and so were able to build an empire.

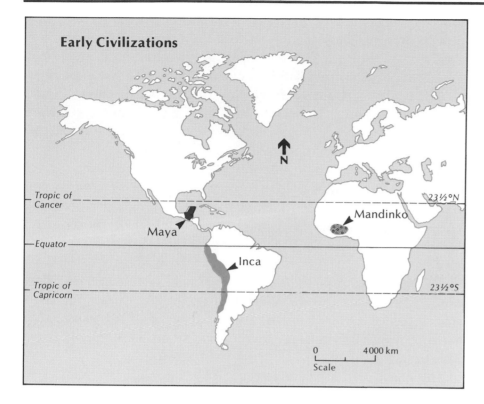

Early Civilizations

The chapters of this unit explore three civilizations which contributed relatively little to our modern way of life. However, each one was important in its own time.

empires. In this "Imperial" stage, the tools, knowledge and customs of a civilization were carried to new peoples.

In the next three chapters we will investigate three other places where a people followed the path of civilization in stages similar to these. One place was the Central American rain forest, home of the Maya people. Another was the Andes Mountains in South America, home of the Inca people. The third was the grasslands of West Africa, home of the Mandinko.

These three places have something in common. They are all tropical environments, closer to the **equator** than the environments we have studied in Unit One. They have different climates, landforms, plants and animals. In each one, good use of the physical environment helped a culture to develop.

Because of their isolation, the Maya, Incas and Mandinko developed cultures that owed little to other peoples. Central and South America were cut off from Europe and Asia by the Atlantic and Pacific oceans, while West Africa was cut off by the huge Sahara Desert. These people lacked the resources for some key discoveries. Neither the Maya nor the Inca invented the wheel. The Maya had no metals and kept no livestock. None of these peoples learned how to travel long distances in ships. Their societies were quite unlike the ancient western ones. Even their cities were different. Mayan cities were more spread out and less concentrated in one site than the ones we know.

However, these three peoples all accomplished some great things. The Mandinko kept accurate records of family and national history without using a written language. Specially trained singers memorized long histories, which were passed on for dozens of generations in the same family, down to the present day.

The Incas had a counting device made of knotted strings. They could perform thousands of calculations on them. Yet their *quipus*, as they were known, are no longer used. The system of writing numbers on paper, which began in Asia, has become almost universal.

The Maya had a calendar that used the stars and planets to keep track of time. Without any telescopes, the Maya learned to count the years as accurately as we can. But their calendars were written in a way that has been difficult to understand, and they have not been used in many centuries.

As a result of their isolation, most of the achievements of these peoples have had little influence on our modern way of life. However, these civilizations are valuable as sources of information about how people master the environment and how they organize into large groups. We will discover that these three civilizations solved their problems differently from the four civilizations we studied in Unit One.

1. In what ways might isolation benefit a group of people?
2. Is writing necessary before a civilization can be considered "great" or important? Write a short paragraph giving your answer and your reasons for it.

Chapter 6

The Maya of Central America

INTRODUCTION

In 1839 A.D. an American explorer, John Stephens, set out into the tropical rain forest of Central America. Accompanied by a British artist named Catherwood, Stephens hoped to find the long-lost cities he had heard were there. Deep in the forest, under the lush growth and soil of centuries, they found large stone pillars and buildings like pyramids. Carved on the pillars were strange human figures with big headdresses. Stephens and Catherwood had come upon the ruins of Copán, an ancient city of the Maya.

The ancient Maya city of Copán as it appears today.

189

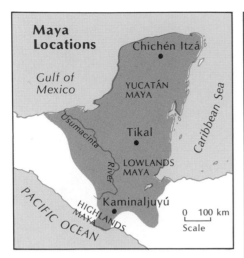

The Maya empire occupied the Yucatán Peninsula and the lands southward to the Pacific Ocean. Name the three distinct divisions within the Maya territory.

The land of the Maya, a native American people, stretches across five countries of present-day Central America. The south-eastern part of Mexico, most of Guatemala (gwät əm ä'lə) and the tiny state of Belize (bəl lēz') as well as parts of Honduras and El Salvador, have been home for the Maya for many centuries.

Maya people began to develop their civilization in Central America more than 3500 years ago. By studying this early period, which spanned about 1500 years, we can see how they grew food crops, mastered the arts of pottery and stone carving, and devised a system of mathematics. As the Maya learned to control their physical environment, they became highly accomplished in many other things.

As the Maya population grew in the lowland rain forests, cities flourished between 250 A.D. and 800 A.D. During this middle period the Maya perfected a system of writing and accurate calendars and produced fine works of art.

Then, mysteriously, the civilization in the rain forest disappeared. Further north, in the Yucatán Peninsula, the Maya civili-

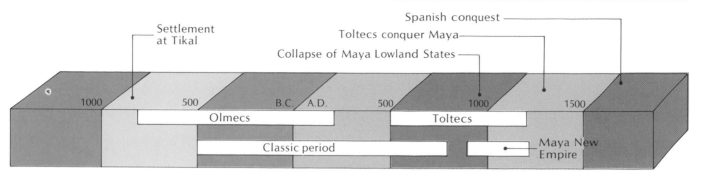

Settlement at Tikal

Spanish conquest

Toltecs conquer Maya

Collapse of Maya Lowland States

1000 500 B.C. A.D. 500 1000 1500

Olmecs

Toltecs

Classic period

Maya New Empire

MAYA CIVILIZATION

zation survived another 600 years, until after 1500 A.D., when Spanish conquerors invaded Central America.

Maya ruins have been discovered in hundreds of places in Central America. Since John Stephens' explorations, workers have cleared away rain forest growth and excavated inside the ruins. From pictures carved in stone and wood, we have learned about Maya customs and beliefs. From their writing, we know the names of some of their gods and rulers. From dates carved on stone pillars, we know a few events in Maya history. Because the Maya are still living in Central America, we can observe their traditional way of life for some evidence of how they used to live.

Maya peoples continue to live in Central America. Some of their traditions, such as open air markets, can be traced to their ancient Maya ancestors. What goods are being sold?

191

Studying the lost cities of the rain forest, we will discover another way a people have modified their physical environment with the tools of their culture. The Maya culture, in turn, was influenced by the rain forest environment to produce a civilization very different from the ancient Western ones.

THE BEGINNING OF MAYA CIVILIZATION

The Environment of the Early Maya

North America and Central America meet at Mexico's narrowest place, the Isthmus of Tehuantepec (tāw än tā pek'). East of the isthmus rise the Sierra Madre de Chiapas (the Chiapas Mountains). Rugged volcanoes rise steeply to peaks over 4000 m above the Pacific Ocean. This is an area of ridges and deep valleys, much of it over 1300 m above sea level. In these highlands, heavy rains fall between May and November–on the Pacific side, more than 4000 mm of rain, more than the rainiest places on the British Columbia coast. Rivers rush down the mountains on both sides. Except for grassy openings the land is covered with leafy trees.

North of the mountains, the land is flat or gently rolling, and the tropical rain forest grows tall and dense. Before the spring rains come, the temperature rises to over 35°C every day. The forest growth includes beautiful trees spreading above several layers of undergrowth. The biggest trees, such as the mahogany, grow more than fifty metres high.

The rain forest teems with life. Jaguars stalk their prey, parrots squawk loudly and howler monkeys swing through the trees. Poisonous snakes slither through the undergrowth. Insects swarm and buzz.

The lowlands further north, in the Yucatán Peninsula, receive less rainfall. Here the forest cover is low and the patches of open land are larger. Rivers and lakes are less common, and water is far below the surface of the ground in many places.

Parrot

Howler Monkey

Jaguar

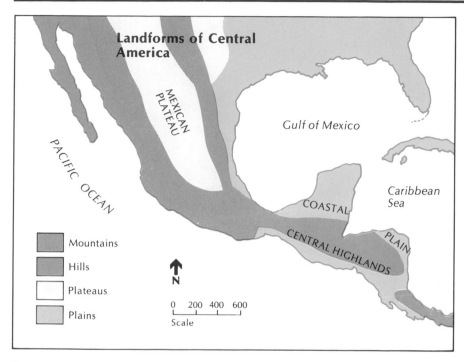

Landforms of Central America

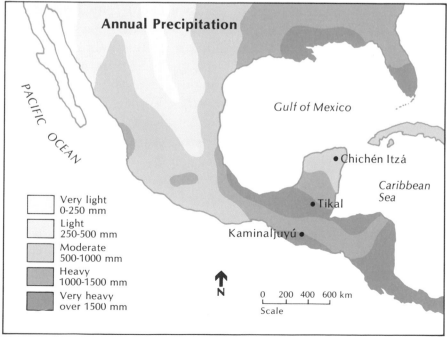

Annual Precipitation

Three ancient Maya cities are marked on the precipitation map. Write a sentence describing the physical environment of each place. Name the present-day country each is found in (see page 190).

This valley in the Central Highlands of Guatemala shows the physical environment of the highland Maya.

Near the end of the last ice age, about 10 000 years ago, native American peoples migrated into Mexico and Central America. They used arrowheads of stone, a sign of a hunting people. Many of these peoples settled west of the Isthmus of Tehuantepec and began their own civilizations. Three of these civilizations figure in the history of the Maya: the Olmecs, early inhabitants of the Mexican Gulf Coast; the people of Teotihuacán from the Valley of Mexico, and the Toltecs who inhabited the same region later. Although all belonged to the racial stock known as Amerindian, each of these peoples spoke its own language, and each adapted to its environment by forming a distinct culture.

As early as 5000 B.C., Maya tribes had settled in the rain forest and established tiny villages where food was in good supply. From the archaeological remains, we know that they hunted turkey, iguana and other reptiles, deer and peccary (a small wild hog). The Maya who settled near lakes and swamps fished, while those who lived near the ocean picked oysters and other shellfish. In the forest they gathered nuts and fruits. They dug edible roots, manioc and sweet potato from the ground and harvested wild squash and other gourds, beans, chili peppers and several kinds of **maize** (a kind of corn).

The tropical environment offered the Maya a bounty they increased by cultivation. These gatherers and hunters learned to plant vegetable seeds near their villages and improve on the natural yield. The planting of seed, especially maize seed, spread throughout the Maya country.

The Maya learned how to grow abundant crops in this rainy environment. One method they used is called **shifting cultivation**. Every spring, before the rains started, the farmers made a few small openings in the forest by cutting down and burning trees. As soon as the rains came, they would plant crops in these open areas. After several years, when the soil became unproductive, they made new openings. Today this is still the most common method of farming in the world's tropical areas.

This method does not require hoes or ploughs. Instead, Maya farmers poked holes in the soil with the tips of fire-hardened sticks and planted the seeds of several vegetables, especially maize, runner beans and squash, in the same field. They weeded out wild grasses to keep them from taking over the fields.

Archaeologists are not sure that shifting cultivation was practiced by all the ancient Maya. It appears that they used a variety of farming methods, depending on the quality of the soil, the amount of rainfall, and the forest cover. Recent evidence shows that some Maya turned wet, low-lying areas into farmland by digging ditches and piling the soil up between them. These raised fields (see top of page 196) were cultivated all year round, and the ditches were used to raise fish. Water from the ditches irrigated the farmland during dry periods.

Most Maya people lived in houses built on low platforms. The walls were made of poles, usually coated with mud and whitewashed, and the roofs were made of palm fronds.

Every home had a pottery griddle on which the women cooked. They ground maize kernels into flour, shaped the dough into flat cakes and cooked them on the griddle. They also made breads out of maize, and for breakfast drank a cornmeal gruel, or soup, flavored with chili peppers. Squash and beans were also important.

The physical environment also provided the Maya with

This is a modern Maya house. Compare it to the description of the homes of the ancient Maya.

In poorly drained areas, ditches were dug to carry water away. The soil from the ditches was piled on the fields to raise the surface higher above the water level. **A** *shows the location of an ancient ditch, and* **B** *identifies raised fields.*

resources they could use to create tools, medicines and clothing. The villagers gathered hard-skinned gourds and used the hollowed-out shells as containers and as floats for their fishnets. They used parts of plants and even animals as medicines. Iguanas (a kind of reptile) were burned and the ash used to make a painkiller for pulling teeth. Some farmers kept orchards and obtained fruits and incense from the trees. Cotton was woven into cloth on hand looms. Some present-day Maya wear loose cotton dresses and blouses made like their ancestors'.

At the harvest time the farmers used strong fibre baskets and bags to carry their produce back to the villages.

From early times, the Maya were excellent potters. They molded clay into pots, bowls, plates and cups, baking them to make them hard. Archaeologists have dug up and pieced together thousands of clay objects.

The Maya found sources where they could obtain resources and goods the local environment lacked. The rain forest villagers sometimes traded their pottery and other wares with villagers from the mountains in order to obtain grinding stones for their maize, and obsidian (a glass-like volcanic rock) for making knives. From coastal areas they obtained colorful sea-shells and the sharp spines of the stingray, which they used in religious ceremonies.

1. How did the Maya use resources from their physical environment to improve their way of life? List a few under these headings: foods; utensils; tools; personal goods.
2. Suggest some reasons why people would domesticate (tame) plants they find in their environment.
3. Suppose you decided to begin domesticating some wild plants. How would you decide which plants to choose? Make a list of the characteristics you would look for.

Early Maya Centres

As far as we can tell, the early Maya villages were governed by local chiefs who likely passed their power from father to son. As the population grew and farmland became scarce, however, centres competed for ownership of the land and for trade. A few powerful chiefs gained control over large areas and the trade routes between them.

The centres of early Maya government were also religious centres. The heads of leading families were priests as well as rulers. Since very early times, people living in outlying areas had travelled to these centres at certain times of year to worship a god or a famous ancestor. Kaminaljuyú, a very old Maya sacred site near Guatemala City, was the largest town in Central America for several centuries, a centre of government, learning and business.

By 150 A.D. Kaminaljuyú was an important Maya centre. Its wealth was a result of trade routes that stretched from modern-day southern Mexico to El Salvador.

A MAYA RELIGIOUS CEREMONY

Even today, religion plays an important role in Maya life. Some Maya still worship the rain gods, the god that they believe makes the maize grow in the earth, the wind gods and hundreds of other guardians and demons of the natural world. Before planting, the Maya make sacrifices to these gods so that rain will fall on their crops. Travellers pray to the North Star god for guidance.

An archaeologist named Wyllys Andrews once witnessed a Maya ceremony near the village of Xkalakoop in Yucatan. Near the village, a long-hidden cave had recently been discovered and contained ancient pottery and incense holders. As Andrews was working in the cave, a young Maya priest came by and asked to hold a ceremony in the cave. The priest said that the ceremony was needed so that the spirits guarding the cave would not take revenge on the visitors who had disturbed them.

On the next day, the priest appeared with thirteen others carrying many goods to offer to the gods: thirteen hens, a turkey, honey, spices, tobacco and maize. They lit thirteen black candles and burned incense as they knelt in the cave, chanting prayers throughout the day and night. Near the end of the ceremony, young boys joined in. While the priests chanted, the boys made sounds like the croaking of frogs and tree toads, animals which tell the Maya when the rains are coming.

After the ritual ended, there was a feast in the village. The turkey and hens that had been sacrificed were wrapped in leaves and cooked in underground ovens. The women provided spicy cornmeal cakes and a drink of maize liquor. After the celebration, the villagers rested, sure that they had satisfied the gods.

In 1959 a Maya shrine was found in a cave at Balankanché. Now the Maya have returned to worship the shrine's god, Tlaloc, the rain god.

The rulers of these centres, and their families, learned how to write and count. By careful observation of the heavens, the priests learned how to follow and predict the movements of the sun, moon, stars and planets and they used these to keep calendars. Archaeologists now think that the Maya might have acquired their writing, arithmetic and astronomy from the Olmecs, an earlier civilization of nearby southern Mexico. Maya writing is very complicated and scholars still have difficulty decoding the symbols.

MAYA WRITING AND NUMBERS

We sometimes use pictures or symbols to represent thoughts, such as signs near a school to tell drivers that pedestrians may be crossing the street. You can probably think of many more symbols and explain what each one means. Maya writing used glyphs, or sculptured symbols, to name things. Some of the Maya glyphs stand for sounds, as the letters of our alphabet do. Unfortunately, we do not know the meaning of all Maya glyphs.

Maya numbers are easier to understand than Maya letters. The Maya wrote numbers with dots and lines. A dot represented one, and a line represented five. The shape of a sea-shell represented zero. The Maya could do arithmetic on paper or even on the ground, using beans for single numbers, sticks for five and shells for zero. By arranging these figures in columns, they could make very large numbers, and add or subtract with them.

Here is how the Maya wrote the numbers

one, two and three: • •• •••

How would four be written?

Here are five and six: —— ——•

How would seven, eight and nine look?

Here are ten and eleven: ══ ══•

Write twelve to fifteen.

Twenty is written:

Write twenty-five.

The early cities of the highlands did not continue to develop and grow, as did their lowland neighbors'. The remains of foreign pottery have led some historians to believe that traders from the great city of Teotihuacán (tā ō tē wä kan') took over the government of the highlands. Meanwhile, the Maya of the central lowlands and the Yucatán Peninsula were building cities in the rain forest and developing a distinctive culture.

1. In what modern countries is the homeland of the highland Maya?
2. Why did some Maya farmers move their fields regularly? What is this method of farming called?
3. How did the Maya use their physical environment for food? List goods under headings: foods grown, gathered, hunted, fished.

4. How did the physical environment of the highland Maya contribute to the development of trading?
5. What subjects would the children of Maya ruling families have learned if they went to school?

THE PEAK OF MAYA CIVILIZATION

The Economy of the Central Lowland Maya

Maya civilization flourished for more than 600 years. When the civilization of the Romans was in ruin, a great number of Maya cities were at their peak in the Central American rain forest. The growth of these cities was fuelled by the Mayas' skill at turning the natural resources of the rain forest into food and wealth.

The lowland Maya developed new food supplies by further changing their physical environment. They created new farmlands in hilly areas by piling up rows of stones across the slopes. The soil that washed down the slopes filled up the flat **terraces** above the stones.

The lowland Maya also cultivated several tree species for food. The breadfruit tree, which produces a heavy growth of starchy, edible nuts, was one of these. Recently, archaeologists noticed thick stands of breadfruit trees growing near the ruins of several ancient Maya cities. It is likely the inhabitants planted the trees handy to their houses and harvested the crop with little effort. By storing the nuts in bins sunk into the ground, they could save food for those years when the maize crops were poor.

With such techniques the Maya population became increasingly concentrated in large centres. Abundant crops freed many people for other activities. While some lowland Maya farmed, others were building cities out of limestone blocks, stucco and wood. They learned how to cement stone blocks together using mortar made by mixing the powder of burnt limestone with sand and water. Temples and other large buildings were constructed

How do you think the breadfruit tree received its name?

Excavations at Tikal suggest that this Maya centre had been established by 600 B.C. Compare Tikal to a modern-day city.

in the cities. These places became the centre of religious life and government. Farmers and artisans brought their goods to the market square to trade for needed supplies, increasing the economic importance of cities. Two cities were even linked with paved roads.

The Maya used their many natural resources to make goods for a host of special uses. From the clay of the lowlands, potters created elaborately painted cups and bowls. Priests and warriors wore ceremonial clothing made from the skins of jaguars captured by rain forest hunters. The wood of the sapodilla tree was carved and used in door frames, while copal gum was burned as incense in religious ceremonies. Cacao trees yield beans with an edible husk. Specially treated, these beans could be ground up into chocolate.

The lowland Maya also traded with people outside their own area. Rich lowland traders sent trains of slaves, laden with baskets of trade goods, such as pottery and carved stone, to the highland centres of the south and to the Yucatán Peninsula. In return, they got such basic goods as salt, as well as luxury items like the bright feathers of the quetzal bird, used by the priests in their religious dress, or jade, from which jewellery was carved.

The Maya of Tikal traded for centuries with the people of Teotihuacán, the great city in the Valley of Mexico. From Teotihuacán, the Maya obtained obsidian and fine pottery. Teotihuacán traders who lived in Tikal even built temples for their own gods there. There were no new temples or other signs of Teotihuacán life in Tikal after about 600 A.D. Therefore, some historians have concluded that the centuries of co-existence between the two cities somehow ended, perhaps because of a period of hardship for Teotihuacán.

Temple at Teotihuacán

1. Compare this Teotihuacán temple with the Maya temple on page 201. How are they different? How are they similar?

2. Imagine you are a rich Maya trader organizing a trading expedition. Decide what you are going to take, where you are going, and what you want to bring back. How will you organize your trip? What will you see along the way?
3. The Mayas increased their food supply by building terraces on hillsides.
   (a) Using a sketch, describe how terraces were built.
   (b) Explain how terraces gave greater crop yields.

Lowland Maya Government

Each Maya community was ruled by a chief or king and a group of nobles, most of whom were also priests. Because religion was so important to the people, priests had great power. They performed rituals and interpreted the calendar, deciding when crops should be planted or harvested, or when trade expeditions should be started. The nobles were in charge of day-to-day activities. They organized work, looked after the use of the land, and kept the cities running smoothly. These rulers lived in luxury, supported by the rest of the population.

Carved stone pillars, some more than ten metres tall, stood in front of many buildings in the Maya cities. The names of rulers and important dates were carved on the pillars. The earliest date found on a pillar and translated into our years is July 6, 292 A.D. The appearance of pillars with names and dates is often considered to mark the beginning of civilized Maya society. They offer the best evidence that well-ordered states had developed, in which highly skilled work forces were ruled by royal families.

Studies of the markings of these pillars have revealed that these families extended their rule over states as large as 15 000 km^2 (a little less than half the size of Vancouver Island). Sometimes the ruling families of two cities intermarried in order to form an alliance. The rulers of Tikal and Uaxactún together organized the eastern area of the lowlands into one state.

It is difficult to tell how rulership of Maya states was passed

Notice that both a bird and jaguar are represented in the glyph. Could you represent your own name in pictures?

on. Some wives and daughters were important enough to have their own carved pillars. A famous member of a family that ruled Yaxchilán for five generations was a man known to us as "Bird-Jaguar." From the carvings on pillars found by archaeologists at Yaxchilán, we know about the dates, marriages and military victories of Bird-Jaguar's family.

When important people like Bird-Jaguar died, they were buried in elaborate vaults. Servants were often sealed in the burial vaults with their masters, to serve them in the afterlife.

1. How were Maya leaders honored? How are people in our society honored?
2. Was it fair that some people, the priests and nobles, were supported by the farmers and artisans in Maya society? Give reasons for your answer.

Life in Ancient Maya

The city of Tikal stood in the middle of the lowland rain forest, in what is now the Petén district of Guatemala. When the Maya civilization was at its height, Tikal was one of the biggest centres in Central America, with perhaps 50 000 people living within five kilometres of its central area.

More than 3000 buildings, including dozens of temples, have been unearthed at the centre of Tikal. The Tikal Maya built large temples over older ones that have been traced to 600 B.C. The largest of all is more than seventy metres high. Some of the temples had big burial chambers hidden inside. Large carved stone altars and pillars stood in front of the temples–more than seventy in the Great Plaza of Tikal. Nearby was a group of buildings more than 200 m long, connected by courtyards. These buildings might have served as homes for Tikal's rulers, as government offices, or as a centre for learning.

Imagine that you live in a small Maya village in the lowland rain forest. Because the planting season has come, you and your family are getting ready to walk to Tikal for the festival of the rain god.

MAYA CALENDARS

This pillar found in Quiriguá in Guatemala records a date in Maya history. Translated into words and numbers, the calendar glyphs say "9.17.0.0.0 13 Ahau 18 Cumku." This refers to a particular day of a certain year. Let us see how the Maya recorded time.

The figures on the right, "13 Ahau 18 Cumku," are called the Calendar Round dates. The Maya priests used them to keep track of the gods' special days and other ceremonies in the course of a year.

The series of numbers separated by dots, 9.17.0.0.0, is called the long count date. It is called this because it adds together the days, months, years and ages from the day the Maya believe the world began. Wherever found, a long count date provides an exact date for some event in Maya history. In translating long count into our calendar, a certain day in the year 3114 B.C. is considered the start of the long count. With this setting, the date 9.17.0.0.0 works out to January 24, 772 A.D.

How was this figure reached? In a long count date, the left-hand number is the largest unit of time, and the right-hand number is the smallest–the latest day since the beginning of time. The Maya names of these five units of Maya time are:

9	17	0	0	0
baktun	katun	tun	uinal	kin

And these are their values:
1 kin = 1 day
1 uinal = 20 kins
1 tun = 18 uinals = 360 kins
1 katun = 20 tuns = 7200 kins
1 baktun = 20 katuns = 144 000 kins

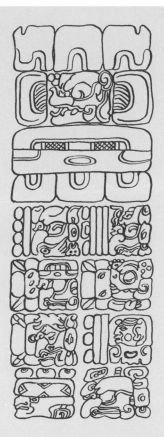

How many days does 9.17.0.0.0 represent? How many of our years of 365 days does that equal?

The last date discovered on a lowland pillar is 10.4.0.0.0 (909 A.D.). It looks as if many Maya cities of the rain forest were deserted and never revived.

1. Calculate how many days are represented by the long count date 8.10.8.0.0.
2. Give reasons why it is important to have accurate methods of recording time.
3. Devise a way of recording long periods of time that is different from our calendar and the Maya calendar.

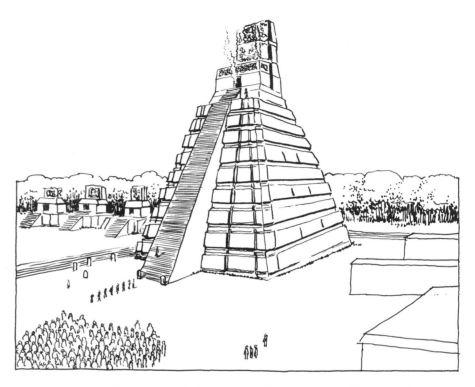

This is how we think the centre of a large Maya city, Tikal, looked. How well do you think the Maya builders used the physical resources of the lowlands?

You travel along a road that runs above swampland and across grassy openings. Then you come to a quarry, where workers are using ropes and levers to lift the blocks of white stone onto rolling logs.

As you approach the middle of Tikal, you see more workers building a new temple. Some are using ropes to draw the stone blocks and buckets of mortar up steep stairs. Other workers are setting the blocks in place. You see some artists chipping away at a pillar. Once they have finished carving the signs of the great lord of Tikal into the stone, the pillar will be placed in front of the temple.

Now you and hundreds of other people are standing in a huge open square. Pyramids of stone with steep stairs running up their fronts tower into the sky all around you. The tops of the buildings, with brightly painted stones, look like huge headdresses. Everyone is waiting excitedly.

WHAT WAS ANCIENT MAYA SOCIETY LIKE?

The ruins of Maya buildings, the buried goods in and around them, the carved pillars, the painted walls and pots and the Maya writing, show there was a privileged ruling class in ancient times. But these remains offer very little information about the lives of the much larger population of ordinary citizens. We do not know, for example, how many people lived in each centre or even in each household. We do not know whether the members of an ordinary family always had enough to eat or whether they had a chance to better their lot in life through learning or hard work. We do not know whether they owned their own land, or whether they could go to court to settle wrongs and disputes.

In order to draw conclusions about the lives of ordinary citizens, historians and archaeologists must make interpretations based on the evidence they find. Discarded tools, remains of houses and types of crops may be pieces in the puzzle. But, the evidence is usually not complete and so the scientist makes an "educated guess," an interpretation. From the clues about the Maya civilizations, we have an idea of some aspects of the lives of average people in that society.

At the top of the steps of the biggest temple, a man appears. Even though he is far away, you can see that he is wearing the spotted skin of a jaguar and a headdress of bright feathers. He holds up a long staff and, as he begins to chant, you join in.

Later, you and others from your village go to a priest to find out about your crops. The priest looks in a book to find out on which days you should offer prayers and sacrifices to the rain god. You also make an offering at a shrine of the god that protects travellers. Women about to give birth also go to worship at the shrine of Ix Chel, the goddess who protects women in childbirth.

After the festival, you sit on the ground in the market, surrounded by baskets of dried chili peppers, pumpkin seeds and other vegetables. You feel thankful to have assured yourself of the gods' protection in coming months.

Sometime before 900 A.D., many of the lowland states collapsed. One after another, centres were abandoned, and farmlands left to grow over. Some were reoccupied only after long periods for which there are no records. By then, it appears that the Maya of the central lowlands had lost their traditions of

A Maya high priest was responsible for training priests, performing ceremonies and making prophecies. What kind of prophecies do you think would have interested the Mayas?

207

calendar-keeping, fine artistry and highly organized government. The reasons for this collapse are a mystery, and we can only suggest what might have happened.

One reason suggested by historians is that the Maya spent more and more time constructing buildings and less and less time on producing food. It is thought that the leading families wanted to increase their own importance in the eyes of neighboring states through the construction of ever-larger temples. With inadequate food supplies, malnutrition and disease may have weakened the Maya population. A second reason may have been invasions of warlike people from Mexico.

These, and other factors, probably contributed to the weakness of lowland Maya society. As trade declined and life became more difficult, the rulers may have lost their authority over the population, and the complicated system of government broke down. As a result of the poor food supplies and the unstable government, people may have abandoned the cities.

1. How is the central lowland area different from the highlands? Organize your answers in a chart using these headings: land formation; climate; vegetation.

2. List the steps that might have been followed in building a Maya temple, and identify the materials that were used. Then, write a sentence or two describing a temple.

3. In what ways did the Maya use the physical resources of the lowland rain forest for food, crafts, dress and religious ceremonies?

4. Describe life in a big Maya centre, using the headings: types of buildings, size, activities, the kinds of people you would meet.

5. Two reasons are suggested for the collapse of the lowland Maya civilization. For each reason, make a list of evidence you might find in Maya ruins that would support that reason.

6. One expert says writing and the calendar were the Maya's greatest achievement. Another says their orderly governments are what made the Maya civilized. A third says their stone carvings, paintings and statues are the best thing they did. What do you think are the most important accomplishments of the Maya? Why?

THE LATE MAYA CIVILIZATION

Late Maya Civilization in the Yucatán Peninsula

Following the collapse of central lowland cities, around 900 A.D., Maya civilization survived for about 600 years in the Yucatán Peninsula. Although close to the Caribbean Sea, the Yucatán has a drier climate than the lowlands, and the peninsula is covered by low, dense rain forest. Months of hot, dry weather follow the spring and summer rains. Much of the rain soaks quickly into the porous limestone earth. During the winter, the few small rivers can dry up altogether.

This is the Temple of Kukulcan at Chichén Itzá (chē chen'ēt sä') greatest of the Yucatán cities. Historians think it was built about 400 years after the main temple of Tikal.

A cenote *is a natural well. It is created when part of the Earth's surface collapses, forming a steep-sided pool of water.*

The jaguar was a symbol of strength and courage. This picture is based on a carving found at Chichén Itzá.

The Yucatán environment provided the Maya with a number of items for their own use, as well as for trade. With fibre from the sisal or hennequen plants, they made strong rope. From the cotton grown in flat fields, they spun thread for clothing. Maya today still grow hennequen plants for the basket trade and cotton for the textile industry. With the salt gathered from oceanside beds, they were able to preserve some foods. Honey and wax came from beehives, built by farmers using twisted grasses. On paper made from the inner bark of the wild fig tree, they wrote and painted, glazing the paper to make it last and then folding long strips to make books. Maya boats carried goods around the shores of the Yucatán Peninsula to Mexico.

Because they could not depend on rains or rivers for year-round fresh water, the Yucatán Maya built their cities near large natural wells called *cenotes*. These wells are found all over the Yucatán Peninsula. They are formed when water seeps into the ground, causing the limestone rock underneath to collapse. Underground springs then flood the large holes.

Divers have explored a *cenote* near Chichén Itzá. At the bottom they found thousands of pieces of jewellery as well as hundreds of skeletons.

As far as archaeologists can tell, the copper and gold in the jewellery came from the lands of the Toltecs, a Mexican people far to the west of the Yucatán. The Toltecs appear to have conquered Chichén Itzá, and ruled it for several centuries.

Researchers suggest that the skeletons are the remains of people thrown into the well as human sacrifices. In times of drought, the Toltec-ruled Maya practiced such sacrifices in order to please the rain gods, who, they believed, lived at the bottom of the *cenotes*. Even today, the *cenote* at Chichén Itzá is known as the Well of Sacrifice.

The Toltecs appear to have left Chichén Itzá during the thirteenth century. After this time, the walled city of Mayapán (mä'yə pán'), to the west, rose up as the Yucatán's most powerful city. It remained as such until about 1450, when fire destroyed it. With the end of Mayapán, the Maya of Yucatán no longer had organized states, only a number of warring peoples.

1. Make a list of the uses for water the Maya would have. How did the need for fresh water influence where centres were located?
2. Suggest reasons why people, and not animals or valuable goods, would be sacrificed during times of great trouble.
3. What other possible reasons could there be for the skeletons and jewellery at the bottom of the *cenote* at Chichén Itzá? Try to think of three alternatives.

Maya Life at the Time of the Spanish Conquest

Still worse troubles came to the Yucatán Maya. Within fifty years, European navigators began sailing across the Atlantic Ocean to explore the American continent. Soon fighting men from Spain, the most powerful state in Europe at the time, came to conquer Mexico and Central America. Their goal was to capture the physical resources of the continent, especially gold and other metals.

Spanish explorers arrived in the Yucatán in 1517. The Maya had never seen ships like the tall wooden Spanish vessels, and they wrote in a book, "On that day, a cloud arises, a mountain arises, a strong man seizes the land, things fall to ruin."

The Spanish invaders marched across Mexico and Central America, subduing the Native peoples. The Aztec rulers in the Valley of Mexico gave up the throne at once, but the Maya fought stubbornly against the Spanish soldiers. Against the steel armor, horses, crossbows and cannons of the Spanish, the Maya had only quilted fabric for armor, wooden spears, bows and arrows. Without leaders, small groups of Maya were free to move about, and some resettled the central lowlands. The Spanish established their first city in the Yucatán in 1542, but the Maya continued to resist Spanish rule for 300 years.

The loss of life from these wars was huge: more than twenty million Mexican and Central American natives are estimated to have died in the first 100 years of Spanish rule. During this time killing diseases struck the native Americans. Spanish settlers

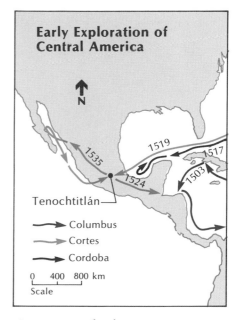

Cortes was the first European to make contact with the Maya. Over a number of years he explored Central America and established Spanish settlements.

imported their ploughs and livestock and changed the Central American environment wherever they set up estates. Ploughing made the soil wash away. Cattle ate the maize shoots growing in forest clearings, and sheep ranged in the Mayas' gardens.

Spanish missionaries set out to destroy the culture of the Maya. They burned the Maya books, described by one such missionary, Friar Landa, as "superstition and lies of the devil." Only three books written in Maya glyphs are left in the world. A page from one of them, a book now in a library at Dresden, Germany, is pictured here. Some of the writing in these books have been translated, and they tell us a great deal about Maya astronomy and religion. Their detailed descriptions of the movements of the planet Venus and of the Moon were probably used by the Maya priests to predict days when good and bad fortune could be expected.

Landa and other missionaries wrote accounts of Maya life. Some Maya writers also learned to write their spoken language in Spanish letters, and they recorded their customs and beliefs. From both these kinds of accounts, we know quite a lot about life in the late Maya era.

From birth onward, a person's life was shaped by custom and ceremony. At birth, most babies had their heads bound between two boards in order to make their foreheads flat. The Maya considered a flat forehead beautiful. Older people tattooed their skins, and young men painted theirs black. The Maya liked to file their teeth and decorated them with glued-on chips of stone.

The parents of newborns went to the priest to find out what the future held for their babies. Children between the ages of twelve and fourteen underwent a religious ceremony to mark their passage into adulthood. During the ceremony, four elders would blow smoke from a pipe into the hair of the youths. Since tobacco was a common offering to the gods, the Maya believed tobacco smoke made the children pure.

After about the age of twelve, Maya boys lived apart from their families and were trained to be soldiers. As recreation, they played a ball game in a court with hoops on two walls.

Girls learned cooking, weaving and childcare at an early age.

A page from the Dresden Codex.

The game illustrated was played in the ball court at Chichén Itzá. The penalties for losing were high: jewellery, goods or sometimes their lives were taken from the losers. Why do you think the game is compared to modern-day basketball?

Although they were not permitted to speak to or play with boys, girls were considered ready to marry at twelve or thirteen. The children's parents arranged the marriage.

Throughout the year the Maya celebrated various religious holidays, the most important of which was New Year. Before the New Year was a five-day period considered very unlucky; everyone stayed indoors in fear. In order to greet the New Year, people swept out their houses and put on new clothes. At this and on other special occasions, they dressed up in cotton garments with bright thread and shining feathers woven in. On New Year's day the priests led processions all around the village to renew the powers of the people's tools and fields.

When a person died, the family filled the body's mouth with food and buried it under the floor of the home, along with the person's possessions. They believed that these possessions would help feed and equip the soul on the journey to the afterworld. Other times, their heads would be dried and preserved in the family shrine. Servants would "feed" them regularly, hoping the dead persons' souls would return the favor.

Today, more than two million Maya people still live in Central America, and they have more than twenty-five native Mayan languages. Some of the Maya live in modern cities, while others are farmers in the rain forest. Some remote tribes even worship their old gods in the temple ruins. But many of their ancestors' skills have been lost for hundreds of years. The ruins they left behind and the traditions that survive only give us clues about their history. There is much that has been lost, probably forever.

1. Compare the civilization of the Spanish explorers to the Maya civilization using these headings: respect for human lives, technology, use of natural resources.
2. Suggest reasons why the Spanish missionaries wanted to destroy the culture of the Maya. What did they hope to gain?
3. Decorating one's body is a practice found in many cultures. Describe the Maya traditions. Describe the practices in our society.

SUMMARY

The Maya people began a civilization in Central America by learning how to grow food crops in the rain forest. They learned how to make pottery, jewellery and other fine crafts. As their population increased, Maya society reorganized. Some of their villages became important centres, with the temples and palaces built around open plazas. Here they worshipped and celebrated solemn occasions.

At its height, Maya civilization flourished in many large centres, especially in the lowlands. Their cities were centres of religion, government and business. Maya government was held by a few powerful families, who ruled over independent states. Priests were also powerful, and skilled at writing and counting. The Maya people relied on them to predict the future and direct their worship to various gods.

The Maya civilization ended after a period during which the people were ruled by warlike Mexican people named the Toltecs. From the Toltecs the Maya learned new habits. They often made human sacrifices and developed a military society. After the Toltecs, there were no leaders who could hold the society together. Next came Spanish explorers and soldiers, conquering all of Central America and Mexico, killing people and destroying many old Maya books. The Maya of today have kept few of their ancient traditions.

Why did the arrival of the Spanish in America almost lead to the extinction of the Maya culture?

Chapter Review: The Maya

NEW WORDS AND IDEAS

1. Unscramble the words listed below. Write a sentence using each word.
   (a) TTOOAT   (e) PHGLYS
   (b) ZEIAM   (f) LLARIPS
   (c) REECASRT   (g) LOECTST
   (d) CNEETOS

2. Who were the Toltecs? What was their origin?

3. For each of the people below, identify their contribution to our knowledge about the Maya civilization:
   (a) John Stephens
   (b) Wyllys Andrews
   (c) Friar Landa.

4. Identify ways in which the Maya used the following items found in their environment:
   (a) gourds   (e) iguanas
   (b) manioc   (f) obsidian
   (c) limestone   (g) cacao beans
   (d) feathers   (h) hennequen plants.

CHECKING YOUR UNDERSTANDING

5. Summarize, in the form of a chart, your knowledge about the three areas in which the Maya lived: the highlands, the lowland rain forest, and the Yucatán Peninsula. Which one is in the south, the centre, and the north? Describe the land, climate, and vegetation in the area.

6. List, in chronological order, the main events of the late Maya era, beginning at about 900 A.D., and ending with the present. Draw a time line using the information.

7. List three resources of the Maya under each of these headings: plants, animals, minerals. Beside each resource, describe how it was used by the Maya.

8. Explain how the Maya used resources from their physical environment to make books. What did they write in their books?

9. Suppose you were a young Maya. Describe the main events in your life. How would these events be different if you were the child of a farmer? a noble? a merchant?

USING YOUR KNOWLEDGE

10. (a) Explain why it is easier for archaeologists and historians to find information about the wealthy and powerful members of a society, than about the common people.
    (b) Do you think that 500 years from now, archaeologists and historians will face the same problems in studying Canada in the 1980s? Explain.

11. Compare the way you celebrate the New Year with the Maya celebration. Time of year, food, dances, clothing, and activities are some of the things you should include in your comparison.

12. Imagine you are a Maya and have been allowed to see the king and queen of Spain to express your concerns about the conquest of the Maya. Sketch a picture to show your meeting with the king and queen.

Chapter 7

The Incas of South America

The Andes Mountains form a high "wall" along the western side of South America. Only short, swift rivers flow to the Pacific Ocean; long, wide rivers drain most of the continent to the Atlantic Ocean. Describe the physical environment of the Inca empire.

INTRODUCTION

The Andes Mountains rise out of the Pacific Ocean like a huge wall. They stretch almost the entire length of the South American continent, with peaks soaring more than 7000 m above the ocean. Volcanoes erupt in these rugged mountains, and earthquakes sometimes shake whole cities to the ground.

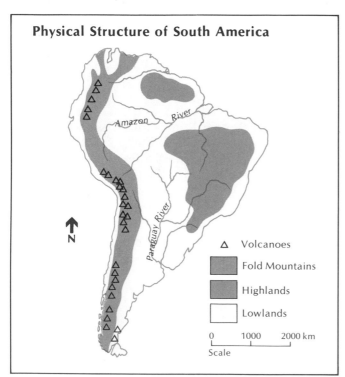

Physical Structure of South America

△ Volcanoes

Fold Mountains

Highlands

Lowlands

0 1000 2000 km
Scale

The Inca Empire

VENEZUELA GUYANA SURINAME FRENCH GUIANA
COLUMBIA
ECUADOR
BRAZIL
PERU
BOLIVIA
CHILE PARAGUAY
ARGENTINA URUGUAY

Inca Empire
Present-day boundaries

0 1000 2000 km
Scale

Descendants of the Incas continue to live in the Andes Mountains of Peru.

The Incas were one of many civilized peoples living in the Andes. To understand their accomplishments, we will first trace the development of civilizations in the Andes Mountains more than 3500 years ago. The early peoples of the Andes were excellent farmers, skilled artisans and hardened fighters. Two thousand years ago they built large cities in the Moche (mo chě') and Nazca (nas'ka) valleys on the coast of present-day Peru. Later civilizations spread from centres in the Southern and Central Andes. We can still learn something about the Andeans' traditional way of life by observing Native inhabitants living there today.

After about 1400 A.D. the civilization of the Incas, a mountain-dwelling native American people, spread up and down South America. Although the origin of the Inca people is a mystery, we know that they imposed their rule over a huge area that includes most of the modern states of Ecuador, Peru and Chile, much of Bolivia and parts of Colombia and Argentina. Under the government of the Inca rulers, and aided by their excellent roads and suspension bridges, the cultures of the Andean peoples mingled in one huge state for a short time.

The Inca civilization lasted only until 1532 A.D. when Spanish conquerors arrived from Central America, seeking gold. With amazing speed, the Spanish took over the rule of the Andean peoples. Although the Spanish were cruel conquerors, their written reports provide a wealth of information about the Inca civilization. By studying the Spanish conquest of the Inca empire, we will also discover what happened when one civilization was destroyed by another.

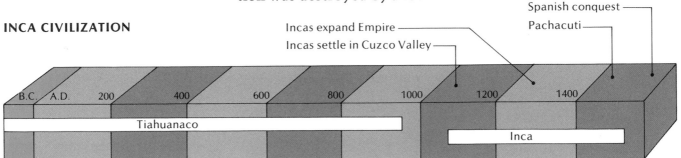

INCA CIVILIZATION

Spanish conquest
Pachacuti
Incas expand Empire
Incas settle in Cuzco Valley

B.C. A.D. 200 400 600 800 1000 1200 1400

Tiahuanaco

Inca

THE EARLY ANDEAN CIVILIZATIONS

The Environment of the Early Andean Civilizations

The environment of the Andes Mountains changes dramatically from west to east. Near the Pacific Ocean is a narrow, flat strip of desert so dry that some people pass their whole lives there without seeing rain. The slopes of the Andes facing the cool winds from off the ocean are also dry, but in summer fog gathers around the mountains, and provides some moisture for plant growth.

Eastward, beyond the first ranges of the Andes Mountains, are flat valleys, many over 3000 m above sea level. These valleys are called *altiplano*, the Spanish word for "high valley." Above these valleys stretch treeless mountain slopes where animals graze and hardy plants grow. Across the Andes, big rivers drain east to the rain forest that covers the huge Amazon River basin.

A Cross Section of the Andes Mountains

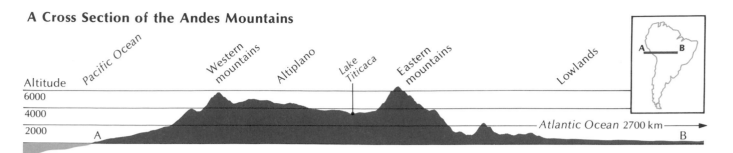

A cross section of the Andes Mountains through Lake Titicaca. About what height is the highest point along this cross section?

According to physical evidence, people first moved into South America from Central America more than 14 000 years ago, and they slowly spread throughout the Andes and onto the coastal plain. Some groups moved back and forth between the lower slopes of the Andes, the ocean shore and the rivers of the desert plain. About 5500 years ago, people began to settle near the coast. They caught anchovies and other fishes in small reed boats, using hooks made of shells and cotton nets. Their catch also included sea lions, shore birds and other forms of life that teem in the cold South Pacific Ocean, one of the richest fishing areas in the world.

Compare this family's use of the mountain slopes with that of the ancient peoples of Peru.

The physical environment of the desert zone could also be coaxed to support human life. In the brief wet season the coastal people gathered the plants and hunted the animals of the desert. Their diet included wild seeds, root plants, foxes, deer, owls and snails.

The coastal settlers learned how to domesticate plants, using the good land near the mouths of rivers to farm. By 1500 B.C. farm crops made up half their food, and included beans, squashes, sweet potato and chilis, gourds and maize. The farming of pineapples, peanuts, cotton, tomatoes and tobacco also developed.

To irrigate the desert soil, the coastal inhabitants channelled water from the rivers.

In the Moche Valley of northern Peru, archaeologists have uncovered many remains of early artisans' work, well-preserved by the dry climate. From these remains, we have learned much about the textiles, pottery and metalwork of the Andean people.

As far back as 1800 B.C., the coastal Andeans were weaving cotton on hand looms. In centuries following, they developed almost every basic method of weaving and needlework, methods such as brocading, crocheting, knitting and tie-dyeing.

The Andeans molded or sculpted pottery, rather than turning it on a potter's wheel. (Like the Maya, the ancient South American civilizations never developed the wheel.) They fired their pottery in open-air bonfires. Priest-artisans made much of the pottery for burials and other religious ceremonies. The remains give us a good idea of the coastal people's everyday lives and their beliefs.

Gold and silver furnished the Andeans with material for jewellery, while copper and tin from the mountains served to make spearpoints and chisels. The Andeans learned how to combine these last two metals in order to make bronze.

In parts of Peru, balsa boats are still used to travel across marshland.

1. Define these words from your readings:

desert	embroidery
artisans	looms

2. How did the coastal peoples of South America use their physical environment for food growing, for religious worship, for clothing and decoration?
3. Read through pages 218-220 once again looking for five phrases that show something about the culture of the people of the coastal plain. Write a one- or two-sentence summary of your findings.

The Andes Mountains were a harsh environment for human life, but settlers learned to survive in the thin air and low nighttime temperatures. They, too, discovered many ways to use their physical environment. After staying on the high plains of the mountains for the growing season, settlers went up higher to hunt herds of llama and alpaca. The meat of these camel-like animals provided them with food, the wool and hides with clothing, and the fat with tallow for candles. The hunters eventually began to capture and domesticate the animals, and they drove herds up and down with the seasons.

The mountain people learned to cultivate most of their food plants. Their staple was the potato, a vegetable native to the Andes that grows at altitudes as high as 5000 m. The Andeans cultivated more than 200 kinds of potato. Maize farming spread through the mountains, and the Andean people began terracing the mountain slopes handy to their villages to make farmland.

Since most of South America is below the equator, its seasons are the reverse of ours. The days are wettest and warmest in December and January. The Andeans planted potatoes in August and most other crops in September and October, the months of their spring. In the field, before planting began, the priests made sacrifices of llamas and food to the gods. Then the men walked in lines, breaking the ground, as the women followed with the seed, dropping it into the soil. A wood and metal hand plough was a later invention that is still used in the Andes.

When the maize shoots started to appear, children with slingshots guarded the fields from birds. In November, the farmers irrigated the crops with water drained from reservoirs and rivers by digging ditches. When the rains started, in Decem-

Even before the Incas' arrival, people in the Andes spun the wool of alpacas and llamas into yarn using hand spindles.

ANDEAN CROPS

The potato was the most important food staple of the Andean people, but maize was cultivated as well. Another staple was the seed of *quinoa*, which the Andeans ground into a nutritious flour. They planted the amaranth, a grain, the bean-like *tarwi* and such root crops as *ulluco*, *oca* and *arracacha*. Few peoples have accomplished as much with as harsh a physical environment as the Andeans.

The ancient Inca markets probably looked just like this modern-day market at Pisco, Peru.

ber or January, the families weeded the soil and banked it up around the potato plants.

By February or March the first potato crop was ready to be dug up. Later the villagers harvested the maize crop and paraded it into town, presenting some of it to the chief. The women made a drink of maize liquor called *chicha* . The valleys echoed with the sound of the flute and the drum as the villagers rejoiced over their successful crop.

During Inca festivals, the people would dance to the music of flutes and drums. List the resources used to make the instruments pictured here.

Since mountain crops can fail easily in freezing weather, the Andeans found ways to store their harvests for long periods. They left potatoes out at night to freeze, put them in the sun to dry out, and then squashed them underfoot to get the remaining moisture out. In this form the potato would keep for months. Strips of llama meat dried in the same way were called *charqui*, the source of our word "jerky." Then, in winter, the crops were stored and irrigation ditches cleared for the next spring's work.

1. Use headings such as land, climate, methods and foods, to compare farming in the Andes Mountains to farming on the coastal plain.
2. The Andeans cultivated maize differently from the Maya. How? Mention the types of land, season of rain, method of planting, types of irrigation and other differences you notice.
3. Explain how moving from place to place helped the settlers of the coast and mountains get the most from their physical environment.

Early Andean Society

Small mountain communities were formed of family groups called *ayllus.* Each community owned farmland, along with the produce and herds on it. This farmland was spread out along a valley, like a chain of long, narrow islands. The individual family's only belongings were its house, gardens and personal goods.

In return for working for the *ayllu*, each family received a share of the community's livestock, produce and water. The local chief made sure each family received its share, and contributed its share of the labor.

This tradition of group ownership among the Andeans still exists. Disagreements between two *ayllus* over the ownership of a pasture or a ditch may go back for generations. During such disagreements, men line up on the edge of their property and shout at the men of the neighboring *ayllu.* Sometimes the shouting turns into a battle of sticks and rocks.

The farmers of this Andean valley continue to practice the same farming methods and grow the same crops as did the Incas. How have these farmers changed the environment to meet their needs?

Coastal communities developed into large states around cities close to the main rivers. As the coastal valleys filled up, the Andeans began moving up onto rocky ridges above the best farming soil. Their irrigation projects are evidence of highly organized people. On some of these ridges, such as those of the Moche Valley, they built pyramid-like buildings from adobe (ə dō′bē) brick. Historians think that these buildings were used as temples. Their leaders were warriors and priests, but even less is known about them than about the early Maya.

Everyday Life in the Andes

Suppose you are a twelve-year old living in the Andes. Since the age of about five, you have been tending your *ayllu's* llama herd. Your unpaid labor is part of your family's contribution to the *ayllu*.

Today you are making a trip to the slopes to bring the llama herd in from pasture. Now that the summer season is just about over, the llamas have to be brought closer to the settlement. You have to get up early to walk the forty kilometres there and back.

Like everyone in the Andes, you have the big lungs and strong heart needed for life in the thin mountain air.

Your family's house is made of adobe brick, with a steep roof of straw and one small window. You have to stoop to pass through the doorway when you go outside to get sticks for the fire. The other families of the *ayllu* made a present of the house to your mother and father when they married. Last year, in the village fields, your sister married a boy from another family in the community, and they were given a house near yours.

Your mother is cooking breakfast in a clay pot on the griddle. You put another stick on the fire before taking some stew of guinea pig and *chuño*. Guinea pigs scuttle about the earthen floor of the house, feeding on leftover cobs of maize. Your mother gives you a supply of food to take with you on your trip: toasted maize, *charqui* and some *quinoa* cakes.

Dressed in your short woollen tunic and heavy cape, you pull on your hat. You take your small spool and a ball of llama's wool with you, in order to spin as you walk.

You pass a field where people of the *ayllu* are harvesting the first potato crops, digging with the *tacllas*. The harvest ceremony will be coming up in a few days.

A family's herd of llamas.

The road winds back and forth above a river bed, gradually becoming higher and higher. You are soon above the fog of the valley, into which the village disappears. The sun appears in the east from behind a mountain, big and shining. You offer a small prayer at a pile of stones. Soon the air warms up. You put your work in your pouch and begin playing a lonely song on your wooden pipes.

High up on a mountainside you catch sight of your *ayllu's* herd of one hundred llamas. As they trot toward you, you count them to make sure the mountain lion has not taken any more. You are glad to see the black llama that you have tended so carefully. The priest will slaughter it for the harvest ceremony. Shouting and whistling, you drive the herd toward the village far below.

1. Describe the Andes Mountains—where they are, how they are shaped, how high, what special features.
2. What are the main physical features of the Andean coast?
3. List the uses of the llama that made it a valuable domesticated animal for the early South Americans.
4. How did the Andeans use metals to enhance their way of life?
5. Why are the farms belonging to an *ayllu* sometimes described as strings of islands?
6. What work skills would a thirteen-year-old Andean have?
7. List some details of everyday Andean life that are different from yours. Mention things like food, clothing and shelter, as well as work, play and any other things that are different.

THE INCA EMPIRE

The Incas and the Andean Environment

Historians are unsure where the people we call the Incas originally came from. Legends say they were a group of tribes that migrated north from the area of Lake Titicaca before 1200 A.D.

to the Valley of Cuzco, in the central Andes. There, they expelled the local inhabitants and began conquering the neighboring ones.

The word "Inca" originally served as a title for the ruler of this people. An Andean legend claims that the first Inca, Manco Capac (mäng'kō kä päk') was the son of the Sun. Like other Andean peoples, the Incas worshipped the sun as a god. The twelve succeeding rulers, who passed their power from father to son, were likewise considered children of the Sun.

According to the legend, the Andean creator-god Viracocha (vir a kō'chä) gave Manco Capac and his sister-wife, Mama Ocllo (mä'mə ok'lo), a golden rod and told them to search for a homeland where they could settle and establish a city. Everywhere they wandered they thrust the rod into the ground to see how deeply it would sink in. The deeper the rod went, the more suitable was the soil for farming. In the Valley of Cuzco, where the rod disappeared into the soil, they decided to settle.

In this valley, they found people living like wild beasts, without proper food or clothing. At the command of Viracocha, Manco Capac and Mama Ocllo showed the people how to farm the fields and how to build with stone. Thus, according to legend, began the royal city of Cuzco.

Reliable accounts of the Incas begin with the ninth, and greatest, of the thirteen Inca rulers. This man took the name Pachacuti (pə shä kut ē), "he who transforms the earth." Between 1438 and 1471 A.D., Pachacuti conquered and ruled all the area of the Andes from Lake Titicaca to the equator. His son Topa Inca and grandson Huayna Capac (wī'nä kä'päk) were also great emperors and conquerors. Within one hundred years the Incas had established the largest empire in the world at that time, imposing a common government and a common language on dozens of scattered peoples.

With few metal tools, no wheels and only their skill building with stones and fibres the Inca architects and engineers constructed vast networks of roads and bridges, as well as great stone buildings, changing the physical environment to suit their need to communicate across huge distances.

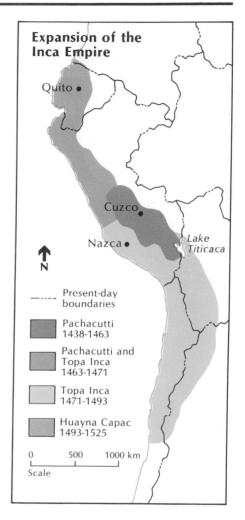

Expansion of the Inca Empire

- Present-day boundaries
- Pachacutti 1438-1463
- Pachacutti and Topa Inca 1463-1471
- Topa Inca 1471-1493
- Huayna Capac 1493-1525

0   500   1000 km
Scale

The information for this map comes from archaeological evidence and oral history.

ROADS IN THE INCA EMPIRE

The roads ran out of the capital city, Cuzco, and went the 4000 km length (a little less than the road distance from Vancouver to Toronto) and 500 km breadth of the empire. The road running north through the Andes was carved through narrow mountain passes. Other routes wound down to the coastal plain, to link with roads six metres across. Their roads were paved with stone over swampy areas.

Where the rivers were narrow, the Incas built bridges of timber. If the rivers were wide, they twined reeds into thick ropes, lashed them to stone foundations and slung them across the gorge. Some of these suspension bridges were made for walking. Others had baskets that could carry people and cargo. Every few years, a crew would rebuild the bridge with new cables. If the river was flat and calm, the crew would lash balsa boats together to make a floating bridge.

Most of the people using the Inca roads and bridges were on government business. Without a good reason for being abroad, people not wearing an official uniform might be questioned and forced to return to their villages. Besides marching soldiers and lords carried in litters by servants, Inca messengers were often seen. A runner on duty at his post would memorize information, run a few kilometres and relay it to another runner. Such messages might consist of requests for more workers on a road construction project or for more blankets for sacrifice at a religious ceremony. Occasionally, the messengers would relay fresh fish from the coast to Cuzco for the royal dinner table. At a slower pace, trains of llama with bundles strapped to their backs carried goods to the capital for the use of the royal family and for offerings to the Sun.

To the Incas, suspension bridges were "little brothers of the road." What does this phrase mean?

Every few kilometres on the roads there was a little stone way-station, with rooms for travellers to stay in, small shrines for offerings to the gods and storage houses filled with food. Some storage centres by the roads had enough food in stock to feed an army on the march or a province whose crops had failed. A centre called Huánuco Pampa (hwän'ūko pam pə) had room to store 40 000 m³ of food. Among the remains are hundreds of large pots used for storing *chicha*, the Andean beer. The Inca lords regularly invited their subjects to such centres for free food and drink.

The cultural life of the Incas led to their engineering more changes to the rugged mountain environment. To grow resources for sacrifice and gift-giving, the Incas cultivated many new mountain valleys. Work parties built stone retaining walls to terrace steep slopes. Most of the new farmland grew maize to make beer for the ruler's use, or to burn as an offering to the Sun. The Incas were also skilful irrigators, diverting creeks into ditches, hollowed-out logs and even huge aqueducts to water their crops.

Write one or two sentences suggesting who these travellers are, and where they might be going.

At the ruins of the Inca town of Machu Picchu, these multilevel terraces remain as evidence of the Incas' farming methods.

This doorway in Cuzco uses a common Inca design.

The centre of this network of roads, bridges and aqueducts was Cuzco, where the Inca ruler had his palace. For over 2000 years Cuzco had been just a small community of sod and brick buildings. Pachacuti imported stoneworkers to rebuild it as a capital city. All the buildings in Pachacuti's Cuzco were a single storey high, usually made of squared blocks fitted snugly without mortar in neat courses. Between the buildings ran narrow cobbled streets with doorways set into thick walls on either side.

The Inca name for their empire means "the Land of the Four Quarters." It was at the Great Plaza in Cuzco that these four quarters met. Most days of the year people gathered for festivals in the Plaza. The nearby Temple of the Sun was the holy centre of the Incas.

The central area of Cuzco was the shape of a puma (mountain lion). The "head" of the puma was the huge fortress of Sacsahuaman (säk sä wä män'), on a hill west of the city. The walls of the fortress were made with some of the biggest stone blocks ever used for building. One is almost ten metres high. The builders used ropes and rollers to haul the blocks up ramps and to fit them properly.

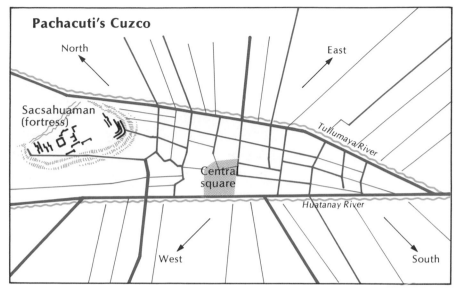

Pachacuti's Cuzco

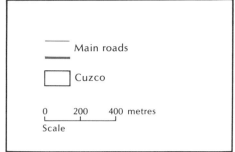

Main roads

Cuzco

0   200   400 metres

Scale

Cuzco is the oldest known Inca settlement. The name means "navel of the world." Why do you suppose it was given this name?

1. According to legend, who were the Incas?
2. Use these headings: transportation, communication, farming, government, to list some ways the Incas modified their physical environment.
3. Design and build a model suspension bridge like the Incas'. First, decide what your materials will be, and then, how large the bridge will be.

The Government of the Inca Empire

The emperor of the Incas had complete control. Atahualpa (ä tə wäl'pä), the last ruler, is reported to have said. "In my kingdom no bird flies, no leaf quivers if I do not will it." The emperor had many privileges. All men of the royal family wore special clothes, but only he could wear a fringe of red fabric over his forehead, and his ear lobes were stretched longer than any other's and pierced with large gold earplugs. He had hundreds of servants who had been taken from their native country to live in Cuzco. The emperor could chose girls to be lifelong servants either to himself or to his court. These girls, called *aclla* ("chosen"), were separated from their families at the age of about ten

231

and went to live in a kind of school. There, they were taught weaving, cooking and beer-brewing. Some lived out their days as workers in the school, others became servants in the royal household.

The royal family included hundreds of wives and children. The emperor's first wife had to be a sister, and to continue the bloodline, he chose one of their children as his successor.

When the emperor died, his body was preserved by being exposed to the cold mountain air, then treated with herbs. The life-like mummy was kept on display in his palace, and his attendants regularly made offerings to the body. Both his palace and the territory he had conquered became the property of his family, while the new emperor built his own palace at Cuzco.

The high priest of the sun-worshipping Inca religion was usually a brother of the emperor. Powerful warriors of the royal family ruled the provinces. With the emperor, the governors of each of the four quarters formed the supreme council of the empire in Cuzco.

Sometimes the emperor raised outsiders to positions of rank. He allowed leaders of conquered groups to keep their powers of local government, giving them the title of *curaca*. A village *curaca* was responsible for 100 households and reported to one ruling 500, and so on, up to the *curaca* ruling a district of 10 000 households. A *curaca* could pass his title on to one of his children. To keep their loyalty, the emperor gave them servants and part of an *ayllu's* fields, and kept their sons at a special school in Cuzco.

All the peoples of the empire owed the Inca **tribute** and yearly **work duty.** If a people did not accept the rule of the Inca emperor, he ordered the people moved by the thousands to another part of the empire. Yet even these people, like everyone else in the empire, were entitled to food, drink and clothing from community stores in times of hardship.

Work duty might consist of service in the army or on a road-building crew in the mountains. Every man over the age of twenty-five had to contribute. Women paid their work duty in the form of woven wool or cotton goods. Every *ayllu* paid

Everyone was expected to help with the Incas' building projects, even these nobles. Was this fair?

tribute, as well. A portion of all produce went to the royal storehouses and palaces, to be consumed by the ruling family, burnt as offerings to ancestors, or given as gifts.

The Incas never used money. In return for the work they performed for their superiors, workers were "paid" by their lords with gifts. Usually this took the form of food and drink, offered to the whole community at regular intervals.

INCA RECORD-KEEPING

Officials in the Inca empire used a clever device to keep track of all the work the villagers performed. Instead of writing numbers down on paper, the Incas made knots in strings and bundled the strings together. Sets of strings, called *quipus*, recorded hundreds of bits of information in an easily carried form. To tell whether the knots on the strings meant a number of people or a number of blankets or something else, the accountant used different knots or wove bits of colored thread into each string.

The Incas used *quipus* for all kinds of accounting. They recorded changes in the work duties and tributes owed by a certain village, for example, as its population increased or fell from year to year. The accountants kept accurate records of the numbers of householders in every corner of the empire. Historians, called

A quipu.

An Inca recorder.

"rememberers," used *quipus* to organize information and passed both their stories and their *quipus* on to their followers. Unfortunately, only a few *quipus* from the coastal desert have survived. Many were destroyed, and the cotton or wool strings of many more decayed in the mountain climate.

Like our system of counting, the Andeans' was based on the decimal. All numbers are based on multiples of ten. The number 4237 is just a simpler way of counting four thousands, plus two hundreds, plus three tens, plus seven ones. The Andeans looked at a series of *quipu* knots the same way. As an example, these symbols, ***** ******* * ******, are another way of writing five thousands, seven hundreds, one ten and six ones, or 5716. Write the following numbers *quipu*-style: 47, 605, 13 364.

The *curacas* upheld the Inca's many laws, aided by officials called "see-alls." These men could enter a home at any time and check on the family's hygiene and furnishings. To discourage stealing, commoners were not allowed to own luxury goods, especially gold or coca leaves. Stealing and dishonesty were serious crimes, sometimes punished by death. Even laziness was punished quickly and severely. It is thought that there was very little crime or idleness in the Inca empire.

1. What were some of the special privileges of the emperor?
2. Who were the *curacas* and what role did they perform in the Inca state?
3. List the various work duties of an Andean man and a woman. What kind of tribute did the *ayllus* have to give to the Inca?

Life for the Privileged in the Inca Empire

Litter bearers approach the city of Cuzco, carrying a young engineer and his first wife from Cochabamba. The couple is excited to be returning to the royal city after an absence of five years. He has an audience with the emperor! She will make an offering at the Temple of the Sun and see her teachers at her old school.

Runners go by them in both directions on the road from the southeast quarter. They stop once to let a regiment of tough-looking soldiers pass. The regiment is guarding the litter of one of the emperor's many sons.

Life has been busy for the engineer since his graduation from the four-year school in Cuzco for sons of the emperor and *curacas*. First he was appointed to plan the road and bridge building in the area where he was born. Then he was given an *aclla* for a wife, as a reward for good work. They now have two children. He was given a special assignment by the governor: to take charge of 5000 settlers brought in to terrace the slopes of the valley in order to begin farming maize for the royal storehouses.

If he is allowed to speak to the emperor, he will be able to report that the first maize crops are now in storage.

The Great Plaza of Cuzco is filled with people celebrating the maize harvest festival. A llama is being sacrificed to the Sun. The engineer and his wife make a short prayer.

Porters carry his gifts to the Inca's palace: packs of coca leaves and costly feathers from the rain forest. He puts on his softest wool robe in preparation for his audience, wondering what the emperor's accountant has reported about him.

The engineer is ushered into the emperor's presence. He removes his sandals and approaches backwards, a sign of respect. He kneels before the emperor who is seated on a low chair near his throne.

The emperor gestures. An attendant thanks the engineer for his good work. The emperor gestures again and servants bring in a small chest containing an elaborately decorated tunic. It is a gift to the engineer. Then the emperor does him a great honor. He has two gold goblets filled with *chicha* brought in. He toasts the engineer. After they have drunk, the Inca makes him a present of the goblets.

The harvest festival began with everyone helping to gather the crops. It ended in a celebration with singing, dancing and feasting.

1. (a) Who made Cuzco the capital city of the Inca empire?

   (b) Explain why the location of Cuzco was suitable for a capital.

   (c) Describe the buildings and activities of the city.

2. Identify four examples of rewards given in the story and explain what each one means.

3. How did people show respect for the Inca? Do you think this was right?

4. Read once again the legend about the first Inca. In a few sentences, explain how this legend shows the relationship between the culture of the Incas and their environment. (Hint: Use the five W words—who, what, when, where, why—to help think about the problem.)

THE END OF THE INCA EMPIRE

The Spanish Arrival in the Andes

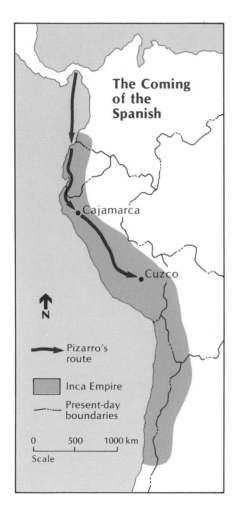

The Coming of the Spanish

Cajamarca

Cuzco

N

→ Pizarro's route

Inca Empire

- - - Present-day boundaries

0 500 1000 km
Scale

In November, 1532 A.D., the Inca emperor Atahualpa met a group of Spanish soldiers. It was the first time an Inca ruler had met men from Europe. We know about the meeting from written eyewitness accounts of the Spaniards.

Atahualpa was camped outside the city of Cajamarca (kä hä mär′kä) in the Andes Mountains with a large army of fierce soldiers and some of his chosen women. He was on his way to the royal city of Cuzco to claim the throne. By royal custom Atahualpa had little right to the throne, because his mother was not Huayna Capac's sister-wife. But Atahualpa was his father's favorite, and he had decided to fight his half-brother, the high priest, for the throne. Just shortly before, Atahualpa's generals had won the final battle, giving him control of the whole empire.

Atahualpa had just had a hot bath and was sitting on a little stool when about fifteen Spanish horsemen rode up to the Inca's camp, led by a man named Hernando de Soto. The Spaniards' upper bodies were cased in light steel armor and they had gleaming steel helmets on their heads. The horsemen sat in their saddles, carrying swords and pikes of hard steel.

Soto rode up to Atahualpa, who had never seen a horse. Reaching down, Soto offered Atahualpa a small gift and invited him to visit the Spaniards' leader in Cajamarca. Atahualpa did not even look at the visitors at first, but he grew curious and accepted the invitation to visit them the next day.

Before leaving, Soto showed Atahualpa his skill on horseback. He spurred his horse straight at the ruler, reining it in only centimetres from him. The horse's foam spattered the god-king. Atahualpa did not move a muscle. Legend has it that soldiers who did flinch were executed that day.

Back in Cajamarca, Soto and the other Spaniards were planning to ambush the Inca. They wanted the Incas' gold. It was because of this gold that they had come at their own expense all the way from Spain, via Central America. With the permission of the king of Spain, their leader, Francisco Pizarro, had been planning this invasion for eight years. Now they were thousands of kilometres from their native country and were outnumbered hundreds of times by fierce Inca soldiers.

Later, a young page wrote a letter to his Spanish parents: "We came here with Governor Francisco Pizarro to the land of this lord where he had 60 000 warriors, and there were 160 Spaniards with the governor, and we thought our lives were finished because there was such a horde of them, and the women were making fun of us and saying they were sorry for us because we were going to get killed."

Atahualpa entered Cajamarca sitting in a gold litter decorated with many-colored feathers. Since this was a time of festival, many of his guard were unarmed, dressed in dark blue gowns, with dazzling gold and silver ornaments on their heads.

With a sudden yell, the Spanish horsemen burst out of hiding and rode into the middle of the Inca troops as their footsoldiers fired cannon. They grabbed Atahualpa off his litter at swordpoint, took him hostage and killed many of his soldiers.

To ransom Atahualpa, the Inca's people brought enough gold to fill a room and enough silver to fill it twice. It is considered the biggest ransom ever paid for the release of a prisoner. But Atahualpa did not go free. After a time, the Spaniards killed him. Within months, the huge Inca empire was controlled by a few Spanish adventurers.

Usually the Inca soldiers wore their fighting garb: heavy tunics and capes, helmets and shields of wood and metal, slings for hurling stones, maces for clubbing and bronze-tipped wooden spears.

Spanish horsemen capture Atahualpa.

A cavalier at the time of the Spanish conquest. Compare the battle dress of this Spanish cavalier with that of the Inca soldier on page 237.

The Inca empire was a huge military power. But it had weaknesses that enabled a few well-armed horsemen to conquer it quickly.

One such weakness was disease. The first Europeans in America had carried smallpox and measles, both of which spread into the Andes even before the Spaniards arrived. Because the South Americans had no contact with these diseases before, and therefore no immunity to them, they died in great numbers.

Civil war also weakened the Inca empire. The rulership of the empire had always passed smoothly from father to son. But Atahualpa's father had died of a disease, probably a European one, before he could choose an heir. In the war to decide which son would rule, thousands more Andeans died.

The Spaniards were ruthless and captured Atahualpa and other leaders by trickery. They even got Atahualpa's enemies, tribes conquered by the Incas, to fight on the Spanish side, so one Andean army was fighting against another.

Their more advanced technology gave the Spaniards a great advantage in battle. Protected by light steel armor and carrying long steel weapons, the Spaniards won almost every battle they fought. Inca soldiers had a reputation for being fierce fighters, but they were not equipped for the Spaniards' fast, daring horseback attacks right into the middle of their ranks. Rearing horses and roaring cannons terrified the Inca footsoldiers.

Finally, the Incas' excellent roads helped the Spanish destroy their empire. The Spanish horsemen already had experience in fighting wars in their own mountainous country. Their horses travelled the Andes' mountain roads much faster than Inca soldiers could. Spanish visitors said that the Inca roads were better than most in Europe at that time, and as good as the old Roman roads in Spain.

1. Describe the weapons of the Spaniards who met Atahualpa. In what ways were these weapons more advanced than the Incas'?
2. List reasons for the conquest of the Inca empire. Which one do you think was the most important?

3. In your notebook, match the terms in the column on the left with the descriptions in the column on the right.

1. Hernando de Soto
   a. an emperor who died without naming an heir

2. Cuzco
   b. the first Inca ruler to meet Spanish soldiers

3. Francisco Pizarro
   c. the leader of the Spanish expedition to South America

4. Huayna Capac
   d. a city the Spaniards had taken over for their camp

5. Cajamarca
   e. the first Spanish officer to meet the emperor

6. Atahualpa
   f. the capital city of the Inca empire.

South American Society after the Spanish Conquest

At first the Spanish conquerors simply divided the wealth of the Incas among themselves and shipped it out of the country. Reports spread of the rich storehouses of Cuzco and of the gold ornaments in the Temple of the Sun. The conquerors found golden maize plants in a garden in the temple, and an eight-sided gold basin for burning offerings of maize and llama meat. In a cave near Cuzco they found a dozen full-sized statues of soldiers, made of gold, guarding a sacred shrine.

The Spanish began to use the Andean economy for their own gain. The first invaders were put in charge of large areas, and their power was called *encomienda*, or custody. For a few years this power passed from father to son, and some of the holdings were enormous.

The Spanish settlers enforced the work duty, as a source of labor. They put native people to work as porters, making them carry heavy loads on their backs until they dropped. The work duty under the Spaniards was much more cruel than under the old Incas.

The Spanish took over the Inca's coca fields in the rain forest. Laborers brought down from the high mountains got sick when forced to work in the low country. The Spaniards began mining the gold and silver of the Andes, using the conquered people as laborers. The only people excepted were those who had migrated out of their native province and were not part of a local *ayllu*. Many natives left their families and homelands to escape the brutal working conditions in the mines or coca fields.

The huge silver mines near Potosí, south of Lake Titicaca, required thousands of new workers every month. Soon the town of Potosi had a population bigger than that of all but the biggest European cities. When mercury, a poisonous metal used for refining silver, was discovered in the Andes, more miners were brought in by force. Many of them died in the mines.

The Spanish collected tribute twice a year from their subjects. Every group had to give a large part of what they produced, as in the old days, but the Spaniards demanded more and more. The natives had to carry most of their maize, potatoes and other goods to the provincial capitals.

A Spanish observer described the life of the people of the Andes during this time:

Even if it freezes or if their cereals and other foods are dried up and lost, they are forced to pay their tribute in full. They have nothing left over from what they can produce. They live the most wretched and miserable lives of any people on earth. As long as they are healthy they are fully occupied only in working for tribute. Even when they are sick they have no respite, and few survive their first illness. They have come to believe that they must continue to work for Spaniards for as long as they or their sons and descendants live, with nothing to enjoy themselves. Because of this they despair; for they ask only for their daily bread and cannot have even that.

Some Spaniards liked to be carried around in litters by the Natives, a privilege of Inca nobles.

Another observer wrote: "The only rule has been to use and exploit the natives according to the greed of each *encomendero*." Even some of the Catholic missionaries took advantage of their positions by using the Andeans as servants.

MANCO INCA

Three years after the conquest of the Inca empire, a young brother of Atahualpa named Manco was crowned emperor in the Great Square of Cuzco. By tradition, the new Inca was crowned by his father, but Manco Inca was crowned by Governor Francisco Pizarro. Every day for thirty days Manco Inca went to the Temple of the Sun and to the palaces of all his predecessors. The mummies of the earlier Incas were borne on litters into the square. There they were set on thrones and attended by servants, who gave them food and drink, while all day the people celebrated the coronation.

Although Manco Inca was their prisoner, the Spanish tried to use him to govern his people. But Manco escaped and formed a rebel kingdom in the forest fringes of the Andes. He assembled all his armies for a surprise attack on Cuzco. They besieged the city again and again but could not take it from the Spanish.

Manco Inca was not the last Inca ruler in the Andes. The Spanish governors continued to give members of the royal family the title of Inca, but these rulers had little power of their own. Slowly, the Spanish Crown established colonial governments in four centres, each with its own administrators and judges. The first such centre, established in 1542, was Lima, the present-day capital of Peru.

The only group of Inca people that kept any power was the *curacas*. They were as happy to serve their new masters, in return for keeping their titles and privileges. Their support helped the Spaniards control the country. To meet the demands of the Spaniards, many *curacas* became as cruel as their masters in getting tribute and labor from their subjects.

While many *encomenderos*, *curacas* and priests unfairly used the Andean people, the Spanish kings tried to stop these abuses. The Viceroy, or king's deputy, appointed protectors of the native Andeans' rights. The Viceroy allowed Andeans to bring complaints into the law courts. But the verdict usually changed nothing. The Spanish argued that they were only following Inca traditions, since it was the Incas who had created hereditary *curacas* and the tributes.

The Spanish viceroy moved farming families from their mountain villages into towns. In 1571 alone, forty-seven such new towns were begun in southern Peru. The Spaniards also hoped to "civilize" the Andeans by destroying their religion.

The Inca people did not vanish with the Spanish conquest. Native Andeans continued to follow traditions linking them with the Inca civilization.

It has been estimated that the population of the empire dropped from at least six million people to less than two million in the fifty years after the conquest. Yet today, the native Andeans again number over five million. They are hardy people, used to life in the mountains. Many of them speak Quechua (kech'wä), a version of the old Inca language, and continue to farm as their ancestors did.

1. How did the Spanish conquer the Inca empire? List four steps.
2. What were the causes for the decline in the native population of the Andes?

3. How did the role of the *curaca*, or Native chiefs, change with the coming of the Spanish?
4. Using the headings, "Incas" and "Spanish," summarize the advantages and disadvantages of living in the Andes under each group of rulers.

SUMMARY

The Andes Mountains have been home to several South American civilizations. Some started in the desert close to the Pacific Ocean, while others started in the high valleys. In both areas the settlers cultivated many crops and fished or hunted. Over 3000 years ago the coastal centres were making textiles, pottery and fine metal objects. The mountain dwellers were organized in family groups called *ayllus* to work on numerous spread out farmlands.

The Inca empire began in the fifteenth century A.D. and quickly grew by conquering most of the Andean peoples. The earliest of the thirteen Inca rulers were legendary, but Pachacuti, who started the system of Inca government, is believed to have ruled from 1438 to 1471. The emperors had many roads, bridges, shelters and storage centres built. They ran the economy, collecting tribute and making most citizens do work duty. They appointed officials to govern the empire. The most important were members of the royal family. The Inca also appointed Native chiefs as local heads. The emperor lived in great wealth, with more privileges than anyone else. He had hundreds of children.

A small group of Spanish soldiers with horses captured the Inca in 1532 and took over the Inca empire to plunder its resources. The conquest was a result of weaknesses in Inca society, as well as of the Spaniards' military skill and ruthlessness. The Spanish turned the empire into a colony, exploiting the natives as workers and suppliers of food. The Andeans suffered under the Spanish, and many of them died.

Chapter Review: The Incas

NEW WORDS AND IDEAS

1. Identify each of the following places, and explain how each is important to a study of the Inca:
   (a) Lake Titicaca   (d) Cajamarca
   (b) Andes Mountains   (e) Potosi.
   (c) Cuzco

2. Explain how each of the following affected the culture of the early Andean and Inca people:
   (a) the physical geography
   (b) cultivated crops
   (c) conquest by new peoples coming to the area.

CHECKING YOUR UNDERSTANDING

3. Copy the following events into your notebook, this time organizing them so that they are in their proper historical order:
   (a) According to legend, Manco Capac settles in the valley of Cuzco.
   (b) The Spanish gain control over the Inca empire.
   (c) People move into South America from Central America.
   (d) Andeans learn how to make bronze.
   (e) Manco Inca leads a rebellion against the Spanish.
   (f) Atahualpa is taken prisoner by Hernando de Soto.
   (g) Permanent villages are established near the mouths of the rivers, along the coastal plain.
   (h) Pachacuti, the ninth Inca ruler, conquers the area of the Andes from Lake Titicaca to the equator.

4. (a) Terracing is an example of how the Incas changed their environment to meet their needs. Using the picture on page 230 as a guide, describe terracing. Include a sketch.
   (b) What would be the benefit of terracing?
   (c) Describe at least one other way the Incas changed their environment.

5. Explain how the Incas preserved potatoes and meat.

6. Give two examples that demonstrate the engineering skills of the Incas.

7. Describe the duties of each of the following members of Inca Society:
   (a) Inca
   (b) priests
   (c) provincial governors
   (d) *curaca*
   (e) "see alls"
   (f) the ordinary men and women.

8. Give three causes for the defeat of the Incas. Which of the three do you think was the most important? Give reasons for your choice.

USING YOUR KNOWLEDGE

9. Draw a twelve month calendar. On it mark the different stages of farming in the Inca civilization. How would this farmer's calendar differ from one for a farmer in your area?

10. There are two isolated villages. One is located on a plateau between two mountain ranges. The second is located on a wide plain, beside a large lake.
    (a) Describe the environment and culture of both villages. Include the climate, vegetation, food, clothing, and shelter.
    (b) One day, members of the two villages meet at the foot of the mountain. How might the culture of the mountain village change as a result of this meeting? How might the culture of the plains village change?

Chapter 8

The Mandinko of West Africa

INTRODUCTION

Stretching across northern Africa, the Sahara Desert covers an area greater than the combined area of Canada's ten provinces. Arab travellers, who have crossed the desert for centuries, compare it to an ocean. Like a trip across the ocean, desert travel can be long and dangerous. Windstorms whip the sand in the air for days, and water is available only in small **oases**.

When underground springs or streams provide enough water, the desert can support plant life, such as the date palm plantation shown here. What is the name given to these green islands in the desert?

African peoples north of the desert have always had a lifestyle influenced by their nearness to the Mediterranean Sea. They have been part of the civilizations that developed around this sea. On the other hand, the peoples of Africa south of the Sahara Desert developed their own civilizations. The great stretches of sand made communication between the two people difficult, but as you will see, not impossible.

Along the southern edge of the Sahara Desert is a flat plain called the Sahel (sä hel'). This is an Arabic word meaning "shore." The Sahel is hot all year, with only enough rain for grass and a few thorny trees to grow. But these trees are a welcome sight to travellers who have just crossed the "ocean of sand" that is the Sahara Desert. This grassland runs in a narrow band beginning at the Atlantic Ocean and extending eastwards across the continent to the Indian Ocean.

Farther south is another zone of grassland called savanna. The land here gets more rain, and the grasses grow thicker. Trees occur more frequently. Farther south of these grasslands, heavy rains encourage the growth of dense rain forests.

The Sahel of West Africa has been the home of many peoples. Some of these peoples belong to a group known as the Mandinko. They are called by this name because they all speak some form of a language called *Mande.* Most Mandinka people (the "o" at the end of Mandinko changes to "a" when the word is used as an adjective) live west of the Niger River.

More than 2000 years ago, civilizations began in the West African Sahel. The Mandinka people developed one of the most important civilizations. They learned to use the difficult physical environment and farmed crops and raised livestock on it, and mined and smelted iron from it. Their empires stretched over large areas of West Africa. Archaeologists have so far found only a few remains of these early empires, but believe they included parts of the modern-day states of Mali (mä'lē), Mauritania (môr i tā'nē ə), Guinea (gin'ē), Guinea-Bissau (gin'ē bis'sou'), Senegal (sen i gôl') and Gambia (gam'bē ə).

By 1400 years ago, traders on camels were travelling regularly across the Sahara Desert to trade with the early Mandinka

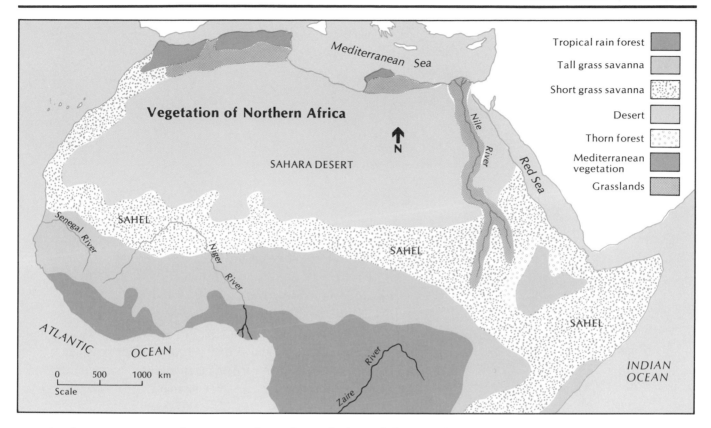

empire known as Wagadu. Most of our knowledge of this civilization comes from the written reports of later Arab visitors.

By 800 years ago, the even larger Mandinka empire of Mali occupied much of West Africa. It was known in Europe and Asia as a strange, far-off place of great wealth. Much of what we know of this empire has come from the writing of travellers who visited Mali. Some of what we know comes from stories that have been passed along by the oral tradition of the Mandinko. Also, many West African traditional customs and beliefs have survived, so we can understand how the Mandinko lived in ancient times by observing their present-day way of life.

In the three sections of this chapter, we will look first at the earliest civilizations of the Sahel. Next, we will examine the Mandinka empire of Wagadu. Finally, we will look at the later Mandinka empire of Mali.

In which vegetation regions is the Mandinka homeland found?

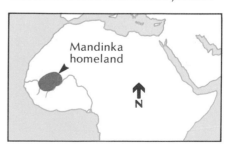

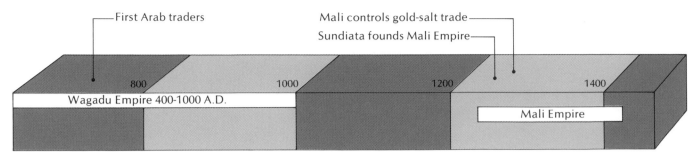

First Arab traders

Mali controls gold-salt trade

Sundiata founds Mali Empire

800   1000   1200   1400

Wagadu Empire 400-1000 A.D.

Mali Empire

MALI EMPIRE

1. (a) Suppose you were travelling southward from the Sahara Desert. Which is the correct order of the vegetation areas you would cross?
   (i) rain forest - Sahel - savanna
   (ii) savanna - rain forest - Sahel
   (iii) Sahel - savanna - rain forest
   (iv) savanna - Sahel - rain forest
   (b) Describe the vegetation of each of the three areas.
2. Explain what is the most important factor in creating the pattern of vegetation in the area south of the Sahara.

THE BEGINNING OF CIVILIZATION IN THE SAHEL

Early Farming and the Environment of the Sahel

People have hunted and gathered food in West Africa for at least 40 000 years. Farming began here about 6000 years ago. The tools, seeds and livestock probably came from Egypt. Year-round, people grew wheat and barley in irrigated fields, but likely depended more on hunting and livestock for food.

Until about 5000 years ago, parts of what is now the Sahara Desert were covered by rivers, lakes, and grasslands. But as the climate gradually turned hotter and drier, these rivers and lakes dried up. The crops in the grasslands failed. The desert grew,

The Sahel

THE MARCH OF THE SAHARA

The Sahara Desert is advancing across West Africa at a rate of two to five kilometres per year. The grasslands are dying and the bare soil is being picked up and carried away by the wind. All that is left behind is bare rock or loose shifting sand. Over the past fifty years, 650 000 km² of the Sahel have been overrun by the Sahara.

What is the cause of this catastrophe? When examined closely, we see this situation has been caused by *people*.

In times past, there were dry periods when the desert advanced somewhat, but eventually more rains came and the desert retreated. When the desert advanced, the people moved to where there was more moisture; they returned when the desert retreated. Nowadays people cannot move so easily. Political boundaries, wars, and private ownership of the land limit where they can go. Often they have to remain in one place in spite of a drought.

A growing population has also been a problem. The fragile environment of the Sahel is being forced to support more and more people.

When people are crowded on the land and cannot move away, they overuse the resources. The few trees and shrubs that grow on the Sahel are cut down for firewood and building materials. Herds feed on the grass faster than it can grow. Wells run dry. Without the trees and grass to hold the soil in place, the wind carries it away.

Scientists think the only way to reclaim the land is to move the people away, maybe for decades. This will give the vegetation a chance to grow. The disruption this would cause for the people would be enormous. Perhaps there is no other solution.

consuming useful farmland on its edges. The desert expanded farther and farther over West Africa.

The Sahara Desert is still expanding. Today the Sahel is too hot and dry to support much food production, except for some bullrush millet and sorghum (kinds of cereal grain). In Kayes, a Sahel city in the Republic of Mali, six months of every year are rainless. This is typical of the Sahel: six months of rain and six months of drought. However, sometimes the rains do not come as expected. Since the early 1970s, the people of the Sahel have suffered long periods of drought and starvation.

But thousands of years ago, when the Sahel was not as dry and hot as it is today, the Mandinka people were able to cultivate the land and grow crops. We do not know whether the Sahel peoples discovered agriculture themselves or whether their crops first came from East Africa. Whatever the case, we think that the earliest farming in the Sahel grew up around underground wells, the major supply of water in the area. Archaeologists think farming methods were much the same in ancient times as they are today.

The farming year began as the dry season ended. The village farmers spread manure on the nearby fields and ridged the soil for the seed crops. The farmers planted their staple crops immediately after the first hard rain, in May or June. The women planted rice while the men planted nuts and millet.

During the summer, the villagers weeded the soil. Young boys watched the growing crops closely to make sure livestock or wild hogs and monkeys did not damage them.

The millet harvest began in August, followed by the harvests of groundnuts, Guinea corn, cowpeas and rice. After these crops had been picked, the villagers set the groundnuts to dry, threshed the grain, cut up fodder for the livestock and set the herds to graze on the farmland.

At the end of the wet season, a winter crop of cassava was planted. As the crop began to grow during the dry season, it had to be watered. The women usually carried out this task, carrying jugs of water from the wells to the fields.

When the dry season began, the farmers used the Guinea corn

Millet is still an important part of the Mandinka diet. How are these women separating the millet from the chaff?

We are used to seeing peanut butter in jars. This girl is rolling peanuts. Later they will be boiled to make a sauce.

stalks to make fences and house roofs. They also harvested tree crops. The bark of the tamarind tree could be used for treating leather, while the seeds of the silk cotton tree could be eaten and its flowers could be used as a medicine.

Cattle, sheep and goats were raised by the farmers. These grazing animals did well on the natural grasses of the Sahel. Their manure helped to enrich the soil, and their milk and meat balanced the vegetables and cereals in the Mandinkos' diet. It is believed that the animals came from Mediterranean Africa and were brought to the Sahel by traders.

1. What important changes have occurred in the physical environment of the area south of the Sahara Desert?
2. List jobs that needed to be done to improve growing conditions in the Sahel.
3. What actions did the people take to try to reduce the effect of a drought?

The Early Society of the Sahel

Ironworking was an important feature of early Sahel society. About 2500 years ago, Sahel tribes whose lands had deposits of iron ore began making iron spears, swords and hoes. Knowledge of **smelting**, the melting of the ore to get the metal out, may have spread to the Sahel from North Africa. People with the knowledge of how to use iron had a great advantage over those who did not have that knowledge. Tribes in the Sahel with iron weapons could easily defeat those tribes which had only wooden clubs and spears. Farmers with iron hoes could till the soil more efficiently than those using wooden hoes. Iron objects were valuable and could be traded to other tribes which had not learned this craft. From this start, the Mandinka people became skilled traders.

Camels were important to the traders of the Sahel. These beasts could travel across the desert for days without water and could carry heavy loads. **Nomadic** tribes of the Sahara used them. They loaded the animals with salt and other goods from the North, then crossed the desert to trade with the communities of the Sahel. The people of the Sahel offered gold and slaves in exchange for the goods from Mediterranean Africa. These were, in turn, traded to tribes to the south of the Sahel.

While camels were useful beasts of burden in the desert and on the Sahel, they were not as good for trading with people to the South. The greater rainfall in the savanna and rain forest caused the soft hooves of the camels to rot. Donkeys were used instead. They carried the trade goods from the Sahel to the forest.

The most common nomadic traders to the Sahel were known as Berbers (bėr'bər). They usually came to trade, but sometimes their visits were hostile. Raids were a feature of life in the Sahel for centuries. The people of most villages built walls for protection against the Berber raids. They also learned to fight using horses and eventually developed large cavalries.

We have no written records to tell us about how the Mandinko organized their activity. Throughout the centuries, however, the people have maintained a traditional way of family life and village organization. By looking at these traditions, we can form

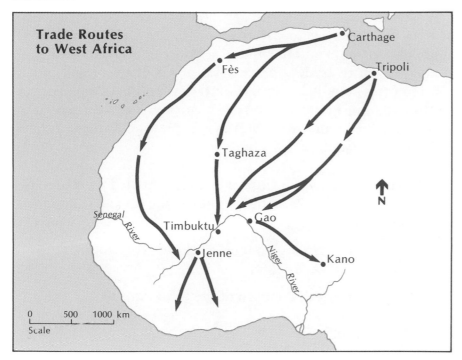

Trade Routes to West Africa

Carthage
Tripoli
Fès
Taghaza
Senegal River
Timbuktu
Gao
Jenne
Kano
Niger River

N

0   500   1000 km
Scale

Traders followed the oases across the desert to get to the land of the Mandinko. Here they traded their goods for gold. The Mandinko also traded with people to the south.

an idea of how the ancient Sahel tribes governed themselves.

In Mandinka villages in Senegal, one man ranks as the head of the traditional leading family. He is called *dugu tigi*, or "master of the land." The villagers believe that the *dugu tigi's* ancestors first cleared the land and learned how to deal with the spirits that inhabit it. The *dugu tigi* supervises the use of the farmland and pasture.

The village is governed by a council made up of men representing all the ranking families in it. The council listens to anyone's advice, including that of visiting strangers. "Strangers make a town prosper" is a Mandinka saying. Musicians, actors, storytellers, blacksmiths, leatherworkers and potters of the village all have a voice in its government. The chief of the village, however, is often its richest, most powerful man.

Some of these chiefs have power over a district of several villages. Such a chief is called *togotigi* or "big man." Often a "big man" is also known as *mansa* or king. There have been hundreds of small kingdoms in the history of the Sahel.

We think these kingdoms developed in several stages. The peoples first learned to use their environment to produce an abundance of food and to support a growing population. Later, as they began to trade with peoples north of the desert, their communities grew. Because of the attacks of desert nomads, they had to become better organized to survive. Horses and iron weapons helped win battles, and the people who possessed them became the most powerful rulers.

1. Describe the relationships the Mandinko had with the tribes of the Sahara and the tribes of the savanna and rain forest.

2. Explain why visitors from other places were both an advantage and a problem.

3. Describe the duties of each of the following:
   (a) *dugu tigi*
   (b) village council
   (c) *togotigi.*

Village Life

Modern civilization is reaching the villages of the Sahel, but enough traditions survive to suggest how the Mandinko lived in ancient times. Imagine that you lived in a village near the upper Niger River long ago.

Each group of mud huts belongs to a family and is enclosed by a low fence of wood or brick. The mud walls of the hut are reinforced with sticks to hold the mud together. They are topped with thatched straw roofs.

Near the entrance of each enclosure is the hut of the head man, and nearby is the hut of his first wife. A man can marry as many women as he can support, and each wife has her own hut. In practice, only a few families have many huts. Smaller round huts are used as granaries. Pigs and chickens run around in the yard, and little children play in the common areas.

A modern Mali village. In what ways have the people of the village made the best use of the environment?

In the middle of the village is the dancing ground. Important occasions such as the planting of crops, the initiation of young people or the death of an elder are celebrated with dancing. The leaders of the dancing sometimes wear masks to represent the invisible powers that they believe rule their lives.

Another important gathering place is the men's lounging area, often the shade of a tree. Here the men gather to talk about the affairs of the village.

At the head of the village, under a tree near the lodge of the village council, the blacksmith works with his bellows, fire and hammers, making and fixing iron tools.

The blacksmith is especially important in the village. He makes weapons and farming tools. The blacksmith is often thought to have magic powers. He controls the four elements: earth, fire, air, and water. His iron comes from the earth, his fire from the forge, his air from the bellows and his water from a bucket which he uses to quench the hot iron. He carves wooden figures to use in rituals that will help the crops grow and help the women produce children.

Just outside the village, a team of workers are threshing the grain. To help them work, the *dieli*, or singer of the village, is playing his *balafon* (xylophone) and drums as he shouts encouragement.

In a secluded grove beyond the village, young boys are preparing for their initiation ceremonies. You can hear them singing songs while beating time on logs: they are chanting words which mean "If an elder tells you something, you must never answer with disrespect." They will stay here, instructed by older men, until they have passed tests of courage and are accepted as adult villagers.

After the initiation ceremonies the boys can join the *ton*, a "youth association." Members of this club volunteer for farming duties and help those in need of food or shelter.

Clubs or secret societies are an important part of village life in the Sahel. Some of these clubs are restricted to boys or men, others to girls or women. Belonging to clubs helps cement bonds of friendship: club members help and support each other. All contribute to the life of the village in some way.

Women have their own clubs, involved with religion and education, led most often by the *muso mansa*, or queen. The *muso mansa* play a leading role at births, marriages and burials. The members of these clubs support each other during difficult times such as illnesses or deaths, and for the day-to-day raising of children. Most of their day, women are busy at the work of raising families and farming.

Some Mandinka groups also have clubs called *Chi Wara*, and *Koré.* Members of the *Chi Wara* make sure the tribal ancestors are remembered and honored through dances at village celebrations. The members of the *Koré* dance in order to make the ground fertile at planting time. They wear animal masks and parade around the fields of the village.

Boys of the same age and girls of the same age form friendships that remain for the rest of their lives.

1. List the three basic kinds of environment in West Africa, south of the Sahara Desert. Write a sentence to describe each one.
2. In what ways were each of the following important to the early people of the Sahel: donkeys, camels, horses?

3. Match the items in column A with their correct descriptions in column B.

A	B
1. *dugu tigi*	a. a Mandinka club of dancers
2. *muso mansa*	b. a Mandinka queen
3. cassava	c. a musical instrument
4. millet	d. the great desert of Africa
5. *balafon*	e. a Mandinka village chief
6. *dieli*	f. a Mandinka chief of several villages
7. *chi wara*	g. area south of the Sahel
8. *togotigi*	h. a Mandinka singer
9. Sahara	i. warlike nomadic desert tribe
10. Berber	j. winter crop of the Sahel
11. savanna	k. summer crop of the Sahel

4. Draw a sketch map of a typical Mandinka village, showing houses, work areas, meeting places and any other features. Label each feature.

THE EMPIRE OF WAGADU

Influences on the Wagadu Empire

For thousands of years, the economy and culture of the Sahel have been influenced by travellers crossing the Sahara Desert. The first empires grew because of the trade routes. The empire of Wagadu, the best known one, developed around the southern end of gold-trading routes that crossed the Sahara Desert from the Sahel to the cities of the Mediterranean Sea. Wagadu was located between the Senegal and Niger rivers. It began in the fourth century A.D. and lasted until about the eleventh century.

Empires such as Wagadu began long before the written history of West Africa. There were no written records or calendars in West Africa until the arrival of Arab traders about 1200 years ago. The Arabs, a people from the desert lands between Egypt

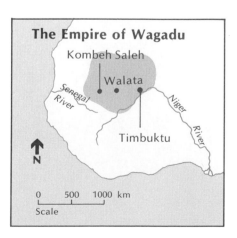

The Empire of Wagadu

and Mesopotamia, took control of the camel routes to the north and east of Wagadu. They lived in the cities of Wagadu and carried oral reports back to their homeland. From these reports, Arab scribes wrote about the geography and history of the empire of Wagadu. They called it "the land of gold." It was not until much later that an account of West Africa was written by someone who had actually visited the area.

Over the centuries, the Mandinko adopted many of the customs of the Arab visitors. Many of them converted to their religion, Islam (is'ləm). The Arabs followed the teachings of Mohammed (mō ham'id), a prophet who died in 632 A.D. People who believe the teachings of Mohammed are called Moslems (moz'ləm), followers of God.

The Economy of Wagadu

It was reported that one Wagadu king had a thousand horses tied up outside his residence, and that another tied his horse up to a huge gold nugget. This gives an idea of the wealth of the Wagadu rulers. Such wealth attracted others to the empire. As many as 20 000 foreigners lived in the gold-trading centre of Kumbi, near the present day site of the town of Kombeh Saleh in Mauretania.

The Arab traders who came to Kumbi never discovered where the gold came from. It was said that it sprouted out of the sand like carrots. We now know the gold actually came from the Bambuk Mountains, beyond the Senegal River. The people who mined it dug small pits or searched the gravel of the rivers for gold nuggets. To protect their wealth, these people did not let outsiders know where their gold fields were. They brought the nuggets down from the mountains themselves.

Besides gold, the Arabs obtained such luxury goods as ivory, and foods such as shea butter and kola nuts. The ivory, from the tusks of elephants, was prized for carving. Shea butter came from the edible oil of a savanna tree. The bitter kola nuts from a rain forest tree were used to flavor foods and drinks.

The Arabs also obtained slaves, captured by the Mandinko during wars with other tribes, and marched them across the desert to be workers in the cities of Europe, North Africa and West Asia.

From the Arabs Mandinka merchants got clothing, copper, pearls and shells. Most importantly, they acquired blocks of salt.

Salt was vital to the health of the people living south of the desert. In the tropical heat, they quickly sweated salt out of their bodies. Lack of salt made their blood "dry out," leading to sudden collapse. To replace the salt they rubbed it on their lips, and licked it when eating. The Mandinko traded the salt to tribes further to the south in the rain forest.

1. Why would the Mandinka gold miners want to keep the location of their mines a secret?
2. Suggest uses the Mandinka people could have had for copper, pearls and shells, goods they got from Arab traders.

Salt is still an important trade item. Here, large slabs are offered for sale at the market at Mopti.

Government of the Wagadu Empire

The early Mandinka kingdoms had no fixed boundaries and few permanent centres. The king of Wagadu ruled over dozens of vassal (servant) kings from whom he collected tributes. Many of these kingdoms had been taken over by force. The king of Wagadu held power only as long as he had the military force to stop rebellions and uprisings. The king often took the sons of his vassal kings as hostages in order to keep the loyalty of the vassals. Some families appear to have ruled Wagadu for generations, only to be overthrown by other family alliances.

Each king had many wives and chose his heir from his huge family.

An Arab named al-Bakrī wrote down travellers' observations of life at the court of Wagadu in the eleventh century. Later writers added more accounts of the wealth and pomp of the Wagadu kings.

Some of these accounts tell how the beat of drummers pounding a long log called the people of Wagadu for an audience with the king. The accounts describe how dogs with collars of gold and silver guarded the gates to the king's chamber. Inside, the king was surrounded by guards armed with gold-mounted swords. On one side were the sons of his princes, dressed in finery, with gold worked into their hair. Seated in front were his advisors.

Wearing rings, necklaces, and a gold cap, the king sat on a throne of ebony wood with huge elephant tusks arching over him on either side. He and his heir were the only people who could wear elaborate clothes in court. Everyone else wore simple robes of cotton.

People who wished the king's help had to humble themselves before him. They put on old robes, holding them above their knees, and bowed as they approached the king. When the king spoke to them, they bared their backs and threw dust over their heads. The writer, Ibn Battūta, who visited Wagadu in the fourteenth century, said this looked like a bather splashing himself with water. "I used to wonder how (it was) they did not blind themselves."

1. List four products of their environment that the Mandinko traded to the Arabs. Explain which ones would be easy to transport and which would be difficult.
2. Who wrote the first accounts of the Wagadu? Where did they get their information?
3. From what we know about Mandinko history and geography, how did the early kingdoms begin?
4. Why was salt so important to the Mandinko?
5. In your own words, describe an audience with the king of Wagadu.

THE EMPIRE OF MALI

The Development of Ancient Mali

Near the head of the Niger River is the homeland of the Malinke (mal'in ke'), a subgroup of the Mandinko. Under the leadership of a powerful clan, the Malinke conquered much of West Africa during the thirteenth century. By the end of the century, the

THE LEGEND OF SUNDIATA

Even today, some Mandinka storytellers can trace their family histories all the way back to the year 1200 A.D. The story of Sundiata, the founder of Mali, has been passed from generation to generation by these storytellers.

According to the legend, Sundiata was born in a terrible thunderstorm in the middle of the dry season. The fortunetellers predicted that he would be a powerful king. He had three powerful family totems (guardian spirits): the buffalo, the panther and the lion. But because of a spell, he could not walk. Sundiata had to drag himself about like a crocodile. His family scorned him. But one day Sundiata astonished everyone by pulling himself onto his feet.

That same day, a huge baobab tree suddenly bore fruit. Fortunetellers said the future king alone could gather and eat the fruit. Sundiata's arm grew long enough to reach the fruit and pluck it. Then he picked up the enormous tree and carried it back to his mother's hut for her.

Later, to save his life, Sundiata was forced to flee from his jealous half-brother, the king. He fled to Mema, near Timbuktu, and lived there for six years. While he was there, his people back home were conquered by Sumaoro, king of the Sosso people. Sumaoro killed anyone who dared to rebel and destroyed the royal city of Niani.

When Sundiata was eighteen, people from his homeland came to him to ask him to be their leader. This was as the fortunetellers had predicted. They asked him to rescue them from Sumaoro.

Sundiata decided to lead his people into battle against Sumaoro's powerful army.

Sumaoro had magic powers, but Sundiata knew that there was a way to take Sumaoro's power from him. He had to strike Sumaoro with an arrow tipped with the spur of a white rooster. When he did this, Sumaoro's power left him and he ran away.

Now ruler, Sundiata enlarged his empire partly through conquest and partly through peaceful means. He called his empire Mali. His people continued to rule this empire for generations.

The baobab is native to Africa. Its thick trunk stores the water needed for growth in Africa's savanna. The baobab provides fruit and medicine, and its soft wood can be used to make canoes and musical instruments.

Malinke ruled most of what had been Wagadu, and much more. The kings of all the grasslands from the Atlantic Ocean to beyond the Niger River paid tribute to the Malinke emperor, whose empire became known as Mali.

Ancient Mali was on a trade route with North Africa. The centre of the empire of Mali was near the gold-bearing mountains of Bure. Its wealth was based on the gold trade with Arabs who crossed the desert on camels. On the Sankarani River, at a crossroad of two trade routes, lay Niani, the royal city of Mali. To judge from recent archaeological digs at Niani, as many as 100 000 people lived there in the fourteenth century.

During the period from about 1200 to 1600 A.D., Mali was the principal source of gold for Europe. Until European sailors discovered sea routes to West Africa in the fifteenth century, all the gold moved through Mali and across the desert.

With so much business, the trading centres of Mali became large and wealthy. Timbuktu was the most famous. Located beyond the Niger River's widest flood line, Timbuktu began as a trading centre. Here caravans with thousands of camels started

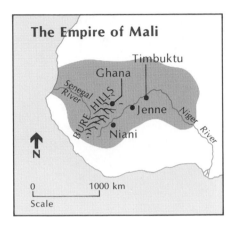

The Empire of Mali

Traders crossing the desert in camel caravans gathered in Timbuktu, making it one of Mali's wealthiest cities.

What resources were used in building Jenne, one of Mali's trading centres?

and finished their journeys across the Sahara Desert. By the end of the fifteenth century, it was a wealthy city. It even became a centre of learning. Europeans imagined Timbuktu as a city of gold-covered houses. In fact, it was like a busy port.

Upstream on the Niger River was another trading centre called Jenne. Jenne was better protected than Timbuktu because it was built on an island and had high walls. Surrounded by lush croplands, it was an agricultural centre as well.

Once a year the Mandinka gold merchants came to Jenne from the Bure hills to buy salt. Moslem traders stored their supplies of salt in Jenne until a deal was finalized. The exchange of gold for salt was then arranged. An Arab observer wrote: "Each trader brings with him one or two hundred black slaves, or even more, to carry the salt on their heads from Jenne to the gold mines, and to bring back the gold."

The markets of Jenne had two kinds of traders. One kind was the long-distance trader who brought goods from far away to

A silversmith at work in modern-day Mali. What is he doing?

Mali. The other kind was the local merchant, who bought and sold foods, leather, metalwork and weaving. The Mandinko used small sea-shells from the Indian Ocean as money.

Leatherworkers, weavers, smiths and other artisans also worked in these centres. Yet most of the Mandinko who made a living in the gold trade did not settle down in one place. If a trade route changed or the nomads began raiding, the traders would move to a new centre. A group of Mandinka traders known as *diula* wandered far and wide across the Sahel to obtain goods.

The empire of Mali lasted about three centuries and then disappeared. Historians think this was because all the separate kingdoms in the empire never really wanted to belong. The Mali rulers always needed to use force to keep the empire together. Eventually, there were too many rebellious kingdoms and the empire fell. An old proverb of the Mandinko says: "It is war that made our kingdom, it is war that ruined it."

1. Give reasons to explain why cities in the Sahel would be important trading centres.
2. Suggest reasons why sea-shells were used as money. What else could they have used instead?
3. Why do historians think the empire of Mali disappeared?

Religion in Mali

Many of the Mandinko kings converted to Islam in the eleventh century A.D. Today it is common for the Mandinko, especially men, to practice both Islam and a traditional West African religion.

Moslem believers follow strict practises. They pray five times a day, kneeling on the ground and facing towards the holy city of Mecca. Mecca is located in Saudi Arabia, across the Red Sea from Africa. Every Friday, Moslems go to the *mosque*, wearing clean white clothes. In the *mosque*, women and girls are separated from the men and boys. In every village where Islam is practiced, an *Imam*, or priest, leads the prayers.

In the Sahel, Moslem mosques are made of wooden beams covered with mud. This is the mosque at Mopti. Every few years the mud exterior has to be rebuilt. The mud is applied like plaster.

Children are made to memorize the *Koran*, the holy book of Islam. An Arab visitor to ancient Mali reported that Mandinka fathers sometimes chained up their children until they learned their daily section of the *Koran*.

265

Children study the Moslem scriptures on stone tablets. How is this class different from yours? How is it similar?

At the same time, the Mandinko follow their traditional religion in some matters. They still look to the village chief for leadership. They believe in the power of invisible spirits to do good or harm. Many West Africans carry charms in leather cases in order to protect themselves against demons.

A Moslem holy man called the *marabout* is a special person in Mandinka villages. People with either Moslem or traditional beliefs visit the *marabout* for advice and help. Moslems entrust the education of their children to him, while those with traditional beliefs seek him to help them combat spells and curses. Because of their training and study of medicinal plants, many *marabouts* are doctors. Because of their ability to sense the presence of animals, many are also expert hunters.

The moslem holy man, the marabout, has learned to serve both the Moslem and the traditional Mandinko.

1. Match the items from column A with their correct descriptions in column B.

A	**B**
1. Jenne	a. royal city of ancient Mali
2. *Koran*	b. enemy of Sundiata
3. Bure	c. trading centre on the edge of the Sahara Desert
4. Timbuktu	d. trading centre on the Niger River
5. Sumaoro	e. mountainous area of gold mines
6. Niani	f. Islamic priest
7. *Imam*	g. holy book of Islam

2. How has the story of Sundiata been kept alive? What evidence can you find in the story that parts of it really happened? What details suggest that parts of it were made up?
3. Suggest reasons why the Mandinko would adopt the religion and customs of the Moslems.
4. In what ways did the physical environment influence the development of the empires of Wagadu and Mali?

SUMMARY

Civilizations developed in West Africa more than 2000 years ago among groups of people we collectively call the Mandinko. The descendants of these people are still known by that name. They inhabited the Sahel, a belt of hot, dry grassland south of the Sahara Desert.

The early peoples of the Sahel planted staple crops such as millet during the wet season. In the dry season, once these crops had been harvested, they planted other crops such as cassava.

Ironworking was an important industry of early Mandinka society. The most powerful Sahel people became those with iron weapons and horse-soldiers. Nomadic tribes crossed the Sahara Desert on camels in order to trade with the Mandinko.

There are no written records to tell us about government in the early Sahel. Therefore, we have to look at the present-day Mandinka way of life, with its traditions that have survived throughout the centuries. This way of life is based on villages which have both local and regional chiefs. Members of the villages often belong to special clubs. The villagers have rituals, such as special dances, to help their crops grow.

The empire of Wagadu was the first great Mandinka empire. It was already well-established when Arab traders first visited it about 1000 A.D. Once written down by Arab scribes, the reports of these traders became our main source of information about Wagadu. The most important items of trade between the Arabs and the Mandinko were gold and salt.

By about 1300 A.D., the Malinke people, a subgroup of the Mandinko, had taken over not only the former lands of Wagadu but also much of West Africa. Their empire became known as Mali. Sundiata was the legendary founder of Mali. Like that of Wagadu, the economy of Mali was based on the gold trade with the Arabs. Timbuktu and Jenne were two important gold-trading centres.

Many Mandinka peoples converted to Islam in the eleventh century A.D. While Islam is still important in the Sahel today, the traditional religious beliefs have also survived.

Chapter Review: The Mandinko

NEW WORDS AND IDEAS

1. Write a sentence identifying each of the following:
   (a) Mali   (d) savanna
   (b) Mandinko   (e) Islam
   (c) Sahel   (f) oasis.

2. (a) Here are some of the titles of people in a Mandinka village. Explain what each person does.

   > *togotigi*   *muso mansa*
   > *dieli*   *dugu tigi*

   (b) List four more occupations found in a village.

3. Explain each of the following sayings, by discussing its importance to a study of the Mandinko:
   (a) "land of gold"
   (b) "strangers make a town prosper"
   (c) "it is war that made our kingdom, it is war that ruined it."

CHECKING YOUR UNDERSTANDING

4. (a) Name the two main seasons of the Sahel.
   (b) List the crops and livestock of the Mandinko.
   (c) Make a calendar to show the year-round activities of a Mandinka farmer.

5. Describe the government of a Mandinka village. Do you think their government is democratic? Explain your point of view.

6. People who developed a knowledge of iron had an advantage over anyone else. Explain this statement by referring to the history of the Mandinko.

7. Suggest four reasons for the growth of the Mandinka kingdoms.

8. Jenne, Timbuktu, and Kumbi were all important centres at one time or another. What did each of these centres have in common? How were they different?

9. Below is a list of items traded by the Mandinko. Beside each one, write where it came from. What did the Mandinko receive in return for their goods?
   (a) kola nuts   (d) ivory
   (b) gold   (e) slaves
   (c) shea butter

USING YOUR KNOWLEDGE

10. What special privileges were given to the Wagadu king? Give some examples of special privileges leaders in Canada receive.

11. For Moslems, memorizing the *Koran* is an important step towards adulthood. It is a time of celebration. Other societies celebrate other events. Draw a time line representing the life of a typical person in Canadian society. Mark on the time line important celebrations that indicate a change in the person's life.

UNIT 3
MODERN TRADITIONAL SOCIETIES

INTRODUCTION

In the first chapter of this book, we saw a world where all groups of people lived from hunting and gathering, moving from place to place in search of food. As time passed, some groups began to live in village groups and to farm. These early people relied on their environment to supply all of their needs, which were very simple.

Later on, descendants of some of these people built the civilizations we have studied. They made better tools and weapons, improved agriculture, built cities, developed writing and mathematics and created works of art. As these civilizations grew, they began to rely less directly on their environment. They traded with people from distant environments to get goods not available in their own area. Different civilizations learned from each other new ways to control and change their environments.

Some groups of people, however, did not build civilizations. They continued to live by hunting and gathering, sometimes combined with growing basic crops. They lived in small villages, and still used simple tools and weapons of wood and stone. Outside their own groups, they had contact with few people.

This Mbuti must depend on his skills as a hunter for his livelihood. The Mbuti are one of a number of peoples that continue to follow a traditional way of life.

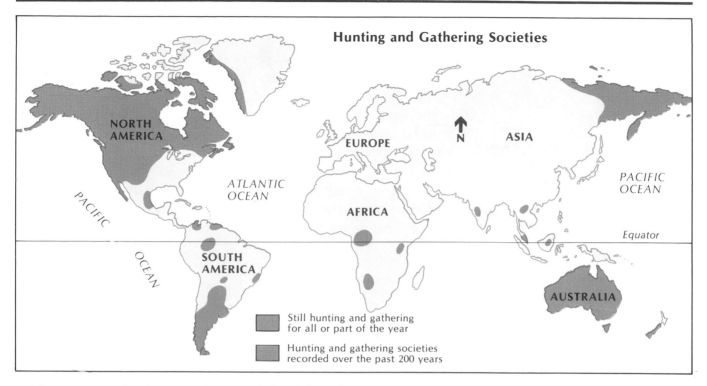

Hunting and Gathering Societies

☐ Still hunting and gathering for all or part of the year

☐ Hunting and gathering societies recorded over the past 200 years

The groups who have maintained this lifestyle are sometimes called primitive societies. Because they continue to live much as their ancestors lived, we will call them **traditional societies.**

European explorers who made expeditions about a century and a half ago found such traditional societies in every part of the world and in every type of physical environment. Most, however, were discovered in rain forests, in deserts, in the Arctic, or on islands.

The environments that traditional societies live in have produced enough resources to support the people. Hunting, gathering and simple farming have provided not only food but also material for housing, clothing where needed and weapons and tools. Yet in most cases, the environments have not provided a great **surplus** of food or other resources.

Because these environments did not provide great surpluses, they were not attractive to explorers or conquerors. Many traditional groups lived in isolated areas, difficult to reach or hard to

Not all peoples who have kept their traditional way of life are hunters and gatherers. Some traditional societies meet their needs, in whole or in part, through agriculture. Where in the world can traditional groups still be found?

traverse. For these reasons, these traditional societies had little contact with outsiders.

For example, about 500 years ago, gold-seeking Spanish conquerors made their way into the South American Andes by way of Inca roads. On the other side of the continent, however, the Portuguese did not try very hard to enter parts of the rain forest away from the major rivers. With no roads, travel promised to be difficult, and there were no tales of riches to lure the Portuguese on. Similarly, in North America, European settlers moved onto the prairies a hundred years before they ventured into the harsh environment of the Canadian Arctic. Even today, the Inuit are almost the only people who live permanently in our Arctic lands.

In the past, the rain forest acted as a barrier between newcomers to the area and the traditional peoples of South America. How has modern technology brought these two groups together?

Groups of people in the same environment have made different choices about the way they will live. For example, both the Mesopotamians and the Bedouins (bed'ü in) lived in the deserts around the Euphrates. Yet the Mesopotamians built a civilization while the Bedouins kept to their simple nomadic lifestyle for thousands of years after the rise and fall of Mesopotamia. In today's world, religious groups in North America, such as the Amish and the Mennonites, have rejected much of modern technology in order to continue living in their traditional manner.

Over the last fifty years, however, almost every traditional group in the world has had to make some changes to its way of life. New methods of transportation have made it possible to reach every corner of the world, so no area remains completely isolated. New technology has made it possible to extract resources, such as oil, from the earth. As easy-to-reach supplies of these resources are used up, searchers are forced to look in more remote places. This means that people are looking for resources in areas that were once ignored.

Many countries are trying to develop these once-isolated areas. Peru and Brazil, for example, are trying to persuade people to settle in the rain forest. All over the world, newcomers are cutting trees, digging mines and sinking oil wells in remote areas where traditional peoples live. These newcomers bring tools, clothing, food and ideas that are unfamiliar to traditional peoples.

Some traditional groups have adopted these unfamiliar ways without completely losing their own way of life. They have found some of the new ways useful, better than their old methods. Other traditional groups have done less well. Many of their members have died in wars with the newcomers or from diseases brought by outsiders. Some traditional groups have disappeared completely.

In this section, we will look at two groups that have survived: the Mbuti (em'büd'ē) of Central Africa and the Yanomami (yan'ō mam'ē) of South America. Although these groups live in similar environments they have quite different ways of life.

They have also reacted differently to the outside world. We will look at both their traditional way of life and at the ways in which they have changed. We will also try to see whether these groups can survive for much longer.

1. What has happened to traditional groups in the last fifty years? Give reasons for your conclusions.
2. Compare your way of life to that of a young person living in a traditional society. Think about the differences that might exist in the ways you and they meet basic needs of food, clothing and housing.

UNDERSTANDING A POINT OF VIEW

Most of our information on traditional groups comes from **anthropologists,** people who visit these groups to study their way of life. Like the rest of us, anthropologists have a point of view, although they try to make their studies as unbiassed as possible.

When we read anthropologists' accounts of life in traditional societies, we must always look for their point of view. The following stories show two different ways of looking at a daily event in our own lives.

The people begin every day with the same ritual. The adult female applies paint to her cheeks, eyebrows, eyelids, eyelashes, and lips. She then inserts metal rings through holes in her ears. During this time, the adult male cuts off all the hair that has grown on his face overnight. Children do not take part in these rituals. The adults drink a liquid made from hot water and dried, ground beans that contain a drug they rely on to prepare them for the day ahead. The woman cooks the meal. She prepares the ova of birds that have not been allowed to hatch. She cooks slices of pig that have been hung in a fire to get a smoky taste; these slices are mostly white fat. She takes slices of white bread full of holes and cooks them until they turn brown on both sides. She spreads on this a covering of yellow animal fat and a thick sweet liquid taken from insects' nests. The adults eat this with more of the brown liquid drug; the children drink mammal milk.

Account by a Martian anthropologist sent to study life in Canada.

Mom put on her makeup and earrings while Dad shaved. Then we had bacon and eggs, buttered toast and honey, coffee and milk for breakfast.

Your account of the same event.

Write an account of another event in your life, as it might be seen by someone from a different society.

Chapter 9

The Mbuti of the Ituri Forest

ENVIRONMENT AND ORIGINS OF THE MBUTI

For many years, outsiders called Africa the Dark Continent, because they knew so little about it. Explorers spent years battling the forests, rivers, mountains and deserts, trying to find routes through the difficult terrain. No place was more difficult than the Ituri forest.

The Ituri, in the country of Zaire (zī'ēr), is almost exactly in the middle of Africa. The forest takes up 130 000 km², about the same size as the total area of New Brunswick, Nova Scotia and Prince Edward Island. It is the home of the Mbuti (em'büd'ē), a traditional people who are believed to have lived in the Ituri forest for over 5000 years.

Since they lie so close to the equator, the Ituri and the other forests around the Zaire River are known as **equatorial forests.** They are among the world's great rain forests, areas where heavy rainfall and high temperatures help create tall, thick masses of trees.

Much of this is still virgin forest; no logger has ever cut trees here. The trees reach high into the sky, as much as fifty metres above the ground. Many of their branches and all of their leaves are near the top. They reach out and interlace with the branches of neighboring trees, forming a leafy **canopy** that keeps the sunlight from shining down onto the forest floor.

The small amount of light that does reach the forest floor is filtered by the leaves, so that it is dim here throughout the day

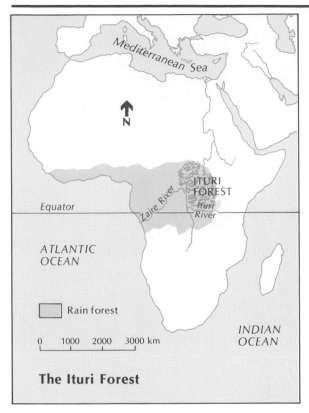

The Ituri Forest

Above: The Ituri Forest is located west of the Zaire River in the heart of the African rain forest.

Above right: Can you explain why the leaves are all at the top of the trees?

and very dark at night. It is cool, shady and pleasant compared to land outside the forest. Only mushrooms, ferns and shrubs can survive in the low light of the forest floor. Vines twine their way up trees to reach the sunlight at the top.

The climate in this area is hot and humid. Temperatures in the direct light of the sun can reach 40°C; they rarely drop below 20°C. The humidity in this area is always close to 95 percent. More than 5000 mm of rain falls here each year. Heavy rain falls most afternoons. Some of the rain is made up of moisture picked up from lakes and oceans far away. Some comes from the forest itself. The trees of the forest breathe water back into the air, to fall once more as rain.

The Mbuti who live in the Ituri forest are part of a larger group we call the Pygmies. The Pygmies are among the smallest people in the world. Adults rarely are more than 140 cm tall or weigh more than 45 kg. Scientists think their size is an adaptation to the environment that has come about over thousands of years. The people's compact size means they can move easily and smoothly through the forest vegetation.

1. Describe the climatic conditions in this part of Africa that produce rain forest vegetation.
2. Some of the last places on Earth to be explored were rain forests. Suggest reasons for this.

Thousands of years ago, the Pygmies were probably the only inhabitants of a huge area stretching from the west coast of Africa to the source of the Zaire River. We first hear of them in the literature of Ancient Egypt, when King Pepi II sent an expedition south along the Nile, to seek the source of the river. In an area the captain of the expedition called the Mountains of the Moon, which we know as the Ruwenzori (rü′wən zō′rē) Mountains, he captured a Pygmy.

When Pepi heard of this, he sent orders that the Pygmy was to be carefully protected and brought back to the king's court. Pepi was fascinated by the idea of this small man who was said to sing, dance and do acrobatics. Unfortunately, our sources do not tell us whether the Pygmy ever arrived at court. Mention of Pygmies also appeared in Greek and Latin literature.

About two thousand years ago, the Pygmies were pushed into a smaller corner of Africa by the arrival of a new people, the Bantu. Taller and heavier than the Pygmies, the Bantu were successful farmers who needed more land for their growing population. They moved south and east from the hump of Africa, squeezing the Pygmies into the forests where they now live. The Mbuti are descendants of the group of Pygmies who occupied the lands of the Ituri forest.

The Mbuti have never had a written language. Until recently, none of the cultures that came into close contact with the Mbuti had a written language. For this reason, we cannot rely on texts to tell us about the history of the Mbuti. Stories and legends of other groups which tell about the Mbuti give some information as do the stories the Mbuti tell about their ancestors.

279

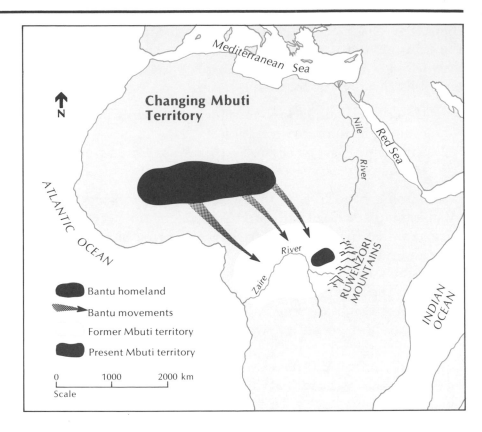

Changing Mbuti Territory

Mediterranean Sea

Nile River

Red Sea

ATLANTIC OCEAN

Zaïre River

RUWENZORI MOUNTAINS

INDIAN OCEAN

N

- Bantu homeland
- Bantu movements
- Former Mbuti territory
- Present Mbuti territory

0   1000   2000 km
Scale

The Bantu people expanded out of their homeland forcing the Mbuti into a smaller and smaller territory. Pressure is now being put on the Mbuti by loggers who want to cut down the forest. How might this affect the Mbuti?

We do know something about their life from the nineteenth century on, from information gathered by explorers, missionaries, doctors and anthropologists. Explorers entering the centre of Africa a hundred years ago wrote descriptions of their meetings with the Mbuti. In the twentieth century, missionaries have tried to convert the Mbuti to Christianity. Doctors have set up hospitals. Government agents also travelled to the forest regions. All these people wrote about the Mbuti.

Most of our information about the present comes from British, German and Japanese anthropologists who have studied the Mbuti in the last thirty years. The anthropologist who has contributed most to our knowledge is Colin Turnbull. Turnbull was born in England in 1924, and studied philosophy in England and India before turning to anthropology. He was twenty-seven years old when he first entered the forests of Africa in 1951. In the 1950s, he lived with the Mbuti for more than a year. He hunted with them, joined in their celebrations, observed their arguments and agreements and filled notebook after notebook with observations on their life.

Since then, Turnbull has returned many times to visit and live with the people he considers his friends. He has provided us with a great deal of information about the Mbuti. Much of the information in this chapter comes from Colin Turnbull's observations.

1. Suggest reasons why the Mbuti were not able to successfully compete for land with the Bantu and so were pushed back into the forests.
2. Anthropologists study groups of people by living near them or with them. What might be some of the problems with this research method?
3. Suppose you were the first anthropologist to ever study the Mbuti. Make a list of five questions you would want answers to before you were finished with your work.

We owe our understanding of the Mbuti way of life to field studies carried out in the rain forest of Zaire.

THE FOREST ECONOMY AND THE MBUTI WAY OF LIFE

The Mbuti call themselves the children of the forest. They say the forest is their father and their mother because it provides for all their needs: food, housing, clothing, water and fire. The Mbuti share in all the gifts of the forest. They relate closely to the physical environment in all their activities and beliefs.

The Mbuti economy centres on the hunt. Some Mbuti groups hunt with bows and arrows, others with nets. The night before a net hunt, men and women gather around a fire to decide where they will hunt in the morning. Early the next day, the group sets out, with the adult male in each family carrying a net made with forest vines. Each net is up to 100 m long. The men and teenage boys go first and fastest. When they arrive at the place chosen for the hunt, they set up their nets. Each net is joined to its neighbor,

Elephant

Woodpecker

Monkey

Antelope

Leopard

Okapi

FAUNA OF THE ITURI FOREST

Some of the plants and animals of the Ituri forest are shown on these pages. In their traditional way of life, the Mbuti depended on the forest for almost everything in their lives. Look at these pictures and read the information. Some questions you should answer are:

1. What might the Mbuti eat?
2. How might they obtain their food?
3. What might their houses be made of?
4. What might they wear? What might their clothes be made of?
5. How might they use vines, leaves, roots and tree bark?
6. How might they use other products they obtain in the forest?

so that a semicircle is enclosed by nets. Since a semicircle must be large to do its job properly, each net-hunting camp must contain at least six families, each with a net.

The women follow, gathering mushrooms, roots, nuts, berries and grubs on the way. They place these in the bark baskets they carry on their backs.

When everyone arrives at the hunting site, the women move quietly out into the forest. For a while, there is no sound. The men stand carefully beside their nets. Then, the noise begins: the women shout and stamp on the ground as they move toward the nets, trying to stampede animals toward the male hunters.

An antelope breaks out of the forest, headed straight for the centre of the nets. It does not see them, and is quickly trapped in the mesh. Three Mbuti stand over it and spear it to death. To left and right, other hunters deal with other game, perhaps another antelope, wild hogs or okapi, that have been chased into the net. At the end of the nets stand the teenage boys; their job is to net or spear any animals that escape the semicircle.

Once the hunt is over, the men cut the meat up into pieces small enough to go into the women's baskets. The villagers divide the meat according to the custom of the village. Usually, the hunter whose net caught the animal receives the best pieces: the heart and the liver. No one goes without; each family receives some of the catch.

Bow hunters usually act in pairs or in groups of three. Pangolin, monkeys and other animals that live in trees must be killed with bow and arrow, since they cannot be stampeded into a net. The arrows are often coated with a poison made from a forest plant, the kilabo. This poison is harmless to people once the meat has been cooked. Bow hunters share the meat with everyone in the camp. Bow-hunting camps are usually smaller than net-hunting camps, since hunting with bow and arrow does not demand the co-operation of many people.

Most often, the Mbuti hunt and kill antelope or some of the smaller animals you saw on page 282. If they are very lucky, hunters may kill an elephant. They do this either by digging a pit trap, then spearing the elephant when it falls into the pit, or by

Suggest one advantage in using a bark tumpline to carry baskets through the rain forest.

At certain times of the year, the Mbuti scour the forest looking for honey trees. When they find one, a man climbs the tree, using a vine to help haul himself upward. He carries with him burning embers wrapped in leaves to smoke the bees into a stupor. He then scoops out the honey. Sometimes he enlarges the hole where the honey is by using an axe to chop away the surrounding wood. Honey combs, dead bees and all are quickly eaten, along with the liquid honey.

creeping up on the elephant and cutting the tendons in its hind legs. When the elephant sinks to its knees, Mbuti hunters rush in to spear it to death. Mbuti do not try to kill leopards or forest buffalo, the fiercest and most dangerous animals in the forest.

Much of the Mbuti diet comes from gathering mushrooms, roots, berries, fruits, nuts and insects in the forest. Both males and females are expert in finding and gathering these resources. Their favorite root comes from the itaba vine; it is sweet-tasting, and can be roasted or stewed. Honey is a great favorite, as are termites. The finding of a termite nest is a special occasion. The termites are toasted over the fire and eaten. To obtain salt, the Mbuti burn the green branches of the "salt tree," then collect and boil the ashes for a day. When the water evaporates, a type of salt remains.

The Mbuti eat birds they shoot with arrows, and occasionally fish, although they prefer meat.

1. List the advantages and disadvantages of hunting with a net.
2. Compare net and bow hunting using these headings: number of people involved, equipment needed, animals hunted.
3. Describe how the Mbuti get salt.

The forest also supplies the Mbuti with clothing. They make their simple clothing from bark, scraped and boiled to make it soft, then decorated with red and black dyes, made from the bark of the nkula (nkü'lä) tree and from the kangay (kan'gā) plant. Adults wear a breechcloth, held up by a fibre belt. They also may wear fibre armbands and necklaces. Children generally go naked.

The forest environment also provides the raw materials for hunters. Nets are woven from the nkusa vine. Women shred the vine, then roll pieces together to make a strong cord that the men can weave into a net. Bows are made from saplings, and spears and arrow tips from wood that has been slowly hardened in a fire. The hunters make a poison from a local plant which they use on their arrows. Pieces of bamboo can be used as cutting tools, and sticks are used to dig honey out of a bees' nest or tree.

Each Mbuti group lives at one site in the forest for only a month, until they have gathered most of the edible plants in the area and animals are becoming scarce. Because they do not have toilets or latrines, their water supply could easily become polluted. When they move to a new site, somewhere else in their section of the forest, and build a new camp, they avoid the problem of pollution. Moving is easily accomplished because they have few possessions, just a few tools and nets. The forest in the new location will supply resources for all their other needs.

Fire is important to the Mbuti, for cooking and for making weapons. Yet the Mbuti do not know how to start a fire. They are careful always to have at least one fire burning, so that they may start new fires from the old. When the camp moves, women carry smoldering coals wrapped in special leaves that do not catch fire. When the group arrives at the new campsite, or when

The Mbuti rely on the forest for materials to meet their needs. How are the Mbuti pictured here making use of their environment?

285

the group stops on the trail for a rest, each woman carefully makes a new fire. To do this, the women add dry twigs to the coal and blow on the twigs until they catch fire.

The Mbuti make their huts from young, straight saplings and the leaves of the mogongo tree. As soon as they arrive at the new site, the women go into the forest to cut down saplings and collect leaves. Usually working in pairs, they quickly drive the saplings into the ground, to make a beehive-shaped framework. Then they tie the large leaves onto the framework, making a waterproof shelter for their family.

Mbuti children have no formal schools; instead, they learn such tasks as fire-building, hunting and hut-building by copying the older people in the village. They play in the *bopi*, a special area just outside the village, away from the adults but close enough for help should trouble occur. Here, they may play in the trees, or pretend to be hunting or building houses.

1. List the foods the Mbuti eat. How do they find their food in the forest?
2. Explain why the forest is so important to the Mbuti. What does it provide them with?
3. Try making a model of a Mbuti house using natural things you find outdoors.

MBUTI SOCIETY

The Mbuti have no chiefs to tell everyone else what to do. Every decision in a Mbuti village is made through discussion and agreement. Everyone, including children, takes part in deciding where to hunt, when to move or where to move to. Some people's views may carry more weight than others. The best hunter in a camp will have more say over where the group should hunt. In some cases, the men may want to hunt in a certain area, but the women will know there are no plants to collect there. The women will then usually persuade the men to hunt elsewhere.

What happens if the group cannot agree? Then the family that does not want to go along with the group may leave and join a

The Mbuti share all the responsibilities of camp life. Here, an elder watches over some of the camp's children.

different group. Disagreements that lead to departures do not often happen. The Mbuti know it is important to have a strong group so that they can hunt successfully.

The Mbuti have no written laws, but they do have many rules and customs. The most important of these make sure that the peace of the forest is maintained. Someone who makes too much noise over too long a time, or who does not share food, has broken the rules. So has someone who cheats during the hunt by setting up his nets in front of everyone else's. These rule-breakers must be dealt with by the rest of the group.

There are no prisons here and no fines. The Mbuti punish rule breakers by refusing to speak to them for a day or more or by making fun of the offender. Mbuti are very sensitive to ridicule and hate being ignored. Often a day's silent treatment will be enough punishment.

Sometimes, someone must be punished more severely, perhaps because he or she continues to make noise or to quarrel. In this case, the young men of a village may run through the village, breaking leaves and branches off the houses and stamping out the fires. Although only one person has offended, everyone is punished. This makes the guilty person feel even more ashamed.

If the crime is very serious, the Mbuti may drive the person out of the village. If the person cannot find a new group to live with, he or she will probably die. Alone in the forest, an individual is at the mercy of the animals.

The Mbuti feel that hunting badly disturbs the peace of the forest, yet they must hunt in order to live. Before each hunt, the older boys in the camp light a fire outside the camp, to warm the forest and ask forgiveness for hunting. The Mbuti tell the forest they will kill only enough animals to feed themselves.

Unlike other peoples, the Mbuti have no need for central government. Each camp looks after its own affairs, and does not interfere in the affairs of other camps. Each group has a part of the forest which by tradition is theirs to live in and hunt in.

People do not marry within their own groups. A newly married couple will generally live with the husband's group. If a man marries a woman from another group, he usually promises his sister or someone else from his group to a man from his bride's group. This arrangement makes sure that no group becomes too small to hunt well. Three to five families in a group are necessary to ensure good hunting.

The Mbuti believe that the forest will always provide for them. They believe in a type of good spirit that is part of the Mbuti and of all the parts of the forest. They often talk of the forest and thank it for its gifts through song and dance. They have special types of song for death, hunting, honey gathering and coming of age. On special occasions, the men of the tribe use the *molimo*, a type of magical musical instrument that can be used to imitate the sounds of the forest. The word *molimo* is also used to mean the special ceremonies the Mbuti hold, whenever they need to solve a difficult problem or put an end to unhappiness in the camp.

Singing and dancing are the Mbuti's way of giving thanks to the forest.

At midday, the older boys go around the camp, collecting food. In the evening, the women go into the huts to sleep, and the men sit around the fire, singing. The boys bring the *molimo* from its hiding place in the forest. The Mbuti in the camp can hear it call, first from one part of the forest, then from another. At last it enters the camp, and the boys dash to and fro with it. Finally they leave to return the *molimo* to the forest, and the men eat. The singing and dancing may go on long into the night. Early in the morning, the sound of *molimo* wakes the camp again.

The *molimo* ceremony goes on each evening for days or even weeks. The Mbuti feel that if something bad, like death or sickness or bad hunting happens, it is because the forest is asleep and not looking after its children. The purpose of the *molimo* ceremony is to wake the forest up, so that everything is well once more.

1. How are the rules of Mbuti society different from the rules of our society?
2. Do you think you would like to live in the way the Mbuti live? Why or why not?
3. Suggest reasons why an individual Mbuti cannot survive alone in the forest.

THE MBUTI AND THEIR NEIGHBORS

The Mbuti's neighbors are the Bantu, a farming people who live in villages at the edge of the forest. Several thousand years ago, other tribes forced some of the Bantu out of the grasslands toward the forest. Ever since then, these Bantu groups have lived on the edge of the forest, cutting down trees and clearing the ground to build villages and grow crops.

The Bantu regard the forest as their enemy. To them, it is dark and fearsome, a place where evil spirits live. Because they need cleared areas for their villages and farm fields, they must always fight the forest. Once the tall trees are cut, vines and new trees and bushes grow quickly in this hot moist area. The Bantu must

Why do you think the Mbuti consider themselves "children of the forest"?

work continually to keep their fields and village sites clear. They can grow crops in the same place for only a limited time before the land is exhausted. For this reason, the Bantu must move their villages to a new site and clear new land every few years.

The Mbuti live most of their lives in the forest. Ever since the Bantu built villages on the edge of the forest, however, the Mbuti have spent some time in these villages. For many years, the Mbuti have brought the Bantu meat, bark for bark cloth and saplings for their house frames. In return they receive plantains, a banana-like crop, and a root crop called manioc (man'ē ok'). Sometimes, they also receive peanuts, rice and palm wine. They trade for metal knives, axeheads, machetes and metal cooking pots. The Mbuti build their own huts near the Bantu villages so they can trade and work for the Bantu, hauling water and wood, and guarding their fields.

Early visitors who saw the Mbuti at work in the Bantu villages thought that the Mbuti were slaves of the Bantu. Important people in the Bantu village said they owned certain Mbuti families. They said the Mbuti had to work when they were told to work and had to bring meat from the forest to the Bantu table.

Later, Colin Turnbull and other anthropologists who talked to the Mbuti instead of to the Bantu got a different story. The Mbuti said they went along with the Bantu and pretended to do as they were told. In this way, they got the food and tools they wanted. When they were bored with life in the forest, they came to the village for a change. When they grew tired of village life, they returned to the forest.

There was another reason for the Mbuti to come to the village. The Bantu wanted meat and other forest products. The Mbuti did not want the Bantu to upset the peace of the forest by coming to hunt and gather food. Since the Bantu did not like the forest, they were happy to stay out as long as the Mbuti provided them with meat.

While they were in the village, the Mbuti lived by some of the Bantu rules. The Bantu tried to tell the Mbuti what to do. They ignored the traditional system the Mbuti had for settling disputes or making decisions, saying that the Mbuti must obey their "owners." As long as they were in the village, the Mbuti pretended they believed in this system. Once they returned to their camp on the edge of the village or to the forest, they forgot all about the village ways.

For example, the Mbuti allowed their sons to go through initiation ceremonies with Bantu boys. The villagers thought this initiation meant that the Mbuti boys would always return to work for the Bantu, and would always follow Bantu customs.

Mbuti went through the ceremonies to keep the villagers happy, but they ignored the village beliefs once they were alone. During the initiation week, for example, the boys are supposed to sleep alone together in a hut and eat only certain foods. They are not to use their fingers to eat, but are to use only knives or spears. When they are with the Bantus, the Mbuti boys follow these instructions. As soon as they are alone, they join their fathers around the fire and eat whatever and however they wish.

1. What do the Mbuti and the Bantu get out of their relationships with each other?
2. The Mbuti and the Bantu view the forest quite differently. Describe how each group views the forest. Do you think you would find the rain forest friendly or frightening? Why?

THE CHANGING LIFE OF THE MBUTI

When Colin Turnbull first went to visit the Mbuti, he travelled along a narrow, twisting muddy trail below the leafy canopy of the Ituri forest. If you travel to the Ituri today, you will go on a hardpacked road with wide, clear spaces on both sides. Many changes have come to the Mbuti along this road.

The road was built when the Ituri was part of the Belgian Congo, a colony of Belgium from 1870 to 1960. The Belgians persuaded the Bantu to start cotton plantations so that cotton could be exported and earn money for the Belgians. But the Mbuti usually refused to work in the plantation fields. The Bantu could not work all the fields by themselves, so the plantations were not very successful.

The Belgians also tried to get the Mbuti to settle down outside the forest and become farmers. They gave the Mbuti seeds so that they would grow crops and produce a surplus that could be sold for cash. The Mbuti, however, could see no reason to plant seeds and wait for food to grow when they could obtain food from the forest or from the villagers. They refused to farm and returned to the forest.

After being a colony for a long time, the native people of the Congo decided they wanted to be free of the Belgians. They wanted an independent country where they could run their own affairs as they wished. After much fighting, they obtained their independence in 1960. The new country was called Congo (in 1971 the name was changed to Zaire). Different groups within the country fought a civil war over who would be in charge of the government.

How have roads built through the rain forest brought change to the forest and to the Mbuti's way of life?

Zaire Today

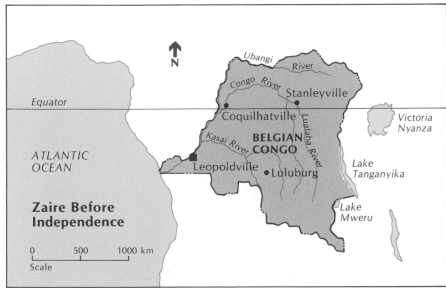

Zaire Before Independence

Once they had independence, the Zaire government changed some of the European names to African names. Why do you think this was done?

These wars caused many problems for the people of the Ituri. Soldiers supporting different groups moved up and down the forest road, battling each other and the local villagers, who supported one side or the other in the dispute. Planes bombed the villages. Many of the Bantu escaped into the forest where the soldiers could not follow. The Mbuti looked after the Bantu, showing them which foods they could eat and teaching them to build houses.

During the fighting, the Mbuti no longer obtained food from the Bantu, worked in the villages or took part in any village events.

After about a year, peace returned and the villagers emerged from the forest and began to rebuild their lives. The group that had won the war formed the government of the new country. This government wanted all the people of Zaire to work together to build a strong economy, so that modern services could be provided for the people. It felt that tribal people such as the Mbuti should take part in this development.

At first, the government encouraged the Mbuti to settle down by the road through the Ituri, clear land and become farmers. It gave the Mbuti houses, clothing, tools and seeds. Each Mbuti group was assigned land for a plantation.

But the Mbuti did not adapt well to life in the hot, sunny clearings. They have fewer sweat glands than other people, so they get heatstroke when they work under the glaring sun. Their muscles are adapted for the quick motions necessary for hunting and running, not the heavy work of farming. No one taught them how to build pit toilets or told them why it would be necessary to keep their new villages clean. Their water supply quickly became polluted and spread disease through the village. Outsiders who used the road and met the Mbuti brought germs to which the Mbuti had not been exposed before. Many Mbuti fell sick and some died from diseases such as measles and influenza.

Because of these bad results, the government of Zaire has given up trying to get the Mbuti to work as farmers. It is now encouraging them to work in the national park in the Ituri. Some Mbuti work as guides, while others sell goods to the tourists who visit the park.

1. Why was there a civil war in the newly independent country of Congo?

2. Give reasons why the government of the new country wanted to change the way of life of the Mbuti.
3. Why did the changes made by the government fail?

In the forest camps, everyone worked together to get food to feed the entire group. Mbuti who work for money, however, see no reason why they should share the money with Mbuti who do not work. This change means that some Mbuti think of themselves more as individuals, and less as members of the group.

The Mbuti used to kill just enough wildlife to feed themselves and to trade to the Bantu. Now they sell game to the newcomers who have settled along the road. They kill more game than they need and dry some to sell or eat later. They are changing from an economy we call **subsistence** (just enough to live on) to an economy we call **surplus** (enough to live on, plus extra to sell).

This changed the Mbuti's relationship to the forest. The Mbuti used to ask the forest's forgiveness for killing its animals. Now they are beginning to look at animals as something that can be sold for money. Some are beginning to see themselves less as "children of the forest" and more as "masters of the forest."

The traditional society of the Mbuti has also begun to change. Administrators were appointed by the government to enforce the laws of the country on both the Bantu and the Mbuti. These officials were from outside the forest and did not understand the Mbuti way of life. Because crime did not exist in the Mbuti idea of the world, the Mbuti could not understand the laws. Ideas such as "theft" did not mean anything to a people who shared their goods. They could not understand why the government fined people or put them in jail when these laws were broken.

For example, the Mbuti saw stealing from the Bantu as a good joke, not as a crime. To the Mbuti, the only things that should not be done were those that disturbed the peace of the forest, and their relationship with it.

Some Mbuti also changed the way in which they met their basic needs. They bought western style clothes, similar to those Canadians wear, and ate food that did not come from the forest. Some began to live in permanent houses instead of temporary huts.

This hunter setting his net illustrates how the Mbuti have adapted to the changes in their environment. What evidence can you find to prove this statement?

Many of the younger Mbuti are particularly curious about school. They come to the villages to learn reading, writing and arithmetic. Most do well in school. Their success sometimes makes them believe they know better than other Mbuti about how their lives should be changed. This brings them into conflict with the older Mbuti, who are convinced the Mbuti should not change their way of life. The older Mbuti want to stay in the forest, because they are sure the forest that has always provided for them will continue to do so.

But the forest itself is changing. Parts of the forest have been cut down in order to widen the road and provide room for plantations. These areas lie open to the hot sun. Heat waves rising from the hot ground push the rain clouds away from the forest, creating a four- or five-month dry season in some parts of the forest. The shortage of water drives game away from these areas and cuts down on the number of plants that can be gathered for food.

Overhunting and capture of wild animals for foreign zoos have also cut the number of game animals in the Ituri. The government tries to regulate when the Mbuti may hunt, making it difficult for them to live their forest camp life year-round. People are also coming into the rain forest to cut trees that can be sawn into lumber, for use in Zaire and for export. The government is trying to reopen gold mines in the forest and start new cotton plantations. The Ituri forest is slowly shrinking.

What will happen to the Mbuti in the future? We do not know. Now that the government of Zaire has agreed that the Mbuti do not have to be farmers, many anthropologists believe that the Mbuti will be able to adapt to a new way of life in the forest. The future of the Mbuti will probably depend on how well they adapt, and on how many changes are made to the forest itself in the next few decades.

1. Under the title "Changes in Mbuti Life" on a page of your notebook, write these headings: hunting, health, work, education. For each heading, write a sentence to describe the changes.

2. Describe how the environment of the Mbuti has changed. In one or two sentences, explain how the Mbuti relationship to the environment has changed.
3. Imagine that you are a young Mbuti. In a paragraph try to explain to your uncle why you want to live at the roadside, go to school and dress in western clothes. Suggest what your uncle will say to you in response.
4. Do you think the Mbuti can preserve their traditional lifestyle? Why or why not?

SUMMARY

The Mbuti, a group of Pygmy people, have lived in central Africa for thousands of years. They now live in the Ituri, an equatorial rain forest in Zaire. Much of what we know about the traditional life of the Mbuti comes from the writings of anthropologist Colin Turnbull.

The Mbuti call themselves the children of the forest, and rely on the forest for most of their needs. They hunt in groups, with nets or bows and gather food from the forest. The forest also provides them with material for housing, clothing, tools and weapons.

The Mbuti live in a society without official leaders, in camps that contain from three to ten families. They have no written laws, but obey rules, the most important of which is keeping the peace of the forest. If the peace is broken, they try to restore it by using a ceremony known as the *molimo.*

The Mbuti spend some time each year living beside their neighbors, the Bantu. The Mbuti work for the Bantu, bring them food from the forest and go along with some Bantu customs. In return, they receive food and trade goods. Most important, the Bantu do not come into the forest.

The Mbuti did not adapt well to the farming life that the Belgians and the government of Zaire tried to persuade them to adopt. Most still live in the forest, keeping some traditional parts of their way of life. However, changes in their economy and beliefs are affecting this traditional way of life.

Carrying spears and a net, these traditional Mbuti are prepared for a day's hunting. However, newcomers to the Ituri forest are bringing change to the Mbuti and their way of life.

Chapter Review: The Mbuti

NEW WORDS AND IDEAS

1. In one or two sentences, explain why the Mbuti are called a traditional people.

2. In your notebook, record the Mbuti's use for each of the following plants:
   (a) kilabo   (e) nkusa
   (b) itaba   (f) bamboo
   (c) nkula   (g) mogongo.
   (d) kangay

3. What are anthropologists? Why are they important to a study of the Mbuti?

4. For each part of this question, identify the classification, or group, the three items belong to. Add one more item to each group.
   (a) antelope, okapi, pangolin
   (b) plantain, manioc, rice
   (c) machete, axehead, metal pot
   (d) bow, net, spear

CHECKING YOUR UNDERSTANDING

5. (a) Make a sketch showing a scene of the Mbuti's life in the Ituri forest. Write one or two sentences to explain what is taking place.
   (b) Make another sketch showing a scene of the Mbuti's life in a Bantu village.

6. (a) Compare the Mbuti and Bantu feelings about the rain forest.
   (b) Explain how the differences in their feelings have encouraged trade between the two groups.

7. Write a paragraph describing the *molimo* ceremony. Why is this ceremony important to the Mbuti?

8. Explain how each of the following events affected the Mbuti:
   (a) The arrival of the Bantu.
   (b) The arrival of explorers and missionaries.
   (c) The formation of the nation of Zaire.

9. (a) List what you think are the five most important resources the rain forest offers the Mbuti. Make a second list giving the resources the rain forest offers newcomers.
   (b) Explain how the two lists are the same, how they are different.

USING YOUR KNOWLEDGE

10. Generalizations are statements about topics that identify relationships or rules. "Forests found near the equator are normally rain forests" is an example of a generalization. Write one generalization to describe each of the following:
    (a) the tools used by the Mbuti.
    (b) food sources for the Mbuti.
    (c) the attitude of the Mbuti towards the Bantu.

11. (a) In the past, the Mbuti have been able to meet their needs by using the resources of the rain forest. Examine ten objects found in your classroom. List the natural resources needed to create each item. Beside each natural resource on your list, indicate if it is found in your area, or outside your area.
    (b) Could the resources available in your area meet your needs? Explain your answer.

Chapter 10

The Yanomami of the Amazon Basin

ENVIRONMENT AND ORIGINS OF THE YANOMAMI

If you look at a resources map of South America, you will see a huge forested area in the northeast. This great rain forest covers large areas of Brazil, Peru and Ecuador and parts of Colombia, Bolivia and Venezuela. Part of this land is drained by the Amazon, the largest river system in the world. The rest is drained by the Orinoco and its tributaries. The traditional people called the Yanomami (yan′ō mam′ē) live where these two river systems meet, in the highlands on the Brazil-Venezuela border.

As many as 300 different kinds of trees grow in this rain forest. The most important are palms and hardwoods. As in the Ituri, the trees of this equatorial forest reach high, sometimes as much as sixty metres tall. A canopy of leaves intertwines near the top, shutting out the light and heat of the sun. The forest floor below this canopy is spongy and damp, made up of layers of leaves that slowly crumble and turn to soil.

Vines curl around the tree trunks, reaching up toward the canopy. **Parasitic plants** that steal nourishment from the trees grow on the trunks. Few other plants can live in the dim light below the forest canopy. The forest is alive with the hum of thousands of insects, the songs of brightly-colored tropical birds, and the chatter of monkeys that swing from tree to tree.

Saplings, bushes and other plants grow in clearings where trees have fallen or been chopped down and along the banks of the many streams.

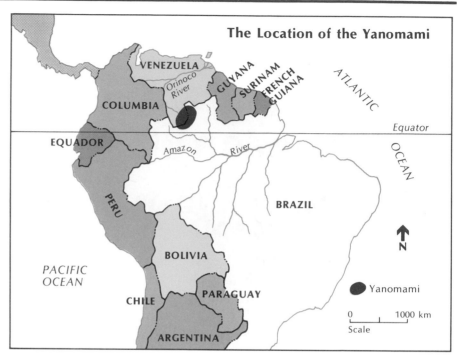

The Location of the Yanomami

The Yanomami live in the rain forest between the Amazon and Orinoco rivers. Their territory straddles the boundary between Venezuela and Brazil.

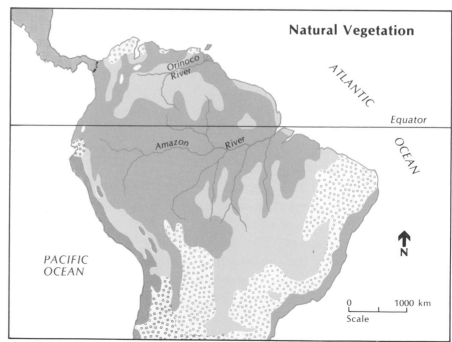

Natural Vegetation

Tropical rainforest

Savanna

Dry scrub forest

Scrub and semidesert

Desert

More than 3600 mm of rain a year fall in this forest: this is over three times as much precipitation as Vancouver gets. The humidity is usually more than 85 percent. Although some months are dryer than others, it is rare for more than a week to pass without rain. Rain storms are often violent, soaking the forest and swelling the rivers. A stream can rise sixty centimetres in less than twenty-four hours.

Temperatures here are warm, averaging 27°C. Daytime temperatures can reach 35°C.

Most of the Yanomami live in the highlands just above the river basins, at altitudes between 300 and 1200 m above sea level. At higher altitudes, night temperatures can be too cool for comfort. At lower altitudes, floods sometimes carry away everything in their path and strip nutrients from the soil.

The streams in these higher lands are narrower and swifter than those at lower altitudes, where the rivers that feed the Amazon spread out into wide, flat channels.

Wildlife in the rain forest.

People in the Rain Forest

When the Inca established their empire five centuries ago, they conquered the peoples of the west coast and the mountains, but did not venture into the rain forest. They thought the land drained by the great eastern rivers such as the Amazon was dangerous and unhealthy, and contained no great riches.

They met few of the tribes who lived in this rain forest. These tribes had lived there for as long as the Inca and their forerunners had lived in the Andes. Historians think that more than eight million native peoples lived in the rain forest at the time of the Inca empire.

The tropical rain forest of South America is the home of the Yanomami.

One of the many tribes, the Yanomami, lived in one of the most remote areas of the rain forest. They occupied the highlands and lowlands that divide the Amazon Basin from the basin of the Orinoco River. Today, they live mostly in the Parima Highlands. Although we cannot be sure, we think that the Yanomami are descendants of some of the earliest residents of South America. They have lived in this area for thousands of years, isolated from all contact with the outside world. They are the largest remaining traditional group in South America. Only in the last fifty years has their world been invaded by people from the outside.

Our information about the Yanomami comes from explorers, missionaries and anthropologists. Journalists, filmmakers and people who want the lifestyle of the Yanomami preserved have also written books and made films about these people.

Because the Yanomami were isolated for so long, there are still many things we do not know about them. For example, because there has been no complete census of this group, no one can say exactly how many Yanomami there are. We think, however, that there are about 21 000 Yanomami living in Brazil and Venezuela. We do not have precise maps of the area where they live. One source says the Yanomami homeland is 75 000 km^2 in size; another says it is close to 150 000 km^2 in size.

1. Go back and read through the description of the South American rain forest on pages 299-301 once again. This time find six words or phrases that best give a feeling of what this environment is like. Write these descriptive words in your notebook.
2. Suggest reasons why rain forests are able to support a greater variety of plant and animal life than other environments, such as a desert or grassland.
3. What kept the Yanomami isolated from the outside world for so long?

THE GARDEN ECONOMY

Looking at the diagram of animals on page 301, you might think that the Yanomami could survive very well from hunting, gathering and fishing. But, in fact, the forest does not provide a good living for its people. Although there are many species in the forest, the animals and plants are not abundant enough to feed the Yanomami easily. Like most other South American rain forest groups, they feed themselves mainly from their gardens.

The economy of the Yanomami centres on these gardens. Their

decisions on where to place their gardens, what to grow and when to move are all based on the forest environment.

Each Yanomami group chooses a village site near a location that can be used for a garden. The Yanomami males look carefully at the altitude of the site, its **drainage**, and its soil. They see whether the site has high and low parts where different crops can be grown before making their decision.

The Yanomami have learned to use their environment to grow a variety of crops. How is this garden different from one found in your community?

Once the garden site is chosen, the men begin the difficult task of clearing the land. The first step is to clear away any underbrush, then pile it up so it can dry and be burned. The next step is to remove the tree leaves that block the sunlight. In the past, some groups of Yanomami did this by cutting down the trees with stone axes. Others cut a circle of bark off all around the tree, then piled brush against the tree and burned it. Although the tree did not fall, it did die and the leaves fell, letting light through to the garden. Now, most groups use metal axes they have obtained from outsiders to cut down the trees.

The frequent rains and high humidity of the rain forest make burning difficult. Yet burning is necessary, because it gets rid of debris (də brē′), destroys pests and weed seeds and provides ash to be used as fertilizer.

YANOMAMI CROPS

Plantains and bananas make up more than one-third of the Yanomami food supply. Banana and plantain plants produce suckers which can be removed from the plant. These suckers are planted, and within a year, become producing plants. Bananas can be eaten raw, but most plantains must be cooked. They are roasted over the fire, or made into a type of soup.

Sweet manioc is the second major crop of the Yanomami. Sweet manioc roots are boiled and eaten, or ground into flour that is made into flat cakes.

A family's storehouse of food is kept on a shelf above their hammocks.

Each male clears his own family patch, getting help from others to remove any particularly large trees. Once the patch is cleared, the soil is broken up using sturdy hoes and crops are planted. Each family has several plots of land in different areas of the garden, each area suitable for planting a different crop. The Yanomami rely most on **plantains**; they also grow bananas, sweet manioc (man'ē ok') ocumo (a root vegetable), yams, and sugar cane. They plant a type of palm much prized for its fruit; cane to make arrow shafts; sharp-leaved reeds that can be used for cutting; and tobacco.

The Yanomami plant some crops together in order to make the most use of their garden plots. They might plant ocumo between the rows of plantain suckers. By the time the plantain leaves are large enough to block the sun, the ocumo is already full grown and ready for harvest.

Gardening is a job done almost completely by the men. But

they do not spend a lot of time looking after their gardens. They may do some weeding if they happen to be nearby.

As the garden is invaded by weeds and the soil becomes less fertile, new garden plots are cleared on the edges of the old ones. Because the old plots continue to bear for several years, they are still harvested. Before the land around the garden is used up, the Yanomami scout neighboring areas and choose a new village and garden site. Once the garden has been prepared and is producing food, the entire village group moves and sets up a new village. But for many years, the Yanomami will visit their old gardens to harvest whatever still grows there.

1. Explain how each of these characteristics could affect the amount of food produced by a Yanomami garden: height or altitude; drainage; soil fertility.
2. Plantains and manioc are staple food crops for the Yanomami. What characteristics would you look for in selecting a staple food?

Though gardens produce much of the Yanomami's food, they provide little protein. Yanomami males hunt to get meat. They hunt with bows and arrows, and spend much time making these weapons perfect. Wherever they think they might find game, like agouti, tapir or peccary, they hunt. They also look for monkeys, birds and other small animals. Sometimes, the Yanomami capture armadillos by smoking them out of their burrows.

Women look after most of the gathering and fishing. They gather palm fruits, Brazil nuts, cashews, termites, caterpillars, and locusts. These foods are useful in the Yanomami diet; termites, for example, contain three times as much protein as the same weight of beef.

The Yanomami use a type of vine poison for fishing. They dam a small stream, then throw some of the poison into the pool that forms. This substance prevents the fish from taking in oxygen and they float to the top where the women catch and kill them.

The Yanomami manufacture many of their tools and weapons out of objects collected from the forest environment. Bows for

Returning from a visit to a neighboring shabono, this woman is carrying all her belongings. This is not an unusually heavy load, for a basket of plantain can weigh more than twenty kilograms.

hunting are made from the wood of the palm tree, which is very heavy and strong. The Yanomami use the very sharp teeth from a wild pig to shape the bow. Fibres from the inner bark of a tree are twisted together to make the bowstring.

The Yanomami make several types of arrow points. One is made from a sharpened splinter of palm wood. Other types of arrow points are made from bamboo and from barbed splinters of monkey bones. The shafts of the arrows, more than a metre and a half long, are made from a type of cane. The ends of the arrows are fitted with wild turkey feathers.

Sometimes, the tips of the arrows are coated with **curare** (kyü rä'rē), a poison made from a vine that grows in the rain forest. The vine and its roots are roasted and ground into a powder which is dissolved in water. The solution is then painted onto arrow points where it dries. When the arrow enters an animal, usually a monkey, the poison makes the muscles relax. The monkey falls out of the tree and can be collected by the

Feathers are fixed to the end of an arrow's shaft to ensure steady flight.

hunter. Curare that enters the bloodstream can kill. Yet the Yanomami can eat an animal that has been killed by a poisoned arrow, because curare is not poisonous in the digestive system.

The Yanomami use tools called fire drills to start fires. The fire drill is made up of two pieces of cocoa wood, one round and one a little pointed, with holes cut in it. The round piece of wood is placed in one of the holes and swiftly twirled. The heat produced sets on fire the dust that is drilled from the hole. The flame is used to ignite some cotton which in turn ignites wood for a fire.

Knives can be made from the long, curved, sharp incisor teeth of the agouti. The end of the tooth is glued into a piece of wood with a resin, and wrapped with fibre. This knife is very sharp, but quite small, and is used mainly to make arrow points.

Canoes are made from the bark of a tree. The men beat the tree to loosen the bark, then carry it back to the village. The ends are heated and folded, to make a rough canoe-shape. The canoe is not very durable, so is usually used for only one downstream trip, then thrown away. Since the Yanomami do not travel much by water, they do not need a better type of boat.

Bark is also used for a type of trough in which soup is made. Razor grass, a reed that grows along the rivers, is used for shaving. Baskets are woven from jungle vines. Hammocks are made from bark strips and liana vines.

One kind of palm fruit grows at the top of trees covered with sharp spines. To get to the fruit, the Yanomami men use two sets of poles crossed in the shaped of "Xs." They loosely tie one set of poles around the trunk of the tree, and climb on to it. Then they place the next set higher up the trunk, hang on to it, move the first set upwards with their feet, and so on until they reach the fruit.

Often, a village specializes in making a certain kind of tool. People in each village trade with other villages, perhaps exchanging cotton hammocks for clay pots. The people in each village could make everything they needed. But they trade instead, because trade is one way of making and keeping friends. A group with many trade ties is more secure than one with only a few friends.

Climbing a peach palm tree is not an easy task. The tree's trunk has protective thorns. How have the Yanomami solved this problem?

1. (a) Copy the list below into your notebook. For each item
      in the list, write the name of the resource used from
      the environment to make the item. The first one is
      done as an example.

ITEM	RESOURCE
bows	wood of palm tree
bowstring	
arrowpoint	
fire drills	
knives	
canoes	

   (b) Add three new items to the list and then complete
      them as before.

2. (a) List ways the Yanomami use their environment to
      ensure they have enough food.
   (b) Explain why this traditional use is not harmful to the
      environment.

3. Why are garden plots abandoned by the Yanomami?

LIFE IN THE *SHABONO*

If you looked down at a Yanomami village from the air, you
would see what looks like a huge mushroom with a hole in the
centre of the cap. This is the *shabono*, the building that houses
all the people who live in a village. Some groups of Yanomami
call this building a *yano*; perhaps the people were named after
the building, or perhaps the building was named after the people.

Each family sleeps and eats in a section of the *shabono*, divided
from its neighbors only by a wall of palm leaves. Hammocks for
every member of the family are strung from poles near the
cooking fire. Smoke from the fires drifts out through the opening in the centre, driving away mosquitoes and other insects that
might disturb the village.

The group lives in the *shabono* for several years, until the roof

While the younger men are hunting, a shabono *elder rests in his hammock.*

is infested with insects. The villagers then burn it down and build a new one, at the same site or at another site.

All village activities take place in the plaza at the centre of the *shabono*. Early in the morning, before dawn, the residents begin to discuss what will be done that day. During the day, the men are usually absent, off hunting or gardening. Women look after the younger children, do housework, weave baskets or aprons or prepare food. Older children play games in the plaza. These games often mimic the activities of the adults. Sometimes they play house or pretend to be hunters and animals.

The Yanomami wear almost no clothing. Men wear only a cotton string around their waists. Women wear fringed, woven, cotton aprons. Children usually go naked. The Yanomami paint their own and their friends' and relatives' bodies with intricate designs. They use a red dye obtained from the bark of a flowering shrub, the urucu, which is grown in their gardens. Just as we dress in special clothes for a party, both Yanomami men and women want particularly handsome patterns on their bodies on special occasions. The men, women and children also decorate

BUILDING THE *SHABONO*

1. When it comes time to move, the Yanomami carefully select a new site for their village. It must provide a good place for a garden, it must be in a place that does not flood in the rainy season and it must not be too near any enemies. Once the garden is bearing fruit, the Yanomami move and begin work on their shelter.

2. The men cut saplings from the forest. Each adult male cuts four main poles (two short and two long) plus other poles for the framework.

3. The men sink the short poles into place on the outside edge of the *shabono* circle, and the long ones about two metres in front of this outside circle.

4. They form a framework by laying more poles across these, at a sloping angle.

5. They string vines along the tops and bottoms of these framework poles.

6. Women collect leaves in the forest. These leaves are tied together and used to build a thatched roof that slopes from the inner circle of poles to the outer circle. The leaves are also used to separate one family's area from the next.

7. The men decorate the *shabono* by hanging fringed bamboo leaves from the front edge of the thatched roof.

The Structure of a Shabono

their bodies with colorful birds' feathers as well as flowers, leaves, twigs and reeds from the forest.

When the men who have been hunting return to the *shabono*, their catch is shared. A successful hunter keeps nothing for himself; he gives all the meat away to other families and to members of his own family. In return, he receives meat from other successful hunters. This exchange of meat strengthens the ties each family has with the other families in the community.

The evening meal consists usually of bread made from manioc flour, cooked plantains, and meat or fish from the day's hunting and gathering. After supper, people chat, then drift to their hammocks to sleep.

1. What are some advantages to living in a large community dwelling?
2. Look at the illustrations in this chapter. Describe the ways the Yanomami have decorated their bodies. Do we have anything in our society to compare with this?

THE SOCIETY OF THE YANOMAMI

The Yanomami divide the world into four groups. The first one is the *shabono*, where everyone is regarded as friends. Each *shabono* contains from thirty to 200 people, with a headman who advises but does not rule the people in it. He is usually one of the wisest and most experienced men. He is expected to tell the people what he recommends and advises; he usually does this in a talk given just before dawn, as people awaken. He might suggest that it is time to plant bananas, or harvest some fruit that has been seen in the forest. He could suggest where the group might hunt that day, or whether it is a good time to go fishing. However, each family makes its own decisions.

Friends who live in other *shabonos* fall into the next group. Each group has alliances with others. Some alliances are based on marriages between people from the two groups. Some are based on trade between the two groups. These people are referred to as "guests," because they may be invited to feasts and celebrations.

The third group is made up of all the Yanomami the *shabono* knows but is not friends with. These people are considered enemies.

The fourth group is "those we do not see": people the Yanomami know exist but have not met.

The Yanomami are hostile toward everyone in the third and fourth groups. They always fear that these people may try to harm them or destroy their home. They are always ready to go to war with them, though they are more likely to try to send spirits to harm the enemies than to fight battles.

Some observers have called the Yanomami the fierce people, because they can seem very hostile towards outsiders. Sometimes, people from one group raid another, trying to steal women. Men from "guest" *shabonos* have contests of strength, wrestling with or hitting each other, to determine who is bravest. Men may also beat their wives, to show how brave they are. A man who has shown his bravery by hitting his wife is respected as someone who will not be pushed around.

Some observers think these displays of fierceness keep the Yanomami from actually having to go to war. A group that has shown its bravery will not be attacked as often as one that is weak. The alliances are necessary for the same reason. A *shabono* with many friends to call on will not be attacked as often as one with no friends.

The Yanomami often hold celebrations and feasts. Sometimes, the celebration will be a party held just because a group feels like

These men were travelling to a local feast when it began to rain. How have they used their environment to solve a problem?

313

a party and wants to invite guests from other *shabonos.* Sometimes it will be held for a special occasion; the most elaborate feast is held when someone dies. At feasts, people eat a great deal, talk and tell jokes.

Yanomami religious beliefs relate very closely to the natural world the people live in. They believe that they are descended from "first beings" who lived in this area many, many years ago. They believe that the world contains many spirits, known as *hekura.* Each person has his own *hekura*, which lives in the body. When the Yanomami draw a picture of a person, they also show the *hekura* dwelling in the body.

The strength of your *hekura* is important to your survival. If it is weak, you may die if someone sends supernatural forces against you. If your *hekura* is strong, you may be able to send forces to injure people in an enemy *shabono.*

Some men in a *shabono* chose to become **shamans** (shä′mən), people who can get in touch with the spirit world. Only adult males can become shamans. They must undergo an initiation during which they are shown by other shamans how to get in touch with the spirit world. To reach this spirit world, they take hallucinogenic drugs called *ebene* and *yakaona*, made from the seeds and bark of trees. During the initiation, the would-be shaman eats nothing for as long as eight days. At the end of the period, he sees the spirits and is beginning to learn how to get into touch with them. It will take him many more weeks before he learns everything he must to be a true shaman.

Shamans can use the spirits in the world to heal people or to make them sick. They also use drugs made from garden plants to heal people. They act as interpreters of the universe to the other Yanomami, speaking of the myths and spirits they alone can know. One writer has called them the explorers of the spirit world.

1. Make a chart showing how each part of Yanomami life relates to the physical environment the Yanomami live in. Your chart should include the headings: food; tools; housing; personal relationships; beliefs.

2. Why do you think the Yanomami view anyone they have not met as an enemy?

3. Explain how looking and acting fierce may help prevent wars among the different groups of the Yanomami.

THE CHANGING LIFE OF THE YANOMAMI

Like the Inca, the sixteenth century Spanish and Portuguese conquerors of South America usually avoided the Amazon rain forest. There were no stories of gold or other riches to attract them. The thick forest that covered the land made settlement and farming difficult. The few explorers who navigated up the broad rivers reported that the native peoples were fierce and hostile.

In the nineteenth century, however, thousands of people entered the forest to tap the rubber trees that grew there. Some were poor people from the Brazilian coast, who hoped to make their fortunes. Some were immigrants from Europe, lured by news of the rubber boom. The next hundred years brought missionaries, traders, miners, farmers, settlers and government officials into the forest. The isolation of the parts of the rain forest where rubber trees grew came to an end.

At first, the newcomers did not reach into Yanomami territory. Unlike the broad, flat rivers used by the explorers and traders, the rivers and streams in the Parima Highlands are narrow and swift and not useful for transportation. There were few rubber trees or other resources for newcomers to exploit. The Yanomami had such a reputation for fierceness that guides from other tribes refused to take people into Yanomami territory.

Yet by 1950, the isolation of the Yanomami was coming to an end as missionaries and anthropologists moved into the area. In the 1970s, both Brazil and Venezuela began to take more interest in the Yanomami area. Brazil had a rapidly growing population, most of it made up of poor people. There was little land along the coast for new settlements. The Brazilian government decided the rain forest must be exploited. Its hardwoods, oil, rubber and land would be used to provide more wealth for the country. Construction began on a road across the rain forest which would link Brazil to countries to the north and west. Part of this road cut across the southern edge of Yanomami territory. Roadworkers and traders set up temporary homes along the new road. Settlers moved in, in order to clear the land and farm.

There were many differences between the traditional life of the Yanomami and the life of the newcomers. Many of these differences had to do with the way the two groups interacted with the physical environment. Almost everything in Yanomami life was tied to the environment. Food, housing, religion, daily life: all had their base in the environment.

The newcomers used little of the rain forest environment. They bought most of their food from traders, hunted with guns, and imported housing materials. The newcomers wore clothing to protect themselves from the sun, the rain and the insects. They believed in a single god in heaven instead of the many spirits of the rain forest. They tried to defeat the environment, not to live peacefully within it.

Some of the things the outsiders brought were useful to the Yanomami. Axes and machetes made it easier to clear spaces for gardens. Matches were easier to use than fire drills. Guns made hunting easier and hunters were more successful than ever.

Trade for new goods changed the Yanomami economy. Before contact with outsiders, each Yanomami family owned the same goods. If needed, goods were shared. Some Yanomami now went to work for the missions or for the government building roads to earn money to buy trade goods. They began to compete with each other to own the best goods. Sharing was no longer as common.

Some Yanomami began to adopt the ways of living of the newcomers. They built cement single-family homes with sheet-metal roofs. Living in these homes ended the old communal way

Newcomers to the rain forest clear large areas, changing the local environment. How are these changes affecting the Yanomami?

of life. Yanomami who were in contact with the newcomers also began to wear western style clothes, even though these clothes were soon wet and clammy in the heat and humidity of the rain forest.

They adopted some of the newcomers' diet. Some groups began to plant bitter manioc, a crop they could sell to the newcomers and use themselves. But this crop did not provide as balanced a diet as the crops they traditionally grew in their gardens. Some Yanomami decided to eat foods such as white bread, canned goods and candy. This new diet did not have the nourishment they were used to.

These Yanomami no longer relied on themselves and the forest. Because they became dependent on goods they could not make themselves, they became dependent on the people they worked for. They forgot how to make bows and used guns instead. They used manufactured containers instead of ones made from bark.

TRADE GOODS

The list below shows which trade goods the Yanomami had acquired by 1970, and by 1980.

1970:	1980:	
steel axes	shotguns and cartridges	threads and needles
machetes	Brazilian-made tobacco	clothing and hats
knives	steel grater boards	thongs and shoes
scissors	aluminum pots	blankets and towels
fishing lines and hooks	soap	candles
combs	toothbrushes	cigarettes
mirrors	whetstones	flashlights and batteries
beads	hammocks	cooking oil
matches	aluminum basins and pans	dishes, cups, spoons
salt	harpoons	plastic containers
	adzes for making dugout canoes	sacks and bags
	hoes and digging tools	suitcases
	rakes	medicine
		files

1. Which traditional tools and technology would the goods in each list replace?
2. Which five items would lead to the greatest change in the traditional way of life? Explain why you select each item.
3. What differences do you see in the sort of goods introduced by 1970, and the new goods introduced between 1970 and 1980?
4. What new items would you expect to see on a list made in 1990?

The Yanomami values were affected by the newcomers. Missionaries wanted to convert the Yanomami to Christianity. They told the Yanomami that they must wear clothes, stop painting their bodies and abandon their belief in shamans and spirits. They wanted the Yanomami to settle down in one place near the mission instead of moving on every few years. Yanomami who did settle down had to depend on the missionaries for food, clothing and shelter.

Many young Yanomami began attending mission schools.

With ideas they learned in school they challenged the traditional Yanomami way of life. They were no longer willing to do things the traditional way.

Diseases such as measles and influenza from the outside world seriously affected the Yanomami. Often when one person in a group caught a disease, so did almost everyone else. Some infected groups fled into the forest, trying to escape from the enemies that had sent spirits to make them sick. Far from medicine and help, many died.

Groups of Yanomami that lived closest to the new highway were the most seriously affected by change. Some groups had moved to live beside the highway. When the highway was finished and the workers left, they could no longer live by trading or working on road building. They had no gardens for food, and there was little game left in the nearby forest because of overhunting.

The Yanomami realized that contact with newcomers was damaging their traditional way of life. A few groups moved farther and farther back into the forest. They chose to do without guns, axes and medicine so that they could continue to live in the old way.

What does the future hold for the Yanomami? Some people are convinced that the traditional way of life is doomed, and that the Yanomami may die out as change makes them less able to survive. Others are more hopeful. The Brazilian government has set aside over seven and a half million hectares that cannot be developed yet and that may become a reserve for the Yanomami. No settlers, miners or other people who want to exploit the forest can enter this area. If the government does not give in to would-be settlers and mining companies who want to use some of this land, there is hope that the Yanomami can survive there.

No one is sure what will happen in Venezuela, where two-thirds of the Yanomami live and where much of the Yanomami territory is still unmapped and untouched. It will be up to the government, the other newcomers and the Yanomami themselves to decide whether there is room in the modern world for a traditional way of life.

1. Why did the Yanomami remain isolated longer than other South American native groups?

2. Write a paragraph to explain how the Yanomami relationship to the physical environment has changed. How has the environment itself changed by the building of the highway, the coming of settlers and the use of guns?

3. In a paragraph, explain why the Yanomami would change their traditional ways and adopt the way of life of newcomers.

4. Suggest reasons why missionaries would prefer the Yanomami to live near the missions rather than spread throughout the forest.

5. Imagine that you are an official of the Brazilian government. Explain why your government wants to exploit the resources of the rain forest. Now imagine you are a Yanomami. Explain to the government official why you feel the section of the rain forest where you live should be left alone.

SUMMARY

The Yanomami, who are descended from some of the earliest people of South America, live on the northern edge of the South American rain forest. Until recently, this rain forest had not been explored by outsiders, and the Yanomami continued to live in a traditional way.

The traditional Yanomami way of life is closely tied to the rain forest environment. Food, housing, tools, technology and beliefs all relate directly to the environment. At the centre of the Yanomami economy are the gardens which provide them with three-quarters of their food. The economy also includes hunting, gathering and fishing.

Traditionally, the Yanomami live in a society centred on the *shabono*. The shabono is the communal building that houses a

The continuation of the Yanomami's traditional way of life depends on the future of the rain forest.

group of Yanomami. All village activities take place in the *shabono*.

The Yanomami form friendships and alliances with other villages. They are hostile toward people in villages outside these alliances. Yanomami beliefs centre on the spirit world and are interpreted to the people by shamans.

Contact with outsiders over the last fifty years has begun to change the traditional Yanomami way of life. Trade goods such as guns and metal axes have replaced some traditional technology such as bows and arrows and stone axes. New beliefs and education are changing the way the Yanomami think about the world. It is too early to tell whether the traditional Yanomami way of life can survive.

Chapter Review: The Yanomami

NEW WORDS AND IDEAS

1. Write a sentence to identify each of the following:
   (a) Parima Highlands
   (b) *shabono*
   (c) "those we do not see"
   (d) shaman
   (e) *hekura*.

2. In your notebooks, match the resource in column A with its use in column B.

A	B
manioc	protein
Agouti incisor	red dye
termites	canoe
palm wood	flour
razor grass	knife
urucu	fire drill
liana vines	bows
bark	shaver
cocoa wood	hammocks

CHECKING YOUR UNDERSTANDING

3. Write a one-paragraph description of the Yanomami's environment. Include the climate, vegetation, landforms and wildlife in your description.

4. (a) Describe how the Yanomami cleared the rain forest to create their garden plots in the past.
   (b) Using the list of trade items found on page 318 as a guide, describe how you think garden plots are cleared today.

5. (a) How do the Yanomami know when it is time to move to a new village site?
   (b) What do they look for when they are selecting a new site?

6. (a) Group the tasks below into those that are carried out by the women of a Yanomami village, and those carried out by the men.

   weeding the garden
   hunting
   gathering berries and roots
   clearing the forest
   fishing
   weaving baskets
   making weapons
   cooking food
   acting as a shaman
   collecting leaves for roofs
   caring for young children
   cutting saplings used for the *shabono*

   (b) Is one set of tasks more important to village life than the other? Explain your answer.

7. Explain how the people of a *shabono* arrive at important decisions, such as the location of the daily hunt.

USING YOUR KNOWLEDGE

8. The Canadian Food Guide suggests that Canadians should eat some fruit, vegetables, dairy products, cereals, and meat in order to have a balanced diet. Classify the diet of the Yanomami using the headings suggested by the food guide. Do you think the Yanomami have a balanced diet? Refer to the classifications to explain your conclusion.

9. The building of the Brazilian Highway brought change to the Yanomami. Imagine a new highway was to be built close to your school. What changes would it bring to your area?

Glossary

A.D.: an abbreviation of the Latin words *anno Domini*, "in the year of our Lord," meaning after the birth of Christ.

anthropologist: a scientist who studies, among other things, traditional societies.

aqueduct: a large channel or pipe built to carry water from a distance.

archaeologist: a scientist who digs up and studies the remains of ancient civilizations.

B.C.: an abbreviation of "before Christ."

barbarian: a term used by the Greeks and Romans to describe the nomadic peoples who lived outside their empires.

borer: a thin, sharp tool which, when turned quickly, makes a hole in wood or other substances.

canopy: an overhead covering which provides a shaded area.

citizen: a person who, by birth or by choice, is a member of a state that gives him or her certain rights.

colony: a settlement which remains governed by the state from which the settlers originally came.

crop: a plant grown or gathered for food or other uses.

curare: a poison made from a vine which grows in the South American rain forest.

democracy: a form of government in which leaders are chosen by a vote of the majority.

dictator: a person neither elected nor leader by right of birth who rules a state with power to make all the decisions.

domestic: tame, not wild, when referring to plants and animals; also means of one's own country, not foreign.

drainage: the system by which water is carried off from land.

drought: a long period of time during which little or no rain falls.

dynasty: a succession of rulers who belong to the same family; the period of time during which this succession rules.

equator: an imaginary circle around the middle of the Earth, halfway between the North Pole and the South Pole.

equatorial forest: a forest found at or near the equator; usually indicates a rain forest environment.

excavate: to uncover by digging.

fossil: the remains of prehistoric plants, animals, or people, preserved in rocks where they have been hardened.

glacier: an enormous mass of ice formed from compressed snow.

gladiator: in ancient Rome, a slave, captive or paid fighter who fought at public shows.

hieroglyphics: a system of pictures used to represent words, ideas or sounds.

invaders: people from one land, city or state who attack and enter another.

irrigate: to bring water to land by means of ditches or channels.

landlocked: completely surrounded by land, without any border on a sea or ocean.

legion: in ancient Rome, a body of soldiers made up of several thousand foot soldiers, and several hundred soldiers on horseback.

lighters: large flat-bottomed boats used for transporting cargo to or from a ship that cannot be berthed at a pier or dock.

majority: the number of people which makes up more than half of the members of a group.

monsoon: a seasonal wind in parts of Asia which brings a great deal of rainfall.

nutrient: substance in the soil which helps food plants to grow.

nomad: member of a group of people which constantly moves from place to place.

oasis: a place in the desert, around a body of water, where food plants can grow.

paleontologist: a scientist who digs up and studies fossils.

parasitic plant: a plant which feeds off other plants.

plantain: an edible plant similar to a banana.

prehistory: the period of time before civilizations, and the invention of writing.

reed: the hollow stalk of a tall, stiff grass that grows in wet places.

republic: a form of government in which the head of state is elected by the citizens.

resources: things that help people meet their needs.

scribes: scholars, sometimes priests, who recorded events, laws, histories.

shaman: in some traditional societies, people who are believed to have special powers allowing them to communicate with the spirit world.

shifting cultivation: the practice of moving crop-planting sites every few years after the soil has become exhausted.

smelting: the process by which ore is melted in order to get the metal out.

species: in biology, a category of classification of plants and animals.

state: an organized political group, occupying a certain territory and having a government.

subsistence: the use of resources to keep alive, with few or no resources left over.

surplus: an amount left over, above and beyond what is needed.

temperate: having a climate without long-lasting, periodic extremes of heat or cold.

terrace: a large, step-like level of land on a slope.

thatching: a process by which a roof or covering is made of straw, rushes or other plants.

traditional society: a society in which much of the way of life of prehistoric ancestors has been kept.

tribute: forced payment of goods, money or services.

work duty: labor provided as a form of tribute.

ziggurat: an ancient Assyrian or Babylonian temple in the form of a pyramid of terraced towers.

Index